CONCLAVE
1559

MARY HOLLINGSWORTH is a scholar of the
Italian Renaissance, and author of *The Medici,
Princes of the Renaissance, The Cardinal's Hat,
The Borgias: History's Most Notorious Dynasty*
and *Patronage in Renaissance Italy: From 1400
to the Early Sixteenth Century.*

CONCLAVE
1559

Ippolito d'Este and the
Papal Election of 1559

MARY
HOLLINGSWORTH

An Apollo Book

First published in 2021 by Head of Zeus Ltd
This paperback edition first published in 2022 by Head of Zeus Ltd,
part of Bloomsbury Publishing Plc

1 3 5 7 9 10 8 6 4 2

A CIP catalogue record for this book is available from the British Library.

ISBN [PB] 9781800244740
ISBN [E] 9781800244726

Typeset by Ed Pickford
Conclave illustration by Jeff Edwards
Front Cover: Cardinal Ippolito d'Este (1509–72), anonymous artist © Bridgeman Images

Printed and bound in Great Britain by
CPI Group (UK) Ltd, Croydon CR0 4YY

Head of Zeus Ltd
5–8 Hardwick Street
London EC1R 4RG

WWW.HEADOFZEUS.COM

To Flora Mary Saywell

CONTENTS

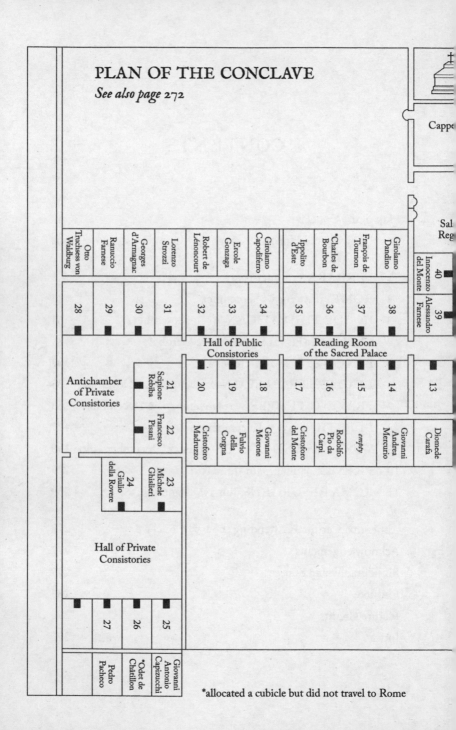

PLAN OF THE CONCLAVE
See also page 272

Cappe

Sal
Reg

Hall of Public Consistories

Reading Room of the Sacred Palace

Antichamber of Private Consistories

Hall of Private Consistories

28	Otto Truchsess von Waldburg
29	Ranuccio Farnese
30	Georges d'Armagnac
31	Lorenzo Strozzi
32	Robert de Lénoncourt
33	Ercole Gonzaga
34	Girolamo Capodiferro
35	Ippolito d'Este
36	*Charles de Bourbon
37	François de Tournon
38	Girolamo Dandino
39	Alessandro Farnese
40	Innocenzo del Monte
21	Scipione Rebiba
20	
19	
18	
17	
16	
15	
14	
13	Diomede Carafa
22	Francesco Pisani
—	Cristoforo Madruzzo
—	Fulvio della Corgna
—	Giovanni Morone
—	Cristoforo del Monte
—	Rodolfo Pio da Carpi
—	*empty*
—	Giovanni Andrea Mercurio
24	Giulio della Rovere
23	Michele Ghisleri
25	Giovanni Antonio Capizucchi
26	*Odet de Châtillon
27	Pedro Pacheco

*allocated a cubicle but did not travel to Rome

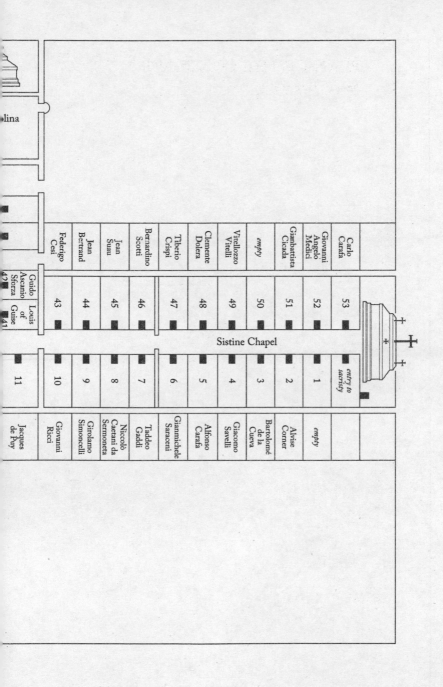

Scudi, Ducats and Florins –
A Note on Money

The relationship between the various currencies that appear in Ippolito's account books is complex. First of all, most states in sixteenth-century Europe had their own silver-based currency. In France, a centralized monarchy, there was a single system based on the *livre* (1 *livre* = 20 *sous* = 240 *deniers*). In Italy each of the peninsula's many independent states had their own local currency. Ferrara, for instance, used the *lira marchesana* (1 *lira* = 20 *soldi* = 240 *denari*); Rome by contrast preferred a decimal system based on the *scudo di moneta* (1 *scudo di moneta* = 10 *giulii* = 100 *baiocchi*). There were also internationally recognized gold currencies, notably the Venetian ducat, the Florentine florin or the gold scudo. The latter appears frequently in Ippolito's ledgers and was evidently used across Europe. These currencies, both gold and silver, fluctuated against each other in response to market forces. The period covered by this book, 1559–65, was one of significant inflation in Ferrara, where the price of a gold scudo rose from 73 to 78 *soldi*; by contrast, in Rome its value remained steady at 110 *baiocchi* over the same period. In France, despite the economic hardship caused by the religious wars, its value rose only slightly from 48 to 49 *sous* over the two years Ippolito spent there, from 1561–3. To simplify this I have translated most of the prices in this book into gold scudi, although I have needed to use the Roman *baiocchi* to clarify relative details about the cost of food.

I

Ferrara

SUMMER 1559

The summer of 1559 had been unusually hot in Ferrara. By the middle of July the broad waters of the Po had sunk to little more than a sluggish stream, barely capable of bearing the barges bringing the newly harvested crops of wheat, barley and spelt down to the granaries in the city. Cardinal Ippolito d'Este sought relief from the sweltering heat in his country villas, entertaining his friends and family at small dinner parties, the tables laden with delicate dishes prepared by his chefs, and plenty of salads and fresh fruit – peaches, figs and melons were all in season, and Ippolito was particularly partial to melons. Their leisurely dining was accompanied by the music of his singers, lute players and flautists, though without Jacques, his sensational castrato who had returned home in May.[1] It was too hot to do anything energetic and Ippolito passed the time gambling at cards, gossiping and making plans with his brother Ercole, Duke of Ferrara, for the autumn hunting season. An enviable life of luxury and ease, you might think, but this idleness was not of Ippolito's choice. Since acquiring his red hat back in 1539, he had worked hard to establish himself as one of the most powerful figures at the papal court. For the last four years his glittering career had been at a standstill after he was abruptly exiled by Pope Paul IV and forced to retire to the provincial backwater of his family estates in Ferrara.

Ercole and Ippolito belonged to Italy's old aristocracy. The eldest sons of Duke Alfonso I and his infamous duchess, Lucrezia Borgia, they had a sister, Eleonora (who was abbess of the convent of Corpus Domini in Ferrara where she had care of the parental tombs), a younger brother, Francesco, and two half-brothers born to their father's mistress whom he married after Lucrezia died. Ercole had been a young man when he inherited the title in 1534; now a staid fifty-one-year-old, he had proved a good, if somewhat cautious, ruler. His father had secured him a prestigious bride: in 1528, he'd married Renée of France, the daughter of Louis XIII and aunt to the present king, Henri II. She had given birth to five healthy children, two sons and three daughters. The eldest, Anna, was married to Francis, Duke of Guise and one of France's premier nobles, whose niece – better known to us as Mary, Queen of Scots – was married to the dauphin. Duke Ercole's heir Alfonso, now twenty-five years old, had recently married Lucrezia de' Medici, the daughter of Cosimo I, Duke of Florence, but in the summer of 1559 he was abroad on an extended visit to the French court, leaving his young bride behind with her family. His younger brother, Luigi – named for their royal grandfather Louis – was destined for the Church. Thanks to the influence of their uncle Ippolito, Luigi had secured the position of Bishop of Ferrara in 1550 at the age of just twelve, but his career too was on hold while the cardinal remained in disgrace in Rome.

Despite the heir and the spare, Ercole and Renée's marriage was not happy. Her royal blood may have cemented the ties between Ferrara and France, and linked her children to the French crown, but she had caused much embarrassment to her husband by converting to Protestantism. In 1554, under pressure from Paul IV and the Inquisition, the Duke had been forced to make her repudiate her heretical beliefs in public, and to insist on her attendance at mass in Ferrara Cathedral on important feast days. She did her duty reluctantly and continued to worship as a Protestant in the privacy of her own apartments; the Duke, worried about her influence on their two young daughters, sent the girls to the care of his sister Eleonora at Corpus Domini. Remarkably, despite his position in the hierarchy of the Catholic Church, Ippolito was far less fazed by his sister-in-law's choice of faith and the two of them, who had been friends for a long time, continued to remain close.[2]

Ippolito himself was a year younger than his brother (his fiftieth birthday, on 25 August 1559, was imminent) and he too was a grandfather. His mistress had borne him a daughter in 1536 and he had named her Renea after his sister-in-law. In 1553 Renea married the lord of Mirandola, a local landowner, and had recently given birth to a daughter whom she affectionately named Ippolita. Among Ippolito's account books is one detailing the expenses incurred in buying Renea's trousseau, which came to the huge sum of 3,000 scudi, more than six months' salary for his household.[3]

Despite his red hat, Ippolito's tastes remained very much those of the aristocratic world into which he had been born.

He certainly enjoyed the company of women – his coach horses were named Beauty, Damsel, Sweetheart and Pet.[4] His wardrobe inventories show his preference for the tight-fitting doublets and hose of the secular world rather than the shapeless robes of the Church. His gloves were perfumed with expensive musk and ambergris, the unmistakable aromas of wealth; he owned as many peacock-feather hats as he did cardinal's birettas and only nineteen cassocks in contrast to over a hundred doublets and thirty-eight pairs of breeches and hose. His wardrobe, like his waistline, was expanding, another sign of age and a hazard with which we too are familiar: in 1559, although he owned the same number of fine linen handkerchiefs as he did as a young man in the 1530s (around 100), he had three times as many coats (120), five times as many pairs of perfumed gloves (73) and seven times the number of doublets (105).[5]

The inventories also reveal other signs of the ageing process. Among the items listed was a pair of silver-rimmed spectacles, suggesting that Ippolito's eyesight had begun to deteriorate; there was also a silver box 'for his stomach powders', implying that his diet of rich meat and red wine had begun to tell on his digestive system. Moreover, although he was generally in good health, he had begun to suffer from occasional attacks of gout, a disease to which the upper classes of the sixteenth century were particularly prone: listed among the cushions were ones specially made by his tailor, filled with strips of fine linen to ease and protect his throbbing toes. The first attack had occurred in June 1551. 'You can imagine how upset I am, but it is the will of God', he wrote philosophically to his brother, who also suffered from the complaint – both men were aware that this disease 'once it has started will never go away'.[6] The gout, however, did not hamper his passion for sport and once the summer was over, he could look forward to hunting expeditions, especially with his peregrines and goshawks, and energetic games of real tennis.

The early part of the summer of 1559 had been dominated by events beyond the Alps. Ercole and Ippolito, together with their courtiers, must have spent many hours discussing the implications of the treaty of Cateau-Cambrésis, which had been signed on 25 April by Henri II of France and Philip II of Spain. Would it really bring an end to decades of war in Europe and herald an era of stability for the small state of Ferrara? More pertinent for Ippolito, there was also the question of what impact it would have on the age-old rivalry between the French and the Spanish cardinals in the papal election that would eventually take place after Paul IV's death.

Then, in early July, a courier arrived from Paris with reports that Henri II had suffered a ghastly accident. The forty-year-old king had been pierced in the eye by a shattered lance while participating, against all advice, in a tournament to celebrate the marriage of his daughter Elisabeth to Philip II, a union designed to cement the peace between the two monarchs. The king lingered in terrible pain for ten long days before his tragic death on 10 July, leaving his sickly fifteen-year-old son, François, as the new king, the kingdom itself in the hands of his inexperienced widow Catherine de' Medici, and the regime under the 'protection' of the uncles of the new queen, Duke Francis of Guise and Cardinal Charles of Lorraine. After her husband's awful accident, Catherine adopted a new personal device, abandoning her joyful rainbow for a broken lance with the motto 'tears from this, from this anguish', or, rather more elegantly in Latin, *lacrymae hinc, hinc dolor.*

Ippolito marked the sombre occasion by giving money to members of his staff, especially to his steward, his sommelier and the others who served at his dining-table, 'so that they can dress themselves in black for the death of the king'.[7] He sent his secretary Montemerlo di Montemerli to France carrying personal letters of condolences to Francis II and the Queen Mother. His shock was evident in a letter to his nephew Alfonso, who was still at the French court. 'The death of the king is truly terrible, an appalling loss to everyone', he wrote, 'for my part I can say I have never felt such grief, but this is God's will and we must accept it.'[8]

Ippolito's friendship with Henri II dated back over twenty years to 1536 when he had joined the French court as a guest of Henri's father, Francis I. Energetic and fun, though perhaps a little naive at first, the young Ippolito had enthusiastically embraced life at what was widely regarded as the most glamorous court in Europe. He hunted with the king, played tennis with the royal princes, gave expensive presents to the princesses, gambled with the courtiers, gossiped with the king's mistress, and enjoyed the banquets, tournaments and other entertainments on offer.[9] Ercole had made an uncharacteristically bold and risky move by sending his brother to France. As the second son, Ippolito was destined for the Church – he had been made Archbishop of Milan at the age of nine – but it was difficult to see how the career of this minor Italian princeling could prosper among the powerful French churchmen at the royal court. Indeed, Ercole's advisors had warned that his brother lacked the political skills needed to survive in this notoriously venomous pit of intrigue and rivalry. But the duke need not have worried: the strategy was to prove astonishingly successful. Within weeks of his arrival, Ippolito had become one of Francis I's favourites, and their close friendship brought greater dividends than even the most optimistic courtiers in Ferrara could have foreseen.

In a move that would transform Ippolito's career, Francis I took the decision to groom his young protégé for the papal tiara, or rather, election to the papal throne. With France at war with Charles V, the powerful ruler of both Spain and the Empire, the king was fully aware that a Frenchman had no chance of election in a college divided by the bitter rivalry between the Habsburg and Valois monarchies. His solution was to promote an Italian candidate but one who owed his wealth and position, and therefore his loyalty, to France. Francis I used his political clout with Paul III to secure a red hat for Ippolito, and showered him with an impressive list of French archbishoprics, bishoprics and abbeys. By the time the king died in 1547, Ippolito had become one of the wealthiest and most influential cardinals in Europe – and he had honed his political skills to become a consummate diplomat, effortlessly manipulating his power with affability and charm.

Ippolito continued to prosper under Francis I's successor, Henri II. The cardinal was one of the very few royal favourites to survive the palace revolution orchestrated by the new king in 1547 and two years later he sent Ippolito to Rome as cardinal-protector of France. This was an important appointment: unlike an ambassador, whose job was to report news and gossip, Ippolito had been given the task of negotiating the interests of the French crown in consistory, the regular meetings between the pope and his cardinals that took place several times a week to formulate papal policy. Moreover, as cardinal-protector Ippolito was now the leader of the French faction in the College of Cardinals and, most significantly, he was

Henri II's choice for the papal tiara. 'All Rome was assembled at the windows and along the streets through which I passed,' he wrote enthusiastically to Henri – in French – giving an account of his formal reception in the city in July 1549.[10] Ippolito's first conclave opened just four months later and, when it became clear that his own chances of election were slight, he proved his political skills by manoeuvring the votes of the French party to support the election of Giovanni Maria del Monte as Julius III (1550–5). The favours with which the new pope rewarded him established Ippolito's credentials at the new papal court.

From the first, Ippolito lived in considerable style in Rome. His main residence in the city was the imposing Palazzo Monte Giordano (now the Palazzo Taverna), a short distance from the Ponte Sant'Angelo and handy for the regular consistories he was obliged to attend at the Vatican. He also had a suburban villa, the Palazzo Monte Cavallo, set high up on the Quirinal hill, with an elegant dining pavilion set in its superb gardens that boasted a panoramic view across Rome to the countryside beyond.* In the middle of the sixteenth century the Quirinal hill was largely undeveloped and it was a highly sought-after location for the villas of the very rich, recommended by doctors for the gentle breezes and fresh air that provided such a contrast to the miasma of the narrow streets and stinking river below. In the summer months, when even the Quirinal was too hot for comfort, Ippolito could escape Rome, as most of his colleagues did, for

---

* The site of Ippolito's villa is now the Palazzo del Quirinale, the official residence of the president of Italy.

his country retreat. One of the favours bestowed on Ippolito by Julius III in gratitude for his support during the conclave was the governorship of Tivoli, where Ippolito now made a start on what would be his most famous artistic project, the sumptuous palace known as the Villa d'Este.

Thanks to the benefices with which he had been endowed by Francis I and Henri II, Ippolito had an income of 75–80,000 scudi a year, making him one of the richest cardinals in the college. During the years 1549–51, for example, in addition to Milan, he was also archbishop of three French sees – Lyons, Narbonne and Auch, the second richest see in France – as well as Bishop of Autun, and abbot of fifteen abbeys including the great Norman foundation of Jumièges and the beautiful abbey of Chaalis, set amid the woods of the royal hunting parks north of Paris.[11] Chaalis alone brought in 10,000 scudi a year, a sum equal to his entire annual income back in 1536 when he had first arrived at the French court. Even then, he would have been considered rich by the standards of the day: a skilled master-builder could expect to earn just 40 scudi a year, a sum that was enough for him to support a wife and family in comfortable, if modest, style.

By the late 1550s Ippolito was spectacularly wealthy. Most of his income came from his benefices – fifty per cent from his French ones and twenty-five per cent from the life interest he held in various family benefices and other concerns in Ferrara. We rarely consider how dependent churchmen were on the weather: benefice income was largely agricultural and it was dictated by the success of the harvest, though large landowners like Ippolito, who had surplus produce to sell, were able to profit from the rocketing grain prices that marked a famine. Rents and taxes produced more regular income. Ippolito received the duty charged on all cows, pigs and sheep brought into Ferrara for sale and, rather surprisingly for an Italian princeling, he was also a landlord in Paris where, as Abbot of Chaalis, he rented out properties to artisans and shopkeepers. Added to these sums was the income he received as cardinal-protector of France, which accounted for some ten per cent of the total and consisted of the charges he levied on all appointments to French benefices – this could be as much as fifty per cent of the taxable value of the bishopric, showing just how difficult it was for an ambitious man to pursue a career in the Church during the sixteenth century without very substantial financial backing.

The prime identifier of rank in Renaissance society was the size of the court that surrounded members of the elite – kings, popes, princes and cardinals. Ippolito was no exception and he assembled a household of courtiers and domestic servants to run his palaces, write his letters, attend to his personal needs, serve at his banquets and groom the horses in his stables. These men – no women, that would have been considered inappropriate in a cardinal's entourage – also provided an escort riding with him through the streets of Rome or travelling further afield. In 1536 this household had numbered around sixty, most of whom accompanied him to France; by 1555, a reflection of his new status, it had more than doubled in size.[12]

The catalyst for this dramatic increase was his appointment as cardinal-protector of France in 1549. At one level the larger entourage gave visual expression to his grander status, but there were also more subtle changes designed to reflect the nature of his new position in Rome. The bulk of the new names were involved in public display. The number of valets, footmen and pages, who formed his escort on official occasions, trebled and there was also a substantial increase in the so-called Officials of the Mouth, the men involved with the other aspect of his public face, his dining-room – Ippolito would become famous for the splendour of his banquets. The number of squires whose job was to present the dishes of food to the guests seated at table trebled and there was a similar rise in the number of chefs, who now included two specialist pastry cooks. He also took on many extra assistants; there were eleven new boys in the kitchen, two of whom had the task of cleaning his silver, and other boys for his stewards, larderers, sommeliers and *credenzieri*. These last were in charge of preparing the dishes for the cold courses from the *credenza*, or sideboard, which alternated with hot courses sent up from the kitchen, and made such a distinctive feature of fine Italian dining of the period.

Several of the new names suggest that he was also deliberately creating a more cultured image for himself. Among the new intake were philosophers, humanists, poets and playwrights; he also took on a full-time antiquarian, Pirro Ligorio, whose map reconstructing the buildings of ancient Rome was to be a landmark in the study of antiquity, though his role in Ippolito's household involved the less edifying task of looking after the cardinal's pages.[13] Patronage of the arts was one of the hallmarks of prestige at the papal court and his strategy seems to have been successful. The humanist who gave his funeral oration was lavish in his praise of Ippolito's court: 'It was an academe, a literary coterie, a world theatre filled with unique talents'.[14]

What is really striking about Ippolito's new household, however, is how he used it to underline his political allegiance to France as well as his position as senior French cardinal in Rome.[15] Many of the new intake were French nationals and, while some were practical appointments – such as the treasurer who dealt with the income from his French benefices, or the secretary in charge of his French correspondence – others were more overtly involved with the display of his political affiliations. The French humanist and poet Marc-Antoine Muret was one of the intellectuals attached to his court, while many of the musicians who played at his banquets were French, as were his sommeliers and three of the nine cooks. His library contained many French books, his cellars were filled with French wines, transported by sea at huge cost from his French benefices; his coachman was French, and so was his tailor. Over half of the coats listed in the inventory of his wardrobe drawn up in 1555 were described as being 'in the French style': it is not entirely clear what exactly identified them as *alla francese* – it was not their length; perhaps it was their collars – but evidently his wardrobe staff had no difficulty in recognizing the style, and presumably this was also obvious to the wider public. Above all, the guests at his famously extravagant banquets would have been left in little doubt of his loyalty to France. They sat in rooms decorated with wall- and door-hangings embellished with Ippolito's own personal emblem of an eagle, embroidered in silver, and the French fleur-de-lys, done in gold; they could even see the two devices stamped on the studs that ornamented their velvet-upholstered chairs.

One of his more splendid banquets was held on 30 March 1550 to celebrate Henri II's recent victory over the English at Boulogne. Among Ippolito's guests were Duke Ercole, who was in Rome with his sixteen-year-old heir Alfonso to congratulate Julius III on his recent election. Also present was the French ambassador Claude d'Urfé and many French cardinals, who had been in Rome for the conclave and were perhaps delaying their journey home until the Alpine passes opened in early summer.

Three of the younger ones had moved into the guest apartments at Palazzo Monte Giordano: Charles of Lorraine (whose brother was married to Duke Ercole's daughter Anna), Louis de Bourbon-Vendôme and Odet de Châtillon. There were also thirteen Italian cardinals present, several of whom were to play significant roles in this story: Guido Ascanio Sforza, Alessandro Farnese and his brother Ranuccio, all grandsons of Paul III, and their cousin Niccolò Sermoneta; the wealthy Venetian Francesco Pisani; Angelo Medici, a Milanese lawyer not related to the Medici of Florence (his nickname was Medichino, or 'little doctor'); and the Roman baron Girolamo Capodiferro.

Ippolito's guests enjoyed a feast not just for their stomachs but also for their eyes and ears. 'The Cardinal of Ferrara [as he was formally known in the documents of the time] is a most magnificent gentleman,' the Florentine ambassador informed Cosimo I, 'and there is hardly another cardinal in the college who can equal his birth, his wealth and his connections', he enthused, 'though there are those who think he likes to show off in too ostentatious a manner.'[16] Ippolito's wealth was conspicuously on display at the banquet. He possessed a splendid collection of silver: his inventories list great platters, ornamental salts and fine cutlery, making a total of some 600 items of tableware, many gilded and all emblazoned with his coat-of-arms.[17] The Florentine envoy described rooms hung with 'very fine and very beautiful hangings' and an amazing silver lamp, six feet high, that appeared to grow out of the ground: 'Its manufacture alone came to a thousand scudi.'[18] The ambassador went on to describe an ingenious little silver fish that thrilled the guests by 'swimming' up the table, with the aid of intricate mechanical devices. 'It moved its head and tail in exactly the same way as if it were a real fish in water,' he wrote in astonishment, 'and when it reached the top of the table it jumped into the air and turned, opening its spine to show not bones but toothpicks, which were picked out by the guests as the fish made its way back down the table.'

Under the leadership of Julius III, Rome increasingly resembled the royal courts of the secular world. The pope himself was an enthusiastic huntsman and gambler, and indulged regularly in the pleasures of the table. He reputedly won 1,500 scudi off Cardinal Ranuccio Farnese in a single afternoon, filled the Vatican with jesters and buffoons, and enjoyed performances of racy Greek comedies.[19] While a cardinal he had picked up a young boy off the streets of Piacenza and persuaded his brother to adopt him. Soon after his election Julius III had scandalized Rome by giving the lad, Innocenzo del Monte, now aged eighteen, a red hat and the important post of secretary of state. The move was profoundly offensive to the growing numbers of reformers who preached the urgent need to stamp out the corruption that was endemic in Rome and to return to the austere simplicity of the early Church. Julius III's lifestyle added fuel to the fire. Cardinal Gianpietro Carafa, the Inquisitor General and leader of the hard-line reformers, made his hostility to the secular character of the papal court abundantly evident. He refused all invitations, insisting on dining only in his own palace and, very conspicuously, refused to attend the banquet at the Vatican hosted by Julius III to celebrate the first anniversary of his election.[20]

Most of the cardinals who attended Ippolito's banquet in March 1550 were guilty in some measure of the abuses that the reformers hoped to eradicate. Guido Ascanio Sforza had been sixteen years old and Alessandro Farnese only fourteen when they received their red hats from their grandfather, Paul III, shortly after his election in 1534 – and there had been an outcry when these teenagers were promoted to the two top jobs in the Church administration, *camerlengo* (or chamberlain) and vice-chancellor, respectively. Their cousin Niccolò Sermoneta had been just ten years old when he was made a cardinal, though Paul III had felt it necessary to keep this promotion secret until the boy reached his twelfth birthday. The French cardinals, at least, were of age and had established ecclesiastical careers behind them when they received their red hats but they, like the papal grandsons, were guilty of pluralism. Thanks to royal or papal patronage, they had all accumulated multiple benefices: Charles of Lorraine was Archbishop of Rheims and Metz, and easily the richest prelate in France; Jean du Bellay's benefices included Bordeaux, Paris and Le Mans; and thanks to his grandfather's bounty Alessandro Farnese outshone even Ippolito in wealth and opulence.

The lavish lifestyles of worldly cardinals caused offence to the ascetic Carafa and the reformers. Carafa himself was a founder member of the Theatines, an order of secular clerics bound by strict rules of poverty and devotion. They were particularly scandalized by Cardinal du Bellay, who showed his lack of respect for the faith by hosting a spectacular public entertainment during Lent to celebrate the birth of a son to Henri II and Catherine de' Medici in 1549.[21] The party, which was attended by many cardinals and prelates, went on until dawn and included bull-fighters, clowns, battalions of soldiers fighting a mock battle, nymphs clad in leopard skins, ballet dancers in grotesque masks, fireworks and a ball.[22]

Indeed, it is easy to forget that these cardinals were princes of the Church. Neither Lorraine, Bellay, Alessandro Farnese,

Sforza, Sermoneta, Medici nor Ippolito had ever been ordained as priests. Many ignored the rule of celibacy, some even lived openly with their mistresses and children, a practice that shocked Catholics and Protestants in equal measure, and appalled Carafa and the reformers, though it should be said in their defence that all of them would have known of the chapel in St Peter's dedicated to St Petronilla, daughter of St Peter, the first pope. Like Ippolito, Alessandro Farnese and Pisani both had mistresses and children; Medici had three illegitimate offspring. Farnese had a portrait of his favourite courtesan painted by Titian – showing her as Danaë seductively receiving Jupiter in a shower of gold – which he hung in his bedroom. His grandfather, Paul III, was cynically lampooned by Protestant reformers in a woodcut that showed the pope as an old ass wearing his tiara and playing the bagpipes, a symbol of sexual incontinence (in a curious twist to this tale, Paul III himself had received his cardinal's red hat thanks to the sex appeal of his beautiful sister, who was the mistress of Pope Alexander VI, Ippolito's own grandfather).

The death of Julius III on 23 March 1555 marked the end of an era – for the Church, for Rome and for Ippolito. The voices condemning corruption and luxury at the papal court had grown louder and the reformers in the college were becoming increasingly influential. The mood in Rome was for a pope untainted by materialism and with the moral authority to spearhead the reforms that were long overdue. Once again, Ippolito entered the conclave as leader of the French party and as Henri II's candidate for election. He did not expect to be chosen himself but he was confident of his ability to engineer the election of an ally. However, things did not go according to plan. Over just four days of voting he was outmanoeuvred by his great rival, Alessandro Farnese, who secured the tiara for his old tutor Marcello Cervini, who chose the name Marcellus II. 'Tonight,' Ippolito wrote to his brother on 9 April, 'a pope has been elected whom I could not more dislike.'[23]

There must have been considerable relief at Palazzo Monte Giordano when Marcellus II died suddenly of a stroke after just twenty-two days in office. Another conclave, another chance: this time, once it was clear his own chances had gone, Ippolito outflanked Farnese, galvanizing the cardinals of the French party to support the election of Henri II's second choice of candidate, none other than the leader of the hard-line reformers, Gianpietro Carafa, who chose the name Paul IV. Ippolito had done his duty by Henri II but it was to prove a serious error of judgement. He should have known that the austere Theatine Inquisitor General would not follow the custom of rewarding those cardinals who had enabled his election. Aged seventy-nine, stubborn and autocratic, the new pope made it his personal crusade to root out heresy and abuses in the Church.

Ippolito was one of the first of several prominent victims of the new regime. Within weeks of the election Paul IV accused him of the crime of simony, in particular of trying to buy votes in the two recent elections. There can be no doubt that Ippolito was guilty as charged. We have letters to show that he entered both conclaves armed with money and promises to oil his quest for votes for a pro-French candidate: 25,000 scudi in gold loaned from his brother Duke Ercole, and French benefices worth a similar sum offered by Henri II.[24] Entries in his ledgers show that he borrowed 4,000 scudi from a group of Roman bankers who, it would seem, had confidence in his ability to influence the election: his ledgers record 1,700 scudi from three bankers on 2 April, three days before the opening of the first conclave, and then another 2,300 scudi on 4 May, three days after the death of Marcellus II.[25]

In late August, while Ippolito was enjoying the fresh air at his villa in Tivoli, rumours started to circulate in Rome that Paul IV was planning to act and a few days later he announced that Ippolito had been sacked from his posts as cardinal-protector and governor of Tivoli, and exiled to Ferrara, with strict orders not to travel via Rome. 'Having recently written a long letter to you in my own hand, I did not expect to have anything more to tell you so soon,' he informed his brother on 7 September, but several friends and members of his household had ridden out from Rome the day before 'to let me know that the pope is angry and has turned against me, that he has issued a brief to appoint another governor here and that I am to leave here without returning to Rome.'[26] He continued that, according to his friends, he had been accused of 'doing everything I could to manipulate the pontificate and to corrupt cardinals in every way that I possibly could, and your Excellency can imagine how strange and unexpected this seems to me', he feigned, all innocence, 'as I am staying in this place and attending to my health and living here so very quietly that I do not see how anyone can accuse me of such things.' It was with a heavy heart that Ippolito packed his possessions and headed home to Ferrara, his career in tatters. The year ended on an even worse note, when his beloved daughter Renea developed quinsy, a septic throat abscess that killed her in late November.

✳

Life in exile in provincial Ferrara, in the company of his brother and family, may not have been quite so exciting as the adrenalin-fuelled rat-race at the political heart of the papal court in Rome, but it did have other advantages. Ippolito's ledgers tell us much about how he enjoyed his leisurely years of exile.[27] There were regular banquets to attend in the ducal castle and plenty more to host in return: Ippolito held one party on an elegantly decorated barge in the river Po, and lost a precious silver platter that a clumsy kitchen boy dropped into the water.[28] He was able to indulge his taste for the chase, often with Ercole. There were fishing expeditions in the marshes of the Po delta – as Abbot of Pomposa, Ippolito owned most of this swampy land, which was famous for its sturgeon, and he had a boat specially made for the annual freshwater fish hunt at one of the towns on the estate. He bought nets to catch partridge, gave tips to villagers who found his lost falcons and bought quantities of herons and rabbits, which he used as bait to train the sparrow hawks, goshawks and peregrines – the latter were particularly prized and a pair of peregrines set Ippolito back 21 scudi, six months' wages for a master builder. Ercole gave his brother a falcon and a pair of peacocks, as well as one of the prized racehorses bred in the ducal stables.[29] He was inundated with presents of horses, hunting dogs and falcons, mostly from the nobles at the ducal court. During 1558 he received no fewer than eleven dogs, including two pointer puppies from a blacksmith, who was tipped 4 scudi for his generosity; and a local barber gave him a 'skylark that sings'.[30]

There was also much gambling in Ippolito's apartments at his palaces and villas, where he spent considerable sums on repairs and renovations – 1,163 scudi in 1558 alone.[31] At Baura, one of his villas on the Pomposa estate, his gardener planted a large orchard filled with fruit trees to produce peaches, apricots, pears, quinces, plums, medlars, mulberries, cherries and almonds for his dining-table.[32] He played a lot of tennis, one of his favourite sports, and rebuilt the court to make the game more exciting (this was not lawn tennis but its ancestor – real, or royal, tennis – a three-dimensional sport using the walls and corners of the court as well as the floor to score points off one's opponent). He had a billiard table made for him, at the cost of 9 scudi, to occupy some more of these long hours of enforced leisure.[33]

Ippolito made just one trip outside Ferrara during his four-year exile, travelling up to Venice for a few weeks in the spring of 1556 to join his cousin Bona Sforza, Queen of Poland and a distant cousin of Cardinal Sforza.[34] The two exchanged presents: Ippolito, on the advice of his brother, gave her a colourful parrot, with which she was delighted, and she gave him the magnificent present of eighty sables in return. Ippolito's tailor made new outfits in black silk striped with black velvet for the eleven pages and seven boy-sopranos who accompanied him, as well as new furnishings for his coach and a special set of hangings to decorate the gondola he rented to travel around the Venetian canals. The tailor also made outfits for the gondoliers themselves, and Ippolito gave them these expensive red satin tunics as presents when he left, which was rather earlier than he had planned because of a sudden and virulent outbreak of plague in the city. Ippolito himself had new outfits for the trip and, significantly, he chose to display his secular prestige on this very public occasion rather than his rank as a prince of the Church. There was no hint of ecclesiastical dignity among the items of clothing made by his tailor for the trip, which included a dark red velvet doublet, scarlet satin breeches and matching hose and a black satin cape, which had been lined with matching silk salvaged from an old cassock. And his hat, the universally recognized badge of social status in Renaissance Europe, was not the plain red biretta of a cardinal but the more elaborate headgear, ostentatiously trimmed with peacock feathers, of a secular prince.

The eight items of clothing made for Ippolito's Venice trip were, in fact, the only clothes his tailor made for him that year – a striking contrast to life in Rome, where the wardrobe staff might stitch the same number of outfits every month. Ippolito seems, very uncharacteristically, to have been cutting back on his personal expenditure. Apart from his boots, shoes, white linen hand-embroidered shirts and under stockings, all of which wore out quickly, he had few new clothes while in exile – when he got back from Venice the gondola hangings were recycled to make a caparison for his mule. His income had been reduced after Paul IV deprived him of his posts of cardinal-protector of France and governor of Tivoli. He certainly saved some money by living in Ferrara, where the cost of living was considerably cheaper than in Rome, and where the wheat, wine, firewood and fodder for his horses could all be sourced from his own estates, but he still had to find over 5,000 scudi to pay the annual salaries for his household. The financial situation worsened in late 1556 when Ippolito was forced by the pope to resign as Archbishop of Milan – and he exacerbated it by fighting for his rights in the law courts, thus incurring even more expense. In July 1557 he was obliged to pawn some of his silver and the following year sold another ninety-eight pieces, which had been given to him by Charles of Lorraine – it is possible, though the inventories are not at all clear on this point, that the cardinal's family had loaned him the silver for this purpose.[35]

Ippolito may have economized on his own personal expenses but he was well aware of the importance of keeping up appearances and it is clear from his ledgers that he made no attempt to stint on the cost of public display. His wardrobe staff were kept busy making plenty of new outfits for the household – he spent huge sums on costly textiles, including 300 scudi on velvets specifically for clothes for his pages, footmen and boy-sopranos, and 934 scudi on velvets, damasks and fringes for new sets of hangings to decorate his reception halls.[36] Moreover, he did not stint on buying lavish presents to curry favour with those in power. He gave the French envoy in Rome four pairs of perfumed leather gloves and sent three valuable falcons with silver hoods to the French court; an unusually large hunting dog with an elaborately studded silver collar went off to Cosimo I, father-in-law of his nephew, Alfonso, and four prized hunting dogs to Giovanni Carafa, Duke of Paliano and nephew of Paul IV.[37]

Above all, Ippolito's ledgers contain almost daily references to letters sent and received, a very poignant reminder of just how far he was from the centre of power. He made strenuous efforts to keep in regular touch with the gossip and intrigue of the papal court. His footmen made regular trips to Codigoro, a town near Pomposa where his letters could join the impressively efficient courier service between Venice and Rome. His post was often delivered in person by a certain Tortello, the official postmaster in Ferrara – in the summer, Tortello was also paid regular sums 'to buy melons every morning' for Ippolito.[38] The postmaster was handsomely rewarded for his exertions: in addition to the standard charges for the post itself, Ippolito gave him an elegant leather game bag from his wardrobe, ornamented with a red silk lining and silver clasps, and a pair of expensive perfumed gloves, as well as large tips for himself and his riders.[39]

The comforts of provincial exile were a marked contrast to the reign of terror that was unfolding in Rome under Paul IV and his unsavoury, unprincipled nephew, Cardinal Carlo Carafa.

Carafa, a hardened soldier with a reputation for debauchery, had abandoned his promising military career to take charge of political affairs for his uncle – his reputation was so bad that the pope had been obliged to issue a formal brief absolving Carafa of all his sins and crimes to date before he could bestow a red hat on this favoured nephew. Paul IV and Carlo belonged to an old Neapolitan family and detested the Spanish who had conquered their city: the 'sperm of Jews and Arabs' as the pope insultingly described them.[40] Using the discovery of a Spanish plot to poison the pope – a fiction devised by Carlo – Paul IV rashly declared war on Charles V, only to suffer a humiliating defeat when the Emperor's armies marched north from Naples and laid siege to Rome. The Romans themselves must have been grateful that the Spanish commander resisted the temptation to allow his soldiers to sack the city but the war caused real hardship. Prices of basic foodstuffs soared after the troops devastated the surrounding countryside, and pilgrims stayed away with disastrous effects on the local economy – like tourism today, Rome relied heavily on the trade these visitors brought to the city. The slump was further exacerbated by the oppressively heavy taxes imposed by the pope to pay for the war. Life in Rome was grim. Paul IV banned dancing and the bawdy, boisterous revelries of Carnival, one of the great pleasures of the Roman year. He expelled all beggars from the city and locked up the Jews, who were forced to wear distinctive yellow hats, to sell their properties and to move into his purpose-built ghetto. The ghetto, constructed on low-lying land regularly flooded by the Tiber, was completely inundated when the river burst its banks in spectacular fashion in September 1557.

Above all, it was the activities of the Inquisition that made Paul IV so very unpopular. Under its new general, Michele Ghislieri – a stern Dominican as rigid in his views as the pope himself – it embarked on a ruthless campaign to reform the morals of the city. One Roman noble was brought before the Inquisition for having a Jewish mistress; a bishop was imprisoned for having relations with a courtesan; a painter was found guilty of heresy for not painting a crucifix in the prescribed manner.[41] Inquisition officials routinely arrested not only those suspected of the merest hint of Protestant sympathies but also blasphemers, simoniacs, rapists, pimps and homosexuals, actors and buffoons, even those who failed to observe the ban on eating meat on a Friday. Paul IV took the unprecedented step of attending the Inquisition's trials in person every Thursday. Those found guilty were tortured, imprisoned or executed, and their property confiscated – one of the few entertainments left to the Romans was the huge number of executions they could watch in Piazza Navona and Campo di Fiore.

While Ippolito was in exile, the Inquisition drew up its infamous Index of Forbidden Books, a list of works which were banned as heretical. Ippolito's own library at Palazzo Monte Giordano was ransacked by Ghislieri's officials, who confiscated a large number of books, including works by Machiavelli, a Bible, tracts on Church reform by Catholic as well as Protestant authors, and his seven volumes of Erasmus's translation and commentary on the New Testament, all bound in gold-tooled leather.[42] Despite the fact that he never renounced his Catholic faith, Erasmus was a severe critic of the corruption endemic in the Church, writing forcefully and articulately about the need for reform, but his scathing censure of the Church authorities made him a heretic in the eyes of Paul IV. Ippolito was fortunate not to have been charged for possessing such controversial writings.

For Ippolito, waiting impatiently in exile and planning for the conclave that would take place when Paul IV died, reports of changes to the College of Cardinals were especially significant. In March 1557 Ercole's ambassador reported that the pope had created ten new cardinals, only two of whom were loyal to France. Among the other eight were Inquisitor Michele Ghislieri and Clemente Dolera, head of the Franciscan order who also served on the Inquisition. Two months later came news that Cardinal Giovanni Morone, a devout lay cleric of unimpeachable moral character, had been arrested on suspicion of heresy, imprisoned in Castel Sant'Angelo and banned from hearing mass. Although he was declared not guilty, Paul IV refused to release him. The pope also widened the definition of heresy to include all those guilty of simony. Ippolito must have been relieved to hear that the college had refused to agree to one of Paul IV's bulls, aimed flagrantly at both Ippolito and Morone, to deprive all cardinals convicted of heresy from voting in future conclaves.

Later that year there were reports of arrests on charges of heresy among the households of Alessandro Farnese and Jean du Bellay, and rumours spread that several cardinals themselves were under suspicion.[43] Giovanni Ricci, who had received his red hat from Julius III as a reward for financial dealings and who lived openly in Rome with his mistress and children, was sacked by the pope on the grounds that he was unfit to hold office. A successful businessman, Ricci had served as papal tax collector in Portugal where he amassed an impressive collection of Chinese porcelain with which he attempted, in vain, to bribe Paul IV to lift the charges against him.[44] Other cardinals were arrested on charges of seditious contact with Spain. Camerlengo Sforza, whose brother was fighting with the Spanish armies, was imprisoned in Castel Sant'Angelo though he was released after paying a fine of 200,000 scudi. Others were able to absent themselves from the city. The lawyer Medici, an outspoken opponent of Paul IV, seized his chance to leave Rome with papal permission – to cure his gout in the hot mineral springs at Lucca – and then failed to return to the city citing urgent family affairs. Ippolito's cousin, Cardinal Ercole Gonzaga, whose five illegitimate children and pragmatic views on Church reform might have attracted suspicion from the hardliners, had a more convincing excuse for avoiding Rome as he was acting as regent for his young nephew, the Duke of Mantua.

The reports got worse as Paul IV's pontificate, and Ippolito's long exile, stretched into 1559. In January came the dramatic news that the pope had sacked his nephew, Carlo Carafa, from his posts and exiled him from Rome. When Paul IV informed the cardinals of his decision, with tears in his eyes, he made no mention of Carafa's scandalous abuse of his position in the Church, nor of the invention of the Spanish plot to poison the pope that had led to war with Spain. What had shocked the old man who, despite his many faults had lived his entire life as a model of monastic abstinence, was the discovery of his nephew's sexual proclivities. 'He sins so abominably, making no distinction between men or women', reported the Cardinal of Lorraine, 'and a man such as this must be detested in the extreme for such monstrous and brutal acts.'[45] The pope sealed off his nephew's apartments in the Vatican and the gossip-mongers in Rome claimed that he intended the drastic step of driving out the devils inside with a formal ceremony of exorcism.[46]

At last, as spring turned to summer in Ferrara in 1559, reports finally began to arrive of the pope's failing health.[47] He was present in St Peter's for Easter mass on 26 March but looked very ill. In early May Ercole's ambassador reported that Paul IV was suffering from dropsy (heart disease) and had had to be carried in his chair to celebrate Ascension Day on 4 May.

However, he continued to attend the trials at the Inquisition on his regular Thursdays, and his doctors expressed their optimism that he would recover, though the ambassador was less sanguine. Ippolito himself must have been very frustrated: funds were running low and at the end of April he had been obliged to sell fifteen gilded silver platters, weighing over 6 kilos.[48] By the beginning of July there was amazement in Rome at how the pope 'keeps going, despite the many ills that afflicts his body and how his spirits remain high even though he is suffering from dropsy, with inflated testicles, failing kidneys, one leg so swollen and useless though they are trying to purge it, and a cough which is troublesome; nevertheless, despite all this, he remains optimistic and says that he will live to the age of his father, who had the same problems for twelve years and was 100 years old when he died'.[49]

Then, on Saturday, 19 August, came the news for which Ippolito had waited four long years – a letter from Rome, carried overnight by a string of horses and couriers, to say that Paul IV had finally died the evening before. More details soon followed in a letter from Ercole II's ambassador: the pope had been ill for several days with vomiting and diarrhoea and 'last night around midnight he got up to use his commode', he explained, 'and had a stroke and he was dead by sunset'.[50] Ippolito's exile was finally over.

Even in the dry records of Ippolito's account books, the sense of excitement is palpable. That same day, Saturday, he wrote several letters to Rome and sent his footman to post them at Codigoro. He then dispatched one of his courtiers to ride fast to Rome, giving him money to pay for post horses and entrusting him with 500 scudi in letters of credit for Provosto Trotti in Rome.[51] Trotti, an old friend of Ippolito's who had been left in charge of the cardinal's affairs during the years of exile, was instructed to use the money to prepare Palazzo Monte Giordano for the immediate arrival of himself and his household. He also wrote a terse note to his nephew Alfonso in France. 'When there is little time it is necessary to use few words,' he scribbled hurriedly, in his own hand, 'and you will agree', he exulted, 'that there could not be better news'.[52]

The weekend must have been impossibly busy for Ippolito's staff. They had less than forty-eight hours to prepare for his departure on the Monday morning and to pack all the items Ippolito would need in the forthcoming conclave. According to custom, the conclave should open on 28 August, ten days after the death of the pope, and there was no time to lose. Meschino and the other chamber servants assembled his fine linen sheets and pillowcases, mattresses and other bedding, as well as his towels, shaving equipment and his commode. Master of the Wardrobe Diomede Tridapalle took Ippolito's ecclesiastical capes, rochets and birettas out of store, and carefully wrapped his silver and other valuables, before packing the items into travelling chests that were fitted with strong padlocks. And the tailor must have spent many hours stitching a doublet for his master, using three metres of dark red silk from the wardrobe stores and two metres of fine linen to line what needed to be a very light garment for the gruelling journey in the steamy August heat.[53]

On Monday, 21 August Ippolito bade a formal farewell to his brother at the gates of Ferrara, where he gave alms to the poor, as was the custom – on this occasion he dispensed 4 scudi – and set off south.[54] He was accompanied by a small party made up of just six members of staff and their servants: his treasurer Francesco Novello; his chief valet Montino Priorato; one of the squires and one of the chamber servants, probably Meschino; René, his French chef; and Francesco, one of the *credenzieri*. These last two would be needed to prepare meals for Ippolito in Rome, initially while he was in residence at Palazzo Monte Giordano and later when he moved into the Vatican once the conclave opened. Also leaving Ferrara that day was Ragno, Ippolito's sommelier, who had the unenviable task of riding with the four heavily laden mules carrying all the clothes, furniture, silver and bedding packed in haste the day before.

With Ippolito gone, the rest of the household could concentrate on packing his remaining possessions – his tapestries, leather wall-hangings and paintings, his furniture that included tables, chairs, benches and beds, as well as all the household mattresses, sheets, pillows and blankets. It was a good time for sorting out – the wardrobe ledgers record over 300 items of linen – tablecloths, sheets, napkins and so on – described as 'too torn to be of any use and given out as alms for the love of God'.[55] The men also prepared for their own journeys south, travelling to Rome in several different groups and not expecting to arrive before the conclave began. The cost of moving himself, his household and his possessions from Ferrara to Rome was astonishingly high. According to his ledgers, he spent over 2,000 scudi on the move, a sum that was equivalent to half his annual salary bill and one that must have added considerably to his financial problems – his own journey, with six men and their servants, came to over 500 scudi, nearly a quarter of the total.[56]

The distance to Rome is 260 miles, a journey that would normally take over two weeks to complete. It took Ragno and the mules that length of time, but Ippolito's party were travelling fast, with regular changes of horses along the road, so were able to average some thirty-five miles a day and complete it in just nine days. On the second day they stopped for lunch in Rimini, where René the cook was sent off to a haberdashery shop to buy two cushions for Ippolito, who had felt the first twinges of an attack of gout on the journey.[57] The party spent that night in Pesaro, in the comfort of the ducal palace belonging to Guidobaldo della Rovere, Duke of Urbino and Ippolito's first cousin – the duke's brother, Cardinal Giulio della Rovere had already left for Rome. Ippolito seems to have spent two nights here, presumably so that he could rest and hopefully stave off the gout, which he knew would make the conclave a nightmare, and finally left Pesaro on 24 August, after handing out 6 scudi in tips to the ducal soldiers and musicians.[58]

That day, back in Ferrara, Ercole played host to their cousin Cardinal Ercole Gonzaga – both had been named for their grandfather, Ercole I d'Este – who was on his way south from Mantua bound, like Ippolito, for the conclave in Rome. 'This morning the Cardinal of Mantua arrived in time for lunch,' the duke wrote to his brother, 'we had expected him yesterday evening but he was delayed because the Po was so low.'[59] Three years older than Ippolito, Gonzaga had been a cardinal since 1527 when his mother Isabella d'Este bought a red hat from Clement VII for her twenty-one-year-old son. Despite his mistress and illegitimate children, he was a serious-minded man and a respected figure at the papal court. However, he was not a supporter of the French party in the college: he had served as legate to the Emperor and had been appointed by Philip II as cardinal-protector of Spain.

On 25 August – Ippolito's fiftieth birthday – he and his party arrived in Foligno, where they were met by Provosto Trotti, who had ridden up from Rome to honour his old friend with a larger, more dignified escort. At Narni, two days later, they were joined by another of Ippolito's courtiers and on Tuesday, 29 August they reached the outskirts of Rome, staying outside the walls overnight to prepare for Ippolito's formal reception by his fellow cardinals and his entry into the city the next day. There would be no peacock-feather hat on show at the Porta del Popolo on that Wednesday morning, nor fancy doublet and hose: Ippolito would don his voluminous red satin cape and his red cardinal's biretta to mark his arrival at the papal court – and his return from the political wilderness.

Rome

31 August–5 September

The sight of a red-robed cardinal making his ceremonial entry into the city escorted by a large cavalcade of courtiers and liveried servants was a familiar one to the Romans but it took on an added layer of significance during the *sede vacante*.* His distinctive red hat, which at other times served to identify him as a prince of the Church, now marked him out as an heir-in-waiting to the papal tiara, the future leader of the Christian world and the ruler of Rome. Ippolito's return after four years of exile would not have gone unnoticed – many would have recognized this influential figure and speculated as to what role he might play in the coming conclave.

Rome was stifling in the late August heat and the atmosphere was ugly. The *sede vacante* was invariably a difficult time in the city: with government offices and law courts closed, anarchy was never far away but the violence that had erupted after the

---

* The *sede vacante*, or empty throne, is the term used to describe the period between the death of a pope and the election of his successor.

death of the detested Paul IV was unprecedented in its scale. With the city in uproar, the nine days of masses and prayers for the soul of the dead pope – the *novendalia* – had been delayed and the services, which should have ended on 27 August, were still in progress when Ippolito arrived in Rome three days later. His cavalcade, guarded by a troop of armed papal guards, made its way into the city through streets swarming with cut-throats and rioters. There were soldiers posted at all public buildings and outside the palaces of the rich. On the Via Ripetta he would have seen the smouldering ruins of the palace of the Inquisition, where hundreds of prisoners – many innocent victims of Paul IV's harsh regime – had been freed when the mob torched the building after hearing the tolling of the great bell on the Capitol that had announced to the world that the pope was dead.

'The people were almost delirious with joy when they heard the news,' reported the French ambassador, the Bishop of Angoulême, Philibert Babou de la Bourdaisière, who had had a lucky escape from the violence:[1]

This morning they broke into the prisons and after lunch they set fire to the palace of the Inquisition which is next door to my residence and it was in great danger... I was with Cardinal Lénoncourt when the officers of the Inquisition sent news that their palace was under attack and asked me to give them all the help I could. I left immediately but I was too late and when I arrived there was nothing anyone could do because there were around two thousand people there and the fire was blazing inside and unfortunately there was a large pile of wood and bundles of sticks belonging to a wood merchant nearby and the mob set it all alight. When I arrived at my house I had an encounter with several men who had escaped from the prison. I told them very loudly that I was a servant of the French king and that I would not admit any Lutheran or any heretic whatsoever and they left.

Released from the reign of terror ruthlessly imposed on them by Paul IV, the Romans had indulged in an orgy of violence directed at the Carafa family, smashing their coats-of-arms and defacing inscriptions across the city. There were fears that the mob might even desecrate the pope's corpse so it was not taken directly to St Peter's, as was the custom, but transferred later to the basilica under the cover of darkness. There was no question of lying-in-state: Paul IV was hastily buried that night and two hundred armed soldiers were ordered to guard the tomb. The rioters vented their anger instead on the life-size statue of the pontiff that had been erected on the Capitol. 'They have destroyed the statue of his holiness,' reported the Ferrarese ambassador, 'they broke off the arm giving the benediction and then removed the head, smashed off its nose and beard and kicked it through the streets of Rome like a football', he explained, deeply shocked at this sacrilegious act; 'at one point someone dressed it in a Jew's yellow hat, and then it was thrown into the Tiber.'[2] Carlo Carafa, who had broken the terms of his exile by returning to Rome the moment he heard that his uncle was dying, had initially taken refuge in the palace of a fellow cardinal, Rodolfo Pio da Carpi, one of Paul IV's staunch supporters, but after two days he was forced to seek the safety of the Vatican where he joined his nephew Alfonso Carafa. Alfonso, who had been made a cardinal two years earlier at the age of sixteen, had been with his great-uncle during the pope's final hours and had taken the opportunity to remove gold and jewels worth 100,000 scudi from the coffers beside the bed of the dying man.

No longer silenced by the threat of the Inquisition, Rome's satirists had a field day hurling insults and poking fun at the Carafa family. Their verses, which appeared regularly, were posted on the 'talking statue' of Pasquino for most of the sixteenth century – and they were published in booklets, which were listed prominently on the Inquisition's Index of Forbidden Books. These *pasquinades* provided much entertainment for those who made the detour to the Piazza Navona to see what Pasquino had to say each morning. Certainly they were widely discussed – during the 1549–50 conclave, Pasquino made some disparaging remarks about Ippolito's health but 'despite everything Pasquino says about me, I am as fit as a fiddle as usual', he informed his brother, 'and the reason so much hair has fallen out of my beard is the terrible heat I suffered during the summer'.[3]

Pasquino's verses provided a cultural counterpart to the brutal violence of the mob – both were equally anarchic – and this irreverent flood of words was a distinctive feature of life in Rome during the *sede vacante*, the only occasion when the Romans had the liberty of free speech. Some were bawdy lampoons, others enraged diatribes; many were scurrilous or treasonable, and all were anonymous, though their authors could be found among the educated intellectual elite of secretaries and bureaucrats employed in the papal administration.[4] 'The big bad fox is dead,' opened one on Paul IV, while another listed the crimes of Carlo Carafa, 'ass, pig, assassin, enemy of Christ, sodomite, scoundrel and traitor'.[5] A third came in the form of an edict banning carafe-sellers from hawking their wares: 'Never again will they shout *caraffe* on the streets', a punning play on the hated family name.[6] There was also a 'letter' written by the dead pope to Alfonso Carafa, using the formal style of papal correspondence complete with the use of the royal 'we'. 'After a long voyage on 18 August', the day Paul IV had died, 'we now find ourselves in hell', it ran, 'where Satan has prepared a place for us at the sign of hypocrisy and tyranny, which well befits our talents.'[7] The pope reported that he had also discovered that a place had already been prepared for Carlo Carafa, 'at the sign of the goat', a reference to the cardinal's sexual proclivities. The letter concluded 'in haste, I will not say more as the great devil is choosing who to devour, but if I manage to escape his gullet, I will write to you again'.

The violence in Rome had begun to abate by the time Ippolito arrived at the end of August, but the hatred towards the Carafa family had been further fuelled with the latest instalment of a particularly offensive and gory scandal.[8] Earlier in the summer, Carlo Carafa's brother Giovanni, the Duke of Paliano, had discovered that his wife was carrying on an affair with one of his stewards – Pasquino, needless to say, made much fun of the cuckolded duke. Under torture, the steward admitted his guilt and this had provoked Giovanni into a frenzied attack: he stabbed the steward twenty-seven times and chucked the corpse down a drain.

Paul IV was informed about the murder and, less disturbed by his nephew's outrageous behaviour, wondered instead why the duchess had not been killed as well. Carlo too had urged Giovanni to act. 'He said that he would not be able to recognize me as his brother unless I erased the shame by killing the duchess', the duke later admitted.[9] But Giovanni was fond of his wife, who was seven months pregnant by the steward, and was reluctant to take this final step so Carlo turned to the duchess's family for assistance and they had taken matters in hand. On 29 August the unfortunate woman was murdered by her own brother and uncle, and all Rome was buzzing with the news when Ippolito arrived in Rome the following day.

Back home at Ippolito's residence, Palazzo Monte Giordano, there was much for his staff to do. There is some evidence that the palace had been attacked by the mob. Ippolito's ledgers record payments for lengths of cloth that were given to a carpenter to use for mending windows, and 88 scudi to a builder for repairs, a sum that suggests a substantial amount of work.[10] He also hired a captain and a squad of soldiers to guard the palace for the duration of the conclave, paying them 315½ scudi for the security they provided.[11] There are no references to any other kind of protective measures, so it seems likely that some of the armoury Ippolito had bought for the 1555 conclaves still remained in the storerooms: on that occasion he had purchased 40 lbs of lead, 12 lbs of gunpowder, 54 lbs of iron chain, four muskets, twenty-four halberds and thirty-six arquebuses – at just over 1 scudo each, the arquebuses were surprisingly cheap, well within the pocket of the Roman shopkeeper or artisan.[12]

With over a hundred men of Ippolito's household on their way south from Ferrara and a conclave to cater for, there was an urgent need to replenish the palace larders and storerooms. As the major-domo and the purveyor were still on the road, it was Ippolito's courtiers who, unusually, were obliged to do much of the shopping in Rome that August. Provosto Trotti was reimbursed for what he spent on oats and barley for the stables, as well as firewood and a large amount of pork fat, while others bought straw for the horses and supplies for the wardrobe.[13] It was also necessary to draw up a contract with a water-carrier to keep the palace cistern filled with water – there were very few wells in Rome and the water-carrier carted the water from up the Tiber in barrels. It was very menial work: he and his assistant shared the modest salary of just 16 scudi a year, though they could augment this pittance with jobs for other patrons.[14]

Despite reports of rampaging mobs and looters in the city, it is clear from Ippolito's ledgers that Rome's shopkeepers remained open for business. Trotti and Romei made arrangements with different tradesmen for regular supplies of meat, poultry and game, milk, fish, vegetables and fruit, as well as for candles, brooms, charcoal, glassware, metalware, glasses and terracotta pots – agreeing, on Ippolito's behalf, to settle the bills of all these shopkeepers every month. Most of them had their shops in the small piazza by the Ponte Sant'Angelo, just a short walk from the palace. There is a nice sense of continuity in the ledgers that reveal many of them – Antonio the butcher, Giacomo the greengrocer, Gianino the fruiterer, Battista the milkman, Luca the broom supplier and Domenico the candlemaker – were the same as those with whom Ippolito had dealt before he went into exile in 1555.[15] Other suppliers were further afield, such as the grocer's shop in Campo dei Fiori and the blacksmith in the Piazza Navona. There were also fewer regular purchases: once he arrived from Ferrara in mid-September, Ippolito's purveyor went out most days to the shops and markets to buy the game birds of which Ippolito was so fond, as well as more mundane items such as string and paper – that October, for example, he spent a total of 4,259 scudi on household supplies.[16] These excursions also suggest that it was not so very dangerous to be out on the streets, at least during daylight hours.

The bulk of the purchases recorded in Ippolito's ledgers in early September were for firewood, wine and wheat to restock the storerooms at Palazzo Monte Giordano, basic necessities that were delivered to the palace in substantial quantities. The first entry in the ledger detailing household expenses in Rome after

Ippolito's arrival was for eighty-four barge loads of logs and 1,500 bundles of sticks, at a total cost of 116 scudi.[17] Wine too was a major priority, not just for the household but also, as we will see, for the conclave. The bookkeeper recorded the delivery of some 573 barrels to the palace during September, and Ippolito spent 1,014 scudi on a particularly large delivery of 338 barrels, which he had bought from the Portuguese ambassador.[18] The bulk of the wine was purchased from Neapolitan merchants trading in Rome, who imported their wines from Ischia and Sorrento, which were subject to an import tax of three per cent that Ippolito had to pay to the customs officials at the port of Rome. The law courts may have ceased to function during the *sede vacante* but these bureaucrats were still assiduously collecting the dues that they charged on all goods entering the city – Ippolito also had to pay a tip of 10 scudi once all the crates, bales and chests containing his possessions arrived from Ferrara and had passed their scrutiny.[19]

The grain harvest had been good that year and the price of wheat in Rome in August was not much above average. During the famine in the winter of 1540, Ippolito had paid 8½ scudi a *rubbio* (a volumetric measure of approximately 200 kg) but in August 1559 the price of the first consignment delivered to the palace, which had been bought by Provosto Trotti, was just over 3 scudi a *rubbio*, affordable to all but the very poor.[20] However, with trade now halted in the Papal States for the duration of the *sede vacante*, the price would rise, and continue to increase until a new administration took office – it had reached 4 scudi by the end of the conclave.[21] Once he had arrived in Rome, the major-domo added to the palace store, filling it with 230 *rubbia* of grain that cost Ippolito over 750 scudi.[22]

One of the courtiers, perhaps Trotti, drew up a contract with a baker Benedetto for the supply of bread. The wheat was handed over to Benedetto in sacks, the weight of which was meticulously recorded in the ledgers – he was given his first sacks, 40 *rubbia* in all, on 26 August, several days before Ippolito arrived in Rome. [23] According to his contract, Benedetto had to arrange for the grain to be milled, though Ippolito paid the cost of this, and then use the flour to produce a range of different products.[24] He was to use the fine white flour to bake the bread for Ippolito's table and for the dining-rooms of his courtiers and officials, and to supply quantities of white flour, though of a slightly lower quality, for the pastry cooks in Ippolito's kitchens. He was also expected to bake batches of coarser brown bread for the lower levels of the household and, finally, to sweep up all the leftover chaff which would be used to fatten the chickens in the palace coop – even the rich in the sixteenth century took care to avoid waste.

Bread was eaten at all levels of society, in substantial quantities – one study has shown that an average of 1,150 grammes of bread (a modern sliced loaf weighs 850 grammes) was consumed every day by each member of Alessandro Farnese's household and this figure is likely to be the standard for the period.[25] The rich, not just the super-rich like Ippolito and Farnese but the urban middle classes as well, ate white loaves made from flour that had been painstakingly sieved to remove the bran. Even the urban poor could afford to buy cheap bread made from brown flour, though wheat was often beyond the pockets of peasants living in rural poverty who baked their bread from flour milled from broad beans, spelt, millet and even chestnuts.

While his household were busy on the domestic front, Ippolito was fully occupied with his official duties. He attended the daily masses of the *novendalia* in St Peter's, followed by meetings in the Vatican, made the customary rounds of visits to colleagues newly arrived in Rome and took his turn serving on the reception committees that greeted each of them at the Porta del Popolo. There was little time for pleasure and amusement but, after four long years in exile, it must have been a thrill to find himself back at the top table. His daily routine took him across Ponte Sant'Angelo every morning past the shops that lined the Via Alessandrina – which had been named for its builder, Alexander VI, Ippolito's infamous Borgia grandfather – and out into the great piazza in front of the half-finished St Peter's. He joined his fellow cardinals inside the basilica, its cavernous interior lit with hundreds of candles and torches that glowed through the clouds of incense, and afterwards they walked across to the palace for their daily meetings. Attendance at these meetings was obligatory, a feature of the *sede vacante* dating back to the Lateran council of 1179, when the ground rules that govern papal elections were established – and they are still largely in force today.

At the death of the pope, the government of the Church passes directly into the hands of the College of Cardinals – there is no deputy pope to take on the mantle of authority and ease the transition between one administration and the next. Although Ippolito and his colleagues did not have the power to formulate policy, there was a lengthy agenda of tasks to be performed: they were required to transact urgent Church business, to fix a date for the start of the conclave, to organize adequate supplies of grain and other foodstuffs in Rome, to liaise with the civic authorities and generally to ensure law and order on the streets. In particular, they had to make practical preparations for the coming election. They gave instructions to the papal master of ceremonies as to the location of the conclave and oversaw the veritable army of builders and carpenters, who now began the work of sealing off a section of the Vatican palace where they constructed the cubicles in which the cardinals would live for the duration of the conclave.

These meetings were chaired by Guido Ascanio Sforza who, as *camerlengo*, was presiding over his third *sede vacante*. His first task had been to smash Paul IV's piscatorial ring and destroy his seals – new rings and seals would be made for the next pope. He then made an inventory of the pope's vestments, jewels, gold and other valuables, and took charge of his papers that would be given to his successor after the election. Sforza also ordered new coins from the mint that were stamped with his own coat-of-arms and inscribed with the words 'sede vacante'. By far his hardest task was chairing the daily meetings of the cardinals, acrimonious and exhausting affairs that were in effect the preliminary skirmishes to the battle that would start in earnest inside the conclave. Often lasting over six hours, the frictions between the cardinals must have been exacerbated by the noise of the loud hammering and sawing, and the bawdy laughter, of the men at work in the halls nearby. Attendance was obligatory for all cardinals in Rome and the dynamics of the group changed daily as more arrived in the city and factional differences rapidly developed into hostile competition. Even the most banal issues were hotly debated as the cardinals lined up behind their leaders, and individuals opened their campaigns for the papal tiara.

At one of their first meetings, the cardinals voted by a very narrow majority – 13 to 11 – in favour of releasing Giovanni Morone from his prison cell in Castel Sant'Angelo, where the cardinal had been incarcerated for over two years on a trumped-up charge of heresy. They also overthrew Paul IV's decree banning this pious intellectual from being elected in the forthcoming conclave. Morone had evidently suffered in prison: 'His sight is so bad that he needs glasses and even so he can only see large letters, and this is because of the dreadful air in the castle.'[26]

More contentious was the issue of the Carafa family. The mood in the streets of Rome was for vengeance but the college voted against removing the cuckolded Giovanni Carafa from his duchy of Paliano, and returning this papal fief to the Colonna family from whom it had been seized by Paul IV. There were also calls to punish both Carafa cardinals, Carlo and Alfonso. Camerlengo Sforza had discovered Alfonso's opportunistic larceny of his great-uncle's money and jewels while drawing up the inventory of the dead pope's possessions. When challenged, the nineteen-year-old insisted that they had been a present and attempted to prove his claim by producing a letter apparently signed by Paul IV on the day of the pope's death – the cardinals were unconvinced but agreed that this issue would be best left to the judgement of the new pope. They also voted against the motion that Carlo and Alfonso should be deprived of their red hats, reluctant to set a precedent by acting so harshly against one of themselves. Carlo, very aware of his precarious position, went out of his way to show great deference towards the college at its meetings, treating the cardinals to the rare sight of him hiding his habitual arrogance behind a mask of humility. On 31 August they voted in favour of lifting his sentence of exile to allow him to vote in the coming conclave, a favour also granted to Ippolito.

Meanwhile, as more cardinals arrived in Rome, the divisions within the college were becoming increasingly clear-cut. At one level, these were political: sixteenth-century popes were not solely spiritual figureheads but also world leaders who occupied a central position on the European stage. Despite the peace treaty signed by

Henri II and Philip II six months earlier, it was evident that the long-standing Habsburg–Valois rivalry had not abated. The old enemies might have laid down their weapons of war but there were other ways of fighting. This papal election, like all the conclaves since 1500, promised to be yet another battle between them, and the daily meetings soon took on the character of preliminary skirmishes between the generals who would lead their armies into the field: Ippolito at the head of the French faction jockeyed for position with Sforza, who was leader of the Spanish.

PARTIES IN THE COLLEGE 31 AUGUST 1559

- French   21 cardinals
- Spanish   18 cardinals
- New cardinals   16 cardinals
- **Total**   55 cardinals

In addition to the French and Spanish factions, there was a third party consisting of the cardinals created by the dead pope who traditionally lined up behind the leadership of his senior cardinal-nephew – in this case, Carlo Carafa. Whatever we might think about nepotism, it was established practice in the sixteenth century and reflected the pope's need to appoint men he could trust to administer his regime.* Carlo was one of many papal relatives in the college – they comprised almost a third of the fifty-five cardinals who would be eligible to take part in the conclave: three grandsons of Paul III, including Farnese and Sforza, as well as two cousins and three men related to the Farnese family by

---

* The term 'nepotism' derives from the Italian *nipote*, which can be translated as either 'nephew' or 'grandson'. This practice of granting benefices, offices and revenues to close family members was outlawed by Innocent XII in 1692.

marriage, one of whom was Medici; three nephews and a cousin of Julius II; and the three members of Paul IV's family.

The divisions between the three parties were further complicated by the fact that each faction contained men of widely differing views on religious issues. This fault line was particularly evident among the party of the new cardinals, that included Inquisitor General Michele Ghislieri and Clemente Dolera, the head of the Franciscan order, two of the most austere and uncompromising members of the college, as well as the wholly unprincipled Carafa. Moreover, this party had become significantly more powerful in late August when Farnese and his supporters decided to join it. Carafa's judiciously humble behaviour towards the college had paid handsome dividends: his party was now large enough to play a key role in the conclave and he would have control over the choice of its candidates. Neither Sforza nor Ippolito had that luxury: they would be following the dictates of their monarchs.

For the Italian princes, the Venetian republic and the great monarchs of France, Spain and the Empire, the choice that the cardinals would make was of paramount importance. For the Romans too – though they had little say in the matter: the new pope would be their ruler and, even though he would pay his bills by taxing their bread, meat and wine, they hoped to profit from his lavish expenditure. On the streets of the city opinion was divided. Shopkeepers and the less well-off favoured the French, while the rich sided with Spain.[27] All but the most pious hoped for a worldly pope, dreading another puritan who would revive the terror of the Inquisition. The rulers of Europe had other priorities and did everything they could to influence the election, communicating their opinions in letters, written in copious quantities that August, to their ambassadors in Rome. And, despite papal legislation dating back to the thirteenth century that threatened excommunication for anyone guilty of interfering in the conclave from the outside, these rulers were to have a considerable influence in this election.

The first to declare his position was Emperor Ferdinand I whose envoy, Francis von Thurm, arrived in Rome on 28 August with instructions that the imperial cardinals were to follow the wishes of Philip II. This was not such a surprising move: the two monarchs had recently inherited the immense Habsburg realm of Charles V, who had died in 1558 leaving the German empire to his brother Ferdinand and Spain to his son Philip, who also received the provinces of the Netherlands, the duchy of Milan, the kingdom of Naples and the Spanish territories across the Atlantic. It was quite a coup for Sforza, however. He was now leader of all those cardinals who held benefices in all the Habsburg lands, not only the Spanish cardinals themselves, but also the Germans and the many Italians whose sees lay in the states of Milan and Naples.

Philip II's own preferences were not so clear cut. He was in the Netherlands when Pope Paul IV died, preferring to wait for the heavy summer gales that were lashing the English Channel to subside before embarking on his voyage home. So, it was not until 8 September when he landed in Spain, after a terrifying voyage across the Bay of Biscay, that he heard the news. Fortunately he had made arrangements for a conclave soon after inheriting the throne from his father, confirming Sforza's role as party leader and sending instructions to his ambassador in Rome to start preparing for the election of a pope who would 'work hard for the welfare and pacification of Christendom' and 'dedicate himself to the much-needed reform of the Church'.[28] Behind these platitudes, however, Philip II was very much a conservative – and he was to use very brutal methods to enforce Catholicism on his Protestant subjects in the Netherlands. Having excluded all the French candidates, in particular Ippolito, he had given his ambassador the names of three possible options: the Franciscan Clemente Dolera and Rodolfo Pio da Carpi, an Italian with benefices in Naples, were both hard-line reformers though Giovanni Morone, his third choice, was more moderate and evidently the king did not agree with Paul IV's judgement that the cardinal was guilty of heresy. Unfortunately for Sforza and his party, not only had Paul IV died but the Spanish ambassador had also just died very suddenly and the king, who received the news shortly before setting sail for Spain, had been obliged to appoint a replacement in a hurry. The new ambassador, Francisco de Vargas, was now on his way south from Antwerp but until he reached Rome it would remain unclear whether there were any new instructions from Philip II.

As the date of the opening of the conclave approached, it was Carpi who began to emerge as the front runner. Philip II's nomination of this fifty-nine-year-old, provided it were still valid, would guarantee the support of the Spanish faction but, significantly, he was also making headway in Carafa's party. Carafa's new ally, Alessandro Farnese, was a close friend of Carpi's. Moreover, during his term on the tribunal of the Inquisition, Carpi had acquired the reputation of being a formidable opponent of heresy, a factor much in his favour with Michele Ghislieri and the other hardliners among Carafa's party. Above all, Carpi had the backing of Carafa himself. Carafa's reasons for backing Carpi were entirely selfish. Issues such as

Protestantism or Church reform were irrelevant to his agenda: in the aftermath of his uncle's disastrous pontificate – and his own unscrupulous term as cardinal-nephew – all that mattered was his own survival. To avoid ruin he needed the support of the next pope; and the best means of ensuring this was to be the king-maker who engineered the election of someone who would be duly grateful. Carpi was the obvious choice for Carafa: despite owning an outstanding collection of pagan antique sculpture, which included several beautiful female nudes, Carpi had been close to Paul IV – it was his palace in which Carafa had sought refuge from the mob after his uncle's death – and he would reward Carafa for arranging his election.

Carpi, however, was anathema to Ippolito and to the French. Long-standing enemies of the Este, Carpi's family had been evicted from their small state by Ippolito's father in the early years of the sixteenth century, and over the years Carpi had done all he could to impede Ippolito's Church career.[29] Nor was Catherine de' Medici a fan of Carpi. 'You must do everything you can to stop Carpi becoming pope,' she informed her ambassador in Rome, the Bishop of Angoulême.[30] Writing in the name of her son Francis II, she also confirmed her intention to continue her husband's wishes by naming Ippolito as the leading French candidate for the papal tiara, a choice that must have had the approval of her protectors, Cardinal Charles of Lorraine and his brother Francis, Duke of Guise, whose wife was Ippolito's niece.

Catherine de' Medici also began canvassing on behalf of Ippolito. In a long letter to her cousin Cosimo I, Duke of Florence, she urged him to use 'the considerable influence that I know you have with many of the cardinals in the sacred college', and asked him 'to do all you can to have my cousin the Cardinal of Ferrara elected pope'.[31] She reminded him, in a postscript written in her own hand, of the recent marriage between his daughter and Ippolito's nephew, 'the alliance that exists between you and my uncle the Duke of Ferrara' – 'uncle' in the rather extended sixteenth-century sense that Henri II had been the nephew of Ippolito's sister-in-law Renée. Ercole, she was sure 'will not fail to do all he can to help his brother the cardinal' and she emphasized the advantages 'of having a man of such birth and standing on the holy throne'. The Cardinal of Lorraine voiced similar views, as reported by the Venetian ambassador: 'The world is fed up and disgusted with popes who come from lowly backgrounds and the Church badly needs a pope who is a prince by birth so that he will have authority with the cardinals as well as with secular rulers.'[32]

The other two French candidates were also from aristocratic backgrounds – more surprisingly, given the overwhelmingly secular character of the college, both these cardinals had been ordained as priests. The seventy-year-old François de Tournon, son of the seigneur de Tournon, was an Augustinian canon with a long career as a diplomat in the service of France and was a much-respected figure at the papal court. Catherine de' Medici's other choice was Ippolito's cousin, Ercole Gonzaga, a choice that astonished the Venetian envoy: 'I would not have believed this if it had not been confirmed by the Mantuan ambassador and by the duke's brother, who is here at court.'[33] Gonzaga was indeed an unlikely choice for the French crown. Not only was Mantua an imperial fief, but Ercole had served as cardinal-protector of Spain. However, he was also first cousin to Ippolito and Duke Ercole and it is likely that the cardinal, acting on the advice of his brother, had persuaded the dowager queen and the Guise brothers to adopt this unusual course of action. Duke Ercole may have been canvassing hard on Ippolito's behalf but he was also a realist. 'If fortune does not come your way,' he urged, 'you must do all that you can to support someone who will manifestly favour our house, and there is no one from whom we can expect more for our family than our cousin.'[34]

Ambition is a powerful stimulant and, despite the attack of gout he suffered on his journey south, Ippolito arrived in Rome full of energy. 'You will have heard about the slight attack of gout that I had on the journey but it was not so bad as to hold up me up for very long and now, God be praised, I am much better,' he informed his brother.[35] Another cardinal afflicted by this painful condition was Medici, who was Cosimo I's choice for the papal tiara. According to Duke Ercole's ambassador in Milan, Medici was seriously ill and would be unable to travel to Rome for the conclave, but this was wishful thinking on the part of the duke and Medici arrived in Rome on 1 September, the day after Ippolito.[36]

Ippolito himself was busy, working tirelessly on schemes to acquire votes in the coming conclave and, above all, to wreck Carpi's chances of election. 'On my arrival here,' Ippolito informed his brother, 'I found that Carpi's campaign was well underway but I hope I have frustrated his plans in such a way that he is no longer a threat.'[37] Ippolito's tactic was to exploit the divisions in the other parties over Carpi, who was not a popular figure in the college. In an attempt to influence the votes of Carafa's party, he urged his brother 'to show special favour and give all proper assistance' to Fabrizio di Sangro, a close ally of the Carafa cardinals who held a benefice in the duchy of Ferrara, 'so that he recognizes that he owes you, and thereby me also, a particular obligation'.[38] Duke Ercole had already canvassed his cousin Ercole's support when the cardinal stopped off in Ferrara on his way to Rome: 'We spoke together after lunch and I found him very well-disposed towards you and resolved to do as you suggested both in the matter of Carpi and the rest.'[39] Cardinal Ercole was not the only one of Carpi's enemies in the Spanish party that Ippolito was able to turn. In a cunning move that further complicated the complex webs of party loyalties, religious attitudes and personal ambitions, Ippolito persuaded Camerlengo Sforza, the leader of the Spanish party, that they should collaborate inside the conclave. They agreed not only to join forces to prevent the election of Carpi but also, in the event of Ippolito's own chances fading, to work together to engineer the election of Gonzaga and, if that proved impossible, for Medici. It was a plan that needed to be kept very, very secret.

From his seat by the Piazza Navona, Pasquino lampooned all the candidates mercilessly. 'Do not lose time, my brother, tell me what animal Jupiter makes them,' he was asked one day.[40] Carpi 'who burns with ambition and desire' was a chameleon, always ready to change his colours to win, while Gonzaga became the terrible dragon who kept a sleepless vigil over the garden of the Hesperides where Jupiter's golden apples were stored, an apt metaphor for the glittering prize of the papal tiara. Carafa, 'murderer and traitor', was a basilisk, a traditional Christian symbol for the devil, able to kill with a single glance, while his young cousin Alfonso was, laughably, 'an indolent giraffe'. Alessandro Farnese was changed into 'an artful elephant', an ironic reference to devious plans and clumsy execution. Bellay was a camel, 'quite clever'. Pasquino was not sanguine about Morone's chances: he was a serpent 'but sadly his poison will not reach the heart of his enemy'. Ghislieri, who was bony and grim from constant fasting, was transformed into a harpy, a hideous female monster 'with sharp teeth that will devour everything'. Cosimo I's candidate, Medici, was sarcastically described as 'full of German eloquence' and turned into a tortoise. Sforza became a vicious tiger 'who kills and destroys with bitter rage'. And Ippolito himself was 'a proud lion who roars so loudly that no one wants to go near him'.

Meanwhile, in the Vatican the builders and carpenters had finished their work in the halls where the conclave was to take place. They were now filled with wooden structures that would become the cardinals' cells. At present, they were all identical, their walls filled with padding and a pallet placed on the marble floor. Over the weekend of 2–3 September, Ippolito and his colleagues gathered together in the Vatican for the allocation of these cells. All the names of those expected to attend had been inscribed on slips of paper that were now drawn by lot from an urn and matched to the number of a cubicle – this was one of the very few occasions in a cardinal's career which he was unable to manipulate to his advantage.

The papal master of ceremonies then drew up a list noting the occupant of each cell – the list would be printed shortly after the conclave opened, although its details were common knowledge in Rome by the end of the day. Several positions were considered particularly auspicious and both betting touts and the diplomatic community took special notice of which cardinals had drawn the cells in the Sistine Chapel under the frescoes depicting Christ giving the keys of the Church to the first pope St Peter, and that of Moses handing the golden rod to Joshua – it was widely believed, with barely a shred of evidence, that these were auspicious omens.[41] We do not know Ippolito's opinion – though he was in the habit of consulting astrologers

– but on this occasion both cubicles were allocated to members of his French party, Niccolò Sermoneta and Federigo Cesi.[42]

In Palazzo Monte Giordano, Ippolito's staff had been busy with the more mundane preparations for the conclave. Ippolito's inventories include a list of fifty-two 'miscellaneous items for use in the conclave', a diverse collection of objects that had been left in store at the palace after the second conclave of 1555 in preparation for the next one. They were now unpacked, repaired and repainted, and clearly marked with Ippolito's coat-of-arms – the sixteenth-century equivalent of school name tapes. The staff also had to find missing items and commission replacements. There is no mention in the list, for example, of the voting desk that Ippolito would need inside the Vatican, nor of the pens, inkwell and paper that would be stored in its drawer. In addition to the special footstools, food baskets and rubbish boxes, the lamps, pots, braziers and fire irons in the list, Ippolito's staff also had to pack his clothes – ecclesiastical garb, of course – into chests, along with clean sheets, pillowcases and mattresses, handkerchiefs, plates, cutlery, silver and glass for his dining-table, and countless other items from his commode and his silver-rimmed spectacles to the needles and thread that the chamber servant would need to repair Ippolito's outfits.

MISCELLANEOUS ITEMS FOR USE IN THE CONCLAVE [43]

- 4 wooden food baskets, painted green
- 5 leather conclave bags
- 3 large stools, painted with the cardinal's coat-of-arms
- 6 small stools
- 3 wooden rubbish boxes for the conclave
- 3 iron braziers

- 2 brass dish-warmers for heating food
- 3 lamps made of crystal
- 1 base belonging to a perfume-burner
- 3 copper water pots
- 1 copper basin
- 2 wine coolers
- 3 earthenware ladles
- 2 brass snuffers for the candlesticks
- 2 wooden bases for the candlesticks
- 2 shovels for the fire
- 4 serving spoons
- 3 large earthenware water pots

Now that the allocation ceremony had taken place, Ippolito's household could start furnishing his cubicle in the Vatican. They had just two days to complete the task and must have been exceptionally busy because they also had to furnish those of the absent Frenchmen, who had no permanent staff in Rome to take care of this job. It seems likely that this was one of Ippolito's obligations as leader of the French party – we know, for example, that his staff outfitted the cells of the French cardinals in both the 1555 conclaves. The first task was to arrange for carpenters to fill the upper parts of the walls of the cubicles with shelves and cupboards of various sizes, all fitted with locks and keys, for the astonishing quantity of items considered necessary for a cardinal's day-to-day comfort in the conclave. In the 1549–50 conclave, when Ippolito had not been responsible for any of his French colleagues, it had taken four porters, making fourteen trips each, to transport all of Ippolito's possessions back from the Vatican after the conclave had ended.[44]

On Monday, 4 September the cardinals gathered in St Peter's for the last of the masses of the *novendalia* in an atmosphere charged with excitement in anticipation of the conclave that would open the following day. For Ippolito at least, the anticipation must have been tinged with anxiety. Only twelve of the twenty-one cardinals in his party had arrived in Rome: those missing were all Frenchmen, only three of whom had arrived so far. Robert de Lénoncourt had been in Rome when Paul IV died and accompanied Sforza to the Castel Sant'Angelo to release Morone on 21 August, and Jean du Bellay had arrived on 24 August. However, Georges d'Armagnac, who had made his entry on 29 August, was now seriously ill and confined to his sick bed, not well enough to enter the conclave. Ippolito received news that Tournon was on his way but it was not known when he would arrive, and there was precious little information about any of the others. Optimistic as ever, Ippolito requested that six of the nine absentees be allocated and he must have been impatient to hear news of their progress.

CARDINALS IN ROME ON 4 SEPTEMBER

- Spanish led by Sforza   16 out of total of 18
- New cardinals led by Carafa   14 out of total of 16
- French led by Ippolito d'Este   12 out of total of 21

Finally, late on Monday evening, Ippolito's French secretary, Abbé Jean Nicquet, arrived at Palazzo Monte Giordano with two letters from France. He had left the royal court at Villers-Cotterêts, north of Paris, on 27 August and, astonishingly, covered the distance of 900 miles to Rome in just nine days.[45] The journey must have been particularly unpleasant in the torrid heatwave that was gripping southern Europe. Another traveller across France that summer was the Venetian ambassador to Philip II, who chose not to travel from the Netherlands to Spain on the fleet specially prepared for the court but to make the trip overland. 'It was a very long and very tiresome journey, and I have endured worse disasters and inconveniences than on any other I have undertaken,' he reported back to Venice, 'due to the unusual and exceptionally high temperatures.'[46] He added that he was 'fed up with staying at uncomfortable and expensive inns' but at least he had avoided the dangers of sea travel. His staff, who did travel by boat, endured much worse hardships, with gales, men overboard and many so sick that they died.

The first letter, from Catherine de' Medici, was the formal announcement of the crown's wishes regarding the conclave – the king's choices of Ippolito, Tournon and Gonzaga, and the exclusion, at all costs, of Carpi. It also contained the information that the royal galleys had been placed at the disposal of the French cardinals in order to hasten their journey to Rome, though it made no mention of who exactly would be travelling.[47] The other letter was from the Cardinal of Lorraine, who explained his reasons for not attending the conclave: 'I would willingly have made the journey to be with you,' he told Ippolito, 'but the king has done me the honour of putting me in charge of his affairs, with which I am fully occupied, and his majesty has not given me leave to go.'[48] He continued, no doubt much to Ippolito's relief, with concrete news that four of the French cardinals were on their way. 'My brother, the Cardinal of Guise, will leave tomorrow by post, and Cardinal Strozzi left yesterday,' Lorraine wrote from Villers-Cotterêts, 'and they will be followed soon by Cardinal Bertrand and Cardinal de Meudon, and they will proceed to Marseilles', where they were expected to board the royal galleys for the voyage to Italy.[49] Ippolito must have been disappointed that Lorraine's letter made no mention of the other three French cardinals – Claude de Givry, Charles de Bourbon and Odet de Châtillon – who had been allocated cubicles that would probably remain empty.

Monday evening and the following morning were very busy. Ippolito had several long conversations with Nicquet, who brought more private news from the French court and, now that he knew that the French cardinals were on their way, Ippolito had to make plans for their arrival. He arranged for one of his valets to travel to Genoa, where he would meet the cardinals and their courtiers with horses, and then escort the party south to Rome – the valet spent a huge sum, almost 150 scudi, on the trip.[50] On Tuesday morning Ippolito wrote a short letter to his nephew in France. 'Nicquet arrived here yesterday evening and he has told me at length of how hard you are working on my behalf,' he wrote in gratitude to Alfonso, adding, 'I am awaiting the arrival of the Cardinal of Guise with great eagerness and although not many others are coming to help in this election, I am happy that Guise is on his way, as I am confident that just having him here will make up for all the others.'[51]

On Tuesday morning, 5 September, dressed in their red robes and all their official ecclesiastical finery, forty cardinals assembled in St Peter's to attend the mass of the Holy Ghost, the ceremony that traditionally marked the start of the conclave. They were seated strictly according to precedence by Giovanni Francesco Firmano, the papal master of ceremonies – or *magister caeremoniarum*, as he himself recorded his proper title. The College of Cardinals was, then as now, a hierarchical body in which the cardinals were ranked according to the titular churches to which they were assigned. Its most prestigious members were the six cardinal-bishops, who were ranked according to the precedence of their bishoprics; they were followed by the cardinal-priests, who were ranked according to their length of service, as was the third group, the cardinal-deacons. Ippolito belonged to the last category, as did Farnese who, as the senior cardinal-deacon, would have the honour of crowning the new pope. By custom, this mass was celebrated by the Cardinal-Bishop of Porto, who was Ippolito's enemy, Carpi. After the service was over, the cardinals lined up, with the master of ceremonies fussing around to ensure they were standing in the correct order of precedence – as we shall see, this official, who would be in charge of running the conclave, had a careful, almost obsessive, eye for this sort of detail. The cardinals now processed out of the basilica and, following the great ornamental papal cross, made their way into the Vatican. The crowds in the piazza in front of St Peter's watched the long red-robed procession disappear inside the palace – their next sight of the papal cross would be the announcement of the election of a new pope.

How long would the conclave last and who would be elected? Ippolito's first conclave after the death of Paul III in 1549 had lasted a gruelling seventy-two days, the longest by a considerable margin for several centuries – of the last twelve conclaves, only two had lasted longer than a week. There were fifty-five cardinals in the college and, strictly speaking, all had a chance of election, though only those inside the conclave had the right to vote. Insofar as anything could be certain, there were two certainties: the new pope would be Italian and over forty years of age, factors that excluded about half the college. Old age was not a barrier but ill health could be, though it could also provide an attractive interim compromise, giving the cardinals another chance at the papal tiara in the near future.

Tuesday afternoon was spent on official business. 'After lunch', the cardinals 'met in the Cappella Paulina to listen as the ambassadors of princes, prelates and the Roman barons all swore their oath of loyalty to the college', the master of ceremonies dutifully recorded in his diary.[52] Later that afternoon, the cardinals submitted to him the names of their conclavists, the men officially allowed to accompany each cardinal into the Vatican, though not of course to vote. Throughout the afternoon and evening the halls were thronged with people – footmen running last-minute errands, servants unpacking bedding and arranging furniture, agents picking up the latest gossip, and the ambassadors making sure that their cardinals fully understood the hopes, and fears, of their princes. There were also crowds of visitors, men and women of all classes curious to see the living arrangements of these great princes – on one occasion there was such a crush that a heavily pregnant woman had to give birth 'in public view' inside the Vatican.[53]

'Then at midnight', the master of ceremonies' account of the first day's events continued, having checked the names of the conclavists in his list, 'a group of cardinals were sent to check the rooms to expel all those unauthorized personnel found hiding in the palace.'[54] That task completed, the door to the conclave was now formally locked and Firmano pocketed the key. The election had begun: 'and I will not fail to let you know what happens', Ippolito informed his brother.[55]

3

❧

Inside the Vatican

6–20 September

Ippolito woke the next morning in the unfamiliar surroundings of the Vatican. He had been allotted cubicle number 35 in the Sala Ducale and it must have come as an unpleasant surprise to discover that Carpi was in the same room, opposite him in cell 16. For the foreseeable future he would have to eat and sleep in close proximity to his old enemy, separated from him by just the narrow passageway that ran the length of the hall. Although the noises were muffled by the padding that lined the walls of his cell, Ippolito would have been able to hear his neighbours as the snores and grunts of the night gave way to the sounds of hawking and spitting, and the filling of pisspots and commodes. Ippolito was woken by his servants, who washed him and dressed him in his ecclesiastical finery. They might have poured him a glass or two of wine in preparation for the day ahead, but breakfast had not yet become a meal in its own right – moreover, snacking (or grazing, as we rather appropriately term it) was considered to be the behaviour of animals, the identifying mark of the labouring classes or gluttons.

The daily routine of the conclave was rigid and demanding, and it is difficult to imagine a greater contrast to Ippolito's years of leisure in exile. The first official event of the day was mass and, on hearing the master of ceremonies ring his bell, Ippolito and his colleagues would crowd into the Sala Regia, from where they were summoned into the Cappella Paolina. They took their places on the high-backed wooden pews lining the chapel walls, which had been allocated by Firmano with his usual pedantic concern for precedence – Ippolito had Camerlengo Sforza on one side of him, and Savelli, one of Farnese's followers, on the other. After it was over, there was a brief break while the conclave servants cleared away the paraphernalia of the mass and laid out the voting table with its red cloth cover and urns for the real business of the day – the papal election. The master of ceremonies bustled about and, once everything was in place, he ushered the cardinals back into the chapel for the morning voting session.

Each cardinal was settled in his pew by his conclavist with his little desk, stocked with pens, ink and paper, in front – the wooden seats must have been hard and no doubt some cardinals brought cushions with them for added comfort. When all was ready, the master of ceremonies left the chapel and formally closed the door and the voting started. The cardinals returned to their cubicles for lunch and to discuss the events of the morning before returning to the Cappella Paolina, summoned again by the master of ceremonies' officious little bell for the afternoon's voting session. In the evening there was dinner, again taken in their cubicles, and the opportunity to scheme and plot for the next day's voting before bed. Firmano rang his 'lights-out' bell at 11.30 p.m., and the cardinals were expected to remain in their cells until morning.

On the first day of the conclave – Wednesday, 6 September – mass was celebrated by Jean du Bellay, Cardinal-Bishop of Ostia and senior member of the college. By tradition there was no voting this particular morning and after the service was over Ippolito and his colleagues moved back into the Sala Regia, where some no doubt remained for a time to chat and gossip, before going back to their cells for lunch. In the afternoon they were back in the Cappella Paolina, taking their places once again on the hard pews to deal with practical matters relating to the conclave. Ippolito had taken part in three papal elections in this chapel, with its decoration redolent of the power and wealth of the Church. On the walls above the pews were expensive silver statues of the apostles and dramatic frescoes of the *Conversion of St Paul* and the *Crucifixion of St Peter*, painted by Michelangelo to commemorate these two pillars of Christianity who had been martyred in Rome for their faith. Set high above the frescoes were large semi-circular windows, and it would be here that the great papal cross would be lifted to announce to the crowds gathered outside in the piazza in front of St Peter's which of them had been elected.

Staged entirely within the great halls of the Vatican against the backdrop of some of the greatest jewels of Renaissance art, sixteenth-century conclaves took place in a setting of exceptional splendour. Both the Cappella Paolina and the Sala Regia had been built by Paul III some twenty years earlier as part of his ambitious scheme of renovations in the palace to provide an impressive setting for papal ceremonial.[1] The massive hall of the Sala Regia, designed for the reception of kings and emperors, was regal indeed. Measuring 110 feet by 40 feet, it was crowned with a stupendous coffered barrel vault that reached 60 feet high and glittered with gilded stuccoes inspired by the monuments of imperial Rome, while the walls and floors of the hall were ornamented with multicoloured marbles pillaged from the ancient ruins of the city – it had cost the pope the enormous sum of 12,000 scudi.[2]

During papal elections, the Sala Regia took on the role of entrance hall and it was the focal point of the conclave. In the courtyard below, squads of Swiss Guards kept watch over the grand staircase leading up to the door that was the only means of access to the conclave. At the bottom of the staircase a team of four bishops, their purple birettas marking them out from the scarlet hats inside, had the onerous task of monitoring everything going into the conclave. Working two-hourly shifts, this episcopal team was on duty all day and all night, and they had their own sleeping accommodation in rooms specially prepared downstairs. One of their main tasks was to check the contents of the food baskets that arrived twice a day with meals for each of the cardinals (see pp. 117–18). Once these baskets, as well as letters and other supplies, had been closely inspected at the bishops' table, the goods could be passed into the conclave by means of two sets of revolving shelves, which the builders had inserted into the wall beside the locked door while preparing the palace for the election.

The ebb and flow of traffic in the Sala Regia echoed the rhythm of the daily routine of the conclave. Filled with noisy anticipation as the cardinals and conclavists crowded by the door into the Cappella Paolina awaiting the start of each voting session, quieter while these were in progress, with the master of ceremonies and his assistants going about their official business and maybe one of the servants sweeping the marble floors. The room was crowded again at meal times as the conclavists milled around, chatting and gossiping while they waited their turn to collect the food baskets from the revolving shelves. It was here in the Sala Regia too that the cardinals gathered at the door to listen to the ambassadors of foreign rulers who were permitted to make formal addresses to the college from the top of the staircase outside. The cardinals could have more private conversations at the door with ambassadors or family, though these were closely monitored by the bishops to make sure that there was no talk of the election. There was also an apothecary's store off the hall, filled with supplies of medicines, spices and wax, as well as a room for the conclave barbers – Ippolito, or his staff, certainly availed themselves of their services and they were rewarded with a tip of 4 scudi after the conclave was over.[3]

The Sala Regia provided access to the master of ceremonies' office, where he dealt with the general administration of the conclave, drafted official lists and documents, recorded the day's events in his diary and kept charge of the key to the door into the Sala Regia. It was his job, for example, to ensure that the candles were replaced in the glass lanterns that hung from the ceilings of all the rooms, and that there were adequate stocks of firewood for the fires that were lit when the weather was cold – not one of his tasks in the present heatwave.[4] He organized builders and carpenters to do any necessary repairs, such as replacing broken locks, resealing doors or mending windows. He also supervised the purchase of the white cassock, red shoes and other vestments which the new pope would don after the election – though there is no mention in his diary of the three different sizes of garments that are prepared today to accommodate the variety of heights and girths of the heirs-in-waiting to the papal throne.

As the focal point of conclave business, the cavernous Sala Regia cannot have been particularly comfortable or quiet for the seven cardinals whose cubicles were at the far end of the hall beside the doors – one leading into the Sistine Chapel and the other into the Sala Ducale – through which their colleagues passed several times a day. Cell number 41 had been allocated to Louis of Guise, who was still on his way from France, while next door in number 40 was Innocenzo del Monte, the toy boy of a besotted Julius III. Arguably the least worthy cardinal in the college, Innocenzo had caused further offence while on his way to Rome for the conclave by murdering two men, a father and his son, because they had offended him. Ippolito was not the only cardinal to be billeted next to his enemy. Camerlengo Sforza in cell 42 and his cousin Alessandro Farnese in 39 had been rivals since their teens when Paul III had favoured the younger boy Alessandro by making him the senior cardinal-nephew. Under the great gilded vault of the Sala Regia, so ostentatiously ornamented with their grandfather's emblems and family coats-of-arms, these two were now scheming for different parties – Sforza for the Spanish and Farnese with Carafa.

The biggest of the dormitories was the Sistine Chapel: at 130 feet by 42 feet, it was slightly larger than the Sala Regia and housed the cells of over a third of the cardinals. This famous chapel was normally used by the cardinals for attending mass with the pope on the major feast days of the Christian calendar, and its magnificence must have been somewhat diminished by its conversion to a dormitory – one contemporary likened it to a hospital ward, a prescient analogy as we shall see. It had been built in the 1470s by Sixtus IV, who had carefully chosen the proportions of the chapel to replicate those of the holy of holies in Solomon's Temple at Jerusalem.[5] The pope had also commissioned a team of artists including Botticelli to decorate the walls with parallel cycles of scenes from the lives of Moses and Christ. Resplendent on the ceiling above, though it would have been hard to see in the murky light of the conclave, was Michelangelo's famous cycle of Old Testament stories painted for Sixtus IV's nephew, Julius II, while on the altar wall was the artist's depiction of the Last Judgement that he had finished for Paul III.

Quite by chance, over half of Carafa's party had been allotted cubicles in the Sistine Chapel. They were easily identifiable from the shield bearing the cardinal's coat-of-arms that hung outside each cell. Moreover, by tradition the cubicles were colour-coded: those belonging to the cardinals who had been created by the dead pope were hung with vivid purple serge curtains, whereas those created by earlier popes were identifiable by contrasting dark green hangings. The hangings were thick, which must have been a welcome boost to privacy, though perhaps not so pleasant in stifling September. Serge was not as expensive as silk or velvet, but neither was it cheap: for his first 'green' conclave in 1555, Ippolito had bought six pieces of the stuff for 50 scudi, a sum that would buy over 500 chickens for his dinner-table, or pay the annual salary of a prosperous master builder.[6]

Among the 'purple' cubicles in the Sistine Chapel was number 5, which belonged to the nineteen-year-old Alfonso Carafa, the youngest member of the conclave; opposite him in number 46 was Bernardino Scotti, who at the age of eighty-one was the oldest. An old friend of Paul IV, he was one of three of Paul IV's hard-line reformers who had 'purple' cells in this hall. In cubicle 48 was Clemente Dolera, the Franciscan minister general, while Bartolomé de la Cueva was in cubicle 3. Despite his illegitimate son, Cueva was a close associate of Ignatius Loyola, founder of the Jesuits. Pasquino had irreverently transformed these three pious cardinals respectively into an ass, a pig and a wild boar caught in a hunter's net.[7] Also in the chapel was their party leader Carlo Carafa, whose cell 53 was next to the altar wall of the chapel, ironically below Michelangelo's depiction of the dead rising from their tombs in the *Last Judgement*.

Michelangelo's fresco had attracted controversy ever since its unveiling in 1541 – some praised it as a work of artistic genius but the majority detested it. The painting was certainly unconventional, not least because it broke with ancient traditions associated with the depiction of this sacred Biblical event. Where was the contrast between the safe order of heaven and the dangerous, frightening chaos of hell, or the comparison of the joys of salvation with the horrors awaiting the damned? The hard-line wing of the Church, determined to uphold Christian tradition, had vociferously attacked Michelangelo's interpretation of the scene and reviled its inaccurate depiction which, for them, verged on heresy. One critic wrote a treatise dedicated to Alessandro Farnese in which he analysed the painting and its accuracy, concluding that Michelangelo had put art before truth.[8] Even moderate progressives criticized the youthfulness of the figure of Christ and the shocking quantity of naked figures: it was even suggested that it would be more appropriate for a tavern or a public bath house.[9] Paul IV himself had demonstrated his dislike by commissioning a painter to cover the nudes with fig leaves and clothe several figures in trousers.[10]

Like the Sistine Chapel, a group of four smaller halls opening off the Sala Regia to the east were also converted into dormitories. In the Sala Ducale, a room used for the reception of princes and dukes, Ippolito and Carpi eyed each other warily across the corridor along with several other French cardinals: Tournon, Catherine de' Medici's second candidate for the papal tiara, would occupy cubicle 37 when he finally arrived. Next door was the Sala del Concistoro, where the pope normally held public meetings with the cardinals, with the cubicles of Ippolito's cousin Gonzaga (33), Giovanni Morone (18) recently released from his cell in the prisons of Castel Sant'Angelo, the Frenchman, Robert de Lénoncourt (32) and Cristoforo Madruzzo (20), Prince-Bishop of Trent and senior imperial cardinal, who would share the leadership of the Spanish party with Sforza. The Camera dei Paramenti, the antechamber to the consistory hall, now contained cubicles for Armagnac (30) once he had recovered from his malady and Lorenzo Strozzi (31) when he arrived from France.

The last of the dormitories was the Camera del Pappagallo, the papal robing room where the pope held private meetings with the cardinals – it was named after the parrot (It: *pappagallo*) that normally lived in the room in an elegant gilded cage. Its occupants included Giulio della Rovere (24), son of the Duke of Urbino who had been made a cardinal at the age of fourteen by Paul III when his brother married the pope's granddaughter; Pedro Pacheco (27), the seventy-one-year-old brother of the Marquis of Villena who had started his illustrious career at the Spanish court as chaplain to Charles V; and Odet de Châtillon (26), born into one of the grandest families in France – though his cubicle would remain empty during this conclave. Sleeping alongside these aristocrats in his hair shirt in cubicle 23 was Inquisitor General Michele Ghislieri, who lacked any drop of noble blood and had been a shepherd before joining the Dominican order. In a society where the walls that segregated the social classes were deeply entrenched, the College of Cardinals was perhaps the only institution in Europe where the rural poor could be found in such close quarters, and share the same status, with the cream of the aristocracy.

One of the real advantages of the Camera dei Paramenti and the Camera del Pappagallo was the fresh air that wafted in through the doors and windows that opened directly onto a long loggia, which all the cardinals were allowed to use for gentle exercise. With its elegant arcades decorated with classically inspired frescoes and stuccoes, and a panoramic view over the city across the Tiber, the loggia must have been a very welcome retreat from the stuffy halls in the sweltering heat of early September. At the far end of the loggia were the communal washing facilities supplied with fresh running water and lavatories. It was here that the conclave doctor had his surgery, and his bed; and he was expected to keep a watch on anyone – cardinals or conclavists – using this secluded spot to communicate with the outside world.[11] There is no evidence of the identity of the doctor on this occasion, but Ippolito's own medical advisor had been the official doctor in the 1549–50 conclave.

On the afternoon of 6 September, after enjoying a good lunch, the cardinals returned to their hard pews in the Cappella Paolina where the main business of that session was to agree on the voting methods they would use to obtain the necessary two-thirds majority to elect the new pope. The most common system was the scrutiny, each cardinal writing the names of his preferred candidates on a slip of paper and placing it in an urn; when everyone had voted, Alessandro Farnese as senior cardinal-deacon read out the names and counted the votes. It was a lengthy process as the cardinals went up to the table in the centre of the Cappella Paolina one by one to drop their ballot papers into the urn. Moreover, the practice of voting for more than one candidate made it difficult to achieve a two-thirds majority for anyone and inevitably prolonged a conclave – it was a tactic Ippolito intended to exploit to make sure this one lasted until his cardinals arrived from France.

Two methods could speed up the procedure. The first, introduced in 1455, was the system of *accessus* that took place immediately after the results of the scrutiny had been announced and allowed a cardinal to add his vote to those for a particular cardinal, and this was especially useful when only one or two votes were needed for election. It was also possible to elect a pope by homage, or 'acclamation', whereby a candidate was announced and his supporters did homage by kissing his foot until the required number had been reached – or not. This could be very exciting theatre. It was crucial to build up momentum in the chapel and, as the magic number approached, members of other parties could be tempted to change sides, and the undecided to take the plunge – both of the conclaves held in 1555 had been resolved in this way. It did, however, tend to be noisy and tempestuous, quite unlike the decorous formality of the scrutiny.

PARTIES ON 6 SEPTEMBER

- Spanish led by Sforza and Madruzzo   16 votes
- New cardinals led by Carafa and Farnese   13 votes
- French led by Ippolito d'Este   11 votes

two-thirds majority needed: 27 votes

That afternoon, while the cardinals debated whether to allow election by acclamation, several members of the Spanish party enacted the correct procedure to be followed for the benefit of those cardinals attending their first conclave by kneeling in turn in front of Carpi. Initially, this appeared to be nothing more than an exercise. But when Carafa's cardinals followed suit, it suddenly became clear to Ippolito and his supporters that this was not some theoretical demonstration but a very real, and extremely underhand, attempt to take advantage of the absence of so many of the French and elect the one pope Ippolito dreaded above all others. In the ensuing uproar it took some time to work out that the attempt had failed. Ippolito had been caught out by an elementary mistake – and it must have been all the more infuriating because he had been warned that something like this could happen. 'It will not be hard, before our cardinals arrive,' Catherine de' Medici had written to Ambassador Angoulême, no doubt on the advice of the Cardinal of Lorraine, for the opposition 'to launch a major coup to elect and create a pope.'[12] Moreover, Ippolito owed his lucky escape to Sforza who, despite being the leader of the Spanish faction, had kept to the bargain the two men had struck before the conclave opened to do all he could to scupper Carpi's election.

After the excitement of that first afternoon, an extraordinary lethargy took hold of the conclave. For the following three days – Thursday, Friday and Saturday – the cardinals remained bogged down in procedure. They listened to the master of ceremonies as he laboriously outlined the minutiae of conclave ritual and explained all the rules governing secrecy.[13] It was forbidden, for example, to write or receive 'letters or messages written on slips of paper', though few of the cardinals observed this particular rule – all Ippolito's letters to Duke Ercole are explicitly signed 'di conclave', from the conclave. Firmano warned that they were forbidden to leave the conclave for any reason except serious illness, in which case they would be formally escorted back to their palaces by a detachment of the Swiss Guards. 'Nor is anyone else allowed to enter the conclave apart from those men who are needed to do necessary work.'

There were strict regulations limiting the number of people accompanying each cardinal into the conclave – the so-called 'conclavists'. According to the bull of Gregory X (1274), they were allowed just two conclavists, though they could also have a doctor if ill enough to require one. This rule had been reinterpreted over the centuries – by the sixteenth century 'three' had become the new 'two': as Firmano cryptically recorded on the official printed record of the conclave, they could have 'two servants to administer to their needs, or rather three as it is now understood'.[14] One of Gregory X's more drastic measures designed to force the conclave into agreement was starvation. If no pope was elected after three days, he had ordered that the cardinals were to be restricted to just one course for each meal, and after eight days only bread, water and wine were to be allowed into the palace. As no proper voting had taken place, apart from the failed attempt to elect Carpi, Firmano was persuaded not to enforce either of these regulations, for the present at least. This must have been welcome news for those like Ippolito who relished good food and wine, though the more ascetic cardinals, like the Dominican Ghislieri and the Franciscan Dolera, would probably not have minded one way or the other (see p. 114).

It was unusual for these procedural issues to take so long to resolve and it is likely that Ippolito and his French party were partly to blame for the delay. The weather also played its part: it was very hot and humid and the Cappella Paolina, with its great semi-circular windows sealed from the air but not from the sunlight, became intolerably stuffy by midday. When Tournon arrived in the conclave on Friday, 8 September he found that his colleagues were waiting until early evening, 'an hour before sunset' as the master of ceremonies recorded, to start their daily meeting in the chapel.[15] Armagnac had recovered from his malady and he too had taken up residence in the Vatican. But the addition of these members of his party coincided with worries about the health of two others: Bellay and Federigo Cesi had both been too weak to make the short walk into the Cappella Paolina that afternoon to swear to uphold the election capitulations. Firmano had been obliged to visit them in their cells, with three cardinals acting as witnesses, to hear them take the oath from their sick beds.

It was not until Saturday, 9 September that the cardinals finally gathered in the Cappella Paolina for the final ritual of the conclave preliminaries, the reading of the bull of Julius II governing papal elections, which had been published in 1510 to halt the practice of buying votes in the conclave – the method by which Ippolito's Borgia grandfather had notoriously secured the papal tiara for himself. Threatening the severest penalties for cardinals implicated in simony, it had been read out at every conclave since its publication, and it had been largely ignored on every occasion – and this election too, as we shall see, was to follow exactly the same pattern. That Saturday afternoon, voting finally started, and then it stopped the next day as no scrutinies were held on the Sabbath. It had taken the cardinals nearly a week to get through the preliminaries. In 1534 Paul III had been elected after just two days inside the Vatican, while the two conclaves held in 1555 had lasted only four and eight days respectively.

As the voting got properly underway in the second week of September, it was evident that the number of names emerging from the voting urns was abnormally high. Out on the streets of Rome there were rumours that as many as twenty cardinals had a good chance of election, and that 'this was causing friction and a considerable degree of disagreement between them'.[16] Ippolito was certainly one of those guilty of this old delaying tactic, informing Duke Ercole that the proliferation of candidates was 'making it possible to drag these negotiations out for as long as one wanted before coming to agreement on the creation of a pope'.[17] As he explained: 'So far I have concentrated on avoiding the election of Carpi... and now it is a question of prolonging the conclave until Guise arrives.' He added, with a hint of desperation, 'I know there is little you can do to help me in this, except to pray to God on whom everything depends in the end, though his divine majesty works with the instrument of men.'

VOTES CAST IN THE SCRUTINIES ON 11 SEPTEMBER[18]

- Cueva   17
- Pacheco   12
- Tournon   9
- Gonzaga   5
- Cicada   5
- Puteo   5
- Crispi   4
- Carpi   4
- Rebiba   4
- Madruzzo   4
- Lénoncourt   4
- Saraceni   3
- Farnese   3
- Cesi   3
- Este   3
- Savelli   3
- Scotti   3
- Dolera   3
- Dandino   2
- Pisani   2

- Diomede Carafa   2
- Ghislieri   2
- Bellay   2
- Capodiferro   2
- Sforza   2
- Ricci   2
- Medici   2
- Cristoforo del Monte   2
- Truchsess   2
- Suau   1
- Alfonso Carafa   1
- Corner   1
- Vitelli   1
- Corgna   1
- Portugal   1

PARTIES ON 11 SEPTEMBER

- Spanish led by Sforza and Madruzzo   17 votes
- New cardinals led by Carafa and Farnese   13 votes
- French led by Ippolito d'Este   13 votes

two-thirds majority needed: 29 votes

On 11 September, as many as thirty-five cardinals received the votes of their colleagues, an unusually high number that reflected the laudable practice of voting for the elderly and high-regarded figures in the college, a gesture that did them the honour of a respectable vote count. The seventy-four-year-old Frenchman Robert de Lénoncourt, for example, received eighteen votes at one scrutiny, while the Spanish grandee Pedro Pacheco got fifteen at another.[19] However, this practice could on occasion cause problems. The attempt to honour the pro-Jesuit Bartolomé de la

Cueva, the sixty-year-old brother of the Duke of Albuquerque, very nearly resulted in his being elected pope. On the afternoon of Monday, 11 September one of the French cardinals, Girolamo Capodiferro, was in the Sala Regia, chatting to some of the new cardinals in Carafa's party while waiting to go into the Cappella Paolina for the scrutiny. On asking who they intended to vote for, he was surprised when they all named Cueva. Surprise turned to alarm when he received the same answer from several other cardinals and he informed Ippolito of his suspicion that it might not be a plan to show respect to Cueva but one to elect him. Capodiferro had indeed discovered a plot, engineered by imperial ambassador Thurm, who claimed to have had promises of thirty-two votes for Cueva. Ippolito circumvented the conspiracy by demanding a secret scrutiny, thus allowing those cardinals who had promised their votes with the intention of honouring Cueva to change their minds in the privacy of their ballot papers – Thurm had good reasons for judging Ippolito to be 'one of the deftest diplomats France ever had'.[20]

It must have been a relief to Ippolito when Guise and Strozzi finally entered the conclave on the evening of Wednesday, 13 September – it had taken them seventeen days to complete the journey from Paris to Rome. Unfortunately, Jean Bertrand had been unable to reach Marseilles in time to board the royal galley: aged seventy-seven and not in the best of health, he nevertheless decided to undertake the arduous journey overland, which would take him at least a month. With his close ties to the French crown, Guise now became Ippolito's second-in-command. 'The arrival of Guise has galvanized and cheered us,' Ippolito's conclavist informed Ercole's ambassador, 'and, though things could be better, we know that even if we cannot do what we want, we shall at least be able to stop others doing what they intend', he added in a coded reference to Carafa and Carpi.[21] Despite their failure to elect Carpi by homage the previous week, it was clear that Carafa, Farnese and the Spanish had not given up campaigning for their candidate.

Over the three days, 15–17 September, the cardinals watched a curious scene staged in the Cappella Paolina. On the first day, Friday, it was decided to reopen the case against Morone and to take a vote on the issue, which resulted, yet again, in Morone being acquitted on all charges of heresy. Reopening the case in itself was odd: not only had the formal trial by the Inquisition already declared Morone innocent of all charges but the cardinals themselves had already agreed on his innocence a month before when they voted to release him from the dungeons of Castel Sant'Angelo. Nor is it clear who suggested this blatant attempt to discredit Morone, who was one of the candidates favoured by Philip II, though the finger points at Carafa. When they gathered in the chapel on Saturday morning, one of Carafa's cardinals, Vitellozzo Vitelli, announced that he had spent the previous evening restudying the documents of the case and was not satisfied with the verdict that had been reached. Carpi immediately stood up to defend Morone. According to the Roman newssheets, he retorted angrily to Vitelli 'what you studied last night, I studied thirty years ago and a man of such standing as Morone should not be treated in this way'.[22]

On the Sunday, Morone himself, acting with considerably more dignity than either Vitelli or Carpi, read out a statement in which he thanked the cardinals for releasing him from Castel Sant'Angelo and for allowing him to take part in the election but, recognizing that many were opposed to his presence, he asked permission to leave the conclave. Supported by a majority of those in the chapel, Bellay refused to accept his resignation but it was clear that Morone's chances were over. The question is *cui bono* – who benefitted from this extraordinary manoeuvre? Carpi, certainly, but also Carafa. By his prompt and robust defence of the highly respected Morone, Carpi had certainly improved his chances of election. For Carafa's part, he had succeeded in eliminating the one Spanish candidate who, after having been locked up by Paul IV for two years in the dungeons of Castel Sant'Angelo, was very unlikely to favour him or his family. Carafa must also have hoped that some of those cardinals who would have voted for Morone would now give their votes to the candidate who had so soundly championed Morone's cause, Carpi – it was not the fairest of play, but it was effective.

Over the next few days Carpi's campaign began to gather pace and Ippolito countered with a bid of his own. On Sunday night, according to the Mantuan ambassador, Ippolito 'began his own campaign with great vigour, and he stormed about for the whole of the next day, even though everyone knows his election is an impossibility'.[23] Whether Ippolito was making a serious attempt at his own election is debatable but it was absolutely essential for the French to make a public display of the strength of their opposition to Carpi. The atmosphere in the Vatican must have been electric on the morning of Wednesday, 20 September when it was discovered that Armagnac had suffered a relapse overnight and was so seriously ill that he had left the conclave to return to his palace in Rome. By lunchtime, the conclave was buzzing with rumours that Carpi was to be elected by homage during the afternoon voting session. In the event, Carpi and Carafa backed down that day but 'it could have been really dangerous', the Mantuan ambassador concluded, 'though the frenzy has now largely abated'. This attempt might have failed but Carpi's bid for the papal tiara was far from over.

Back in his cubicle, Ippolito reported his account of the events of the last few days to his brother: 'I have had your letter and the coded one you sent to your ambassadors,' Ippolito wrote, full of gratitude for all he was doing for him.[24] He denounced the 'evil disposition' of Carafa's 'character and nature' and informed the duke that 'I am keeping a close eye on Carpi about whom rumours are flying around in here and in the city... however, I have never been afraid of him, and I am not frightened now, and I hope that he ends up with his hands full of air'. What Ippolito had learned, however, was that the French party would have a say in the election: he might not have rated his own chances but he was confident that 'at least it will not be possible to elect a pope without us, indeed that our party will play a large part in it'.

4

❦

Cubicle Life

In their headquarters in Ippolito's cubicle in the Sala Ducale, the French party schemed and planned, with a man on guard outside to dissuade eavesdroppers – especially those who might take advantage of the empty cell next door, which had been allocated to the absent Bourbon. Inside, the atmosphere emanated luxury and wealth – Ippolito, as ever, went out of his way to impress his guests with material evidence of his considerable prestige. Ushered in by the guard from the dim corridor outside, they entered a brightly lit space, sweet with the aroma of expensive white candles made from beeswax and the scent of costly fragrant resins issuing from the perfume-burner. There is no record of the purchase of these candles in his ledgers, so it is likely that he had brought a large supply of quality Venetian beeswax with him from Ferrara – during the 1549–50 conclave he spent over 107 scudi on white wax in the apothecary shops in Rome in a single month.[1] Beeswax was expensive: it cost four times the price of tallow, the wax made from animal fats that was used by most people. The candles in the Cappella Paolina

81

were white wax but it was tallow that lit all the other conclave halls as well as the communal washing facilities down at the end of the loggia.[2] The unpleasantly greasy and rancid smell left by the yellow tallow must have permeated the conclave, and made Ippolito's cubicle all the more inviting to his guests.

At 13 feet by 11 feet, the cubicle was not large but the bare wooden structure had been transformed into a sumptuous tent, with carpets on the floor and walls festooned with lengths of costly green silk to match the green serge on the outside. Ippolito's staff had covered the walls with 200 yards of silk – the total length of the wall space measured just 16 yards, which gives some idea of how thickly these curtains were draped, and a further 50 yards of the material had been used for the ceiling canopy.[3]

With the beeswax candles burning in silver candlesticks, the guests took their seats on comfortably cushioned wooden stools – Ippolito owned ninety-one cushions, made of taffeta, damask, velvet, satin or cloth-of-gold, even leather, some perfumed and others lavishly encrusted with pearls.[4] His men offered sweetmeats from gilded silver plates, and poured wine from silver carafes hung with chains bearing his coat-of-arms into elegant gilded silver cups engraved with leaves and birds.[5] There was little evidence of the religious nature of the occasion – Ippolito does not appear to have brought any devotional images into the Vatican, though one of his missals was covered with red velvet in early October, perhaps for the conclave.[6] Significantly, he had made no attempt to replicate the visual effect of his palace interiors: there were no tapestries, for example, nor any of the sets of gilded leather wall-hangings that ornamented his rooms at Palazzo Monte Giordano; nor were there any of his antique statues and *objets d'art* – just the gilded silver, in conspicuously large quantities.

There was an amazing amount of stuff inside this tiny conclave cell – Ippolito was fortunate that Bourbon's cubicle next door was empty and provided him with extra storage space. In addition to the scrutiny desk, the food basket, the perfume-burner, the silver, the various pieces of the bed, the ladder, the chests of clothes and the commode, space also had to be found inside the cubicle for larger items such as Ippolito's nine footstools, all painted green and decorated with his coat-of-arms, wooden buckets for rubbish and copper basins for washing. The overhead lockers were filled with supplies of every kind, luxurious and utilitarian – clean bedding, writing paper, boxes of sweets to offer guests, bundles of beeswax candles, a sewing kit for Ippolito's servant to mend his clothes, cleaning rags, a dustpan and brush, fire irons, a wine cooler, cups, plates, dishes, glasses and cutlery, and probably one of the three clocks he owned, though perhaps not his hour glass.[7]

It is evident from other sources that Ippolito was not alone in cramming his cubicle with equipment and furnishings – a good conclave servant must have had a cabin-trunk mentality, and would have had to work hard to keep the place clean and tidy. An earlier master of ceremonies, Paris de Grassis, made a list of the items a cardinal would need inside his cubicle:[8]

The following are to be brought to the conclave by the cardinals: two food baskets, one of which will be in the conclave, the other outside; green serge hangings to cover the walls and ceiling, in purple for those cardinals created by the dead pope; one portable couch 6 x 3.5 feet; the cardinal's bed with its bedding; two wooden boards and bedding for the conclavists, who will sleep on the floor of the cardinal's cubicle; one trestle table 3.5 feet long; two pisspots; one commode; two napkins for the cardinal's dining-table; two cloths for the cardinal's table; two napkins for the conclavists; two or more pieces of cloth for wiping lamps; three carpets for the floor; one box for the cardinal's clothes, and shirts, surplices, towels for washing the face and handkerchiefs; one coat, or rather cloak with its cap; sweetmeats, biscuits, cakes, cookies, march panes, and a loaf of sugar; one inkwell with its set of cutters, pens, ink and red wax; one ream of writing paper; jug, bowl, cups, dishes, small dishes, plates, one salt cellar filled with salt, knives and bread knives for the cardinal's table... two water bowls and a stone for washing, one or two brooms, one dustpan, one small ladder, a hammer, keys, string, needle and thread; the Decretals of Gratian, of Gregory IX, of Boniface VIII and Clement V, and other books of the cardinal's choice, breviary, missal and... clock, bed cap and nightshirt.

Despite the grand furnishings, living conditions in all the cubicles must have been astonishingly cramped. It was not just the cardinal who occupied the space but also his conclavists as well as a menial servant, all of whom slept in the room, ate their meals here, and washed and dressed and used the commode. The Dominican Ghislieri and the Franciscan Dolera might have been used to life in a spartan monastic cell but rich aristocrats like Ippolito and Guise, or Farnese and Sforza, were all accustomed to a suite of four or five large rooms, with their own bathroom and an army of servants to look after their needs. After his evening guests had left, Ippolito's cubicle had to be refitted for the night, the task of Meschino, or whichever of the chamber servants was on duty that day in the conclave. He made up Ippolito's bed, draping it with more green silk

Anon, *Cardinal Ippolito d'Este*, 1537 (Liverpool, Walker Art Gallery). Grandson of the Borgia pope Alexander VI (1492–1503), Ippolito used his family contacts and powerful friends to establish himself as one of the most influential figures at the papal court in mid sixteenth-century Rome.

'From the Conclave on the 16 December 1559', written in Ippolito's own idiosyncratic and untidy scrawl.

Niccolò dell'Abate, *Ercole II d'Este* (Private Collection). Ippolito was close to his elder brother Ercole. The two hunted together, jousted against each other, played tennis, gambled, gossiped and squabbled; and Ercole was Ippolito's most loyal ally in the race for the papal tiara.

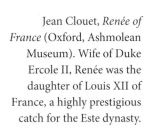

Jean Clouet, *Renée of France* (Oxford, Ashmolean Museum). Wife of Duke Ercole II, Renée was the daughter of Louis XII of France, a highly prestigious catch for the Este dynasty.

Der Bapst kan allein auslegen
Die Schrifft : und irthum ausfegen
Wie der Esel allein pfeiffen=
Kan : und die noten recht greiffen;
Mart. Luth. D. 1545.

Paul III as an ass playing the bagpipes, 1545 (London, British Museum), attributed to Martin Luther. The printing press provided the Protestant reform movement with a powerful and cheap means of disseminating its criticism of the abuses in the Church, not least the dynastic ambitions of several Renaissance popes.

Francesco Rossi, *Cardinal Rodolfo Pio da Carpi*, c.1545 (Vienna, Kunsthistorisches Museum). The intense dislike that existed between Ippolito and Cardinal Carpi had its origins in a dispute between the two families but came to a head during Ippolito's years in France owing to Carpi's jealousy of his high standing with Francis I.

Titian, *Cardinal Alessandro Farnese*, 1545–6 (Naples, Museo di Capodimonte). As the eldest son of a modest baronial family, Alessandro had hoped for a secular career but was obliged to become a cardinal after his father's election as pope.

Ruota del Conclaue

Mazzieri

Cocina

Tauola, done li Scalchi
presentano le uiuande delli
R.mi, Alli reueditori

Scala di ritorno

A woodcut depicting the arrival of meals at the conclave door (from Scappi's *Opera dell'arte del cucinare*). The bishops seated at the table are checking the contents of the baskets for prohibited items before they are placed on the revolving shelves to be passed into the Sala Regia behind.

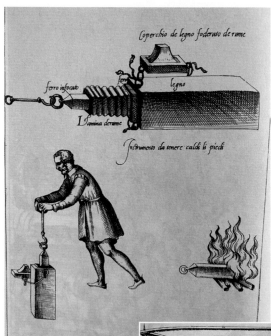

A footwarmer of the kind used by the cardinals attending the conclave (from Scappi's *Opera dell'arte del cucinare*). It consists of a wooden box lined with copper into which a large ingot of red hot iron was inserted.

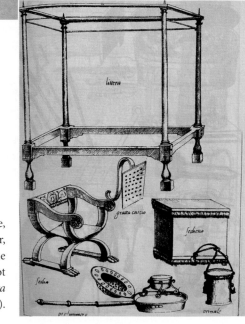

The cardinal's bed frame, a chair, cheese grater, commode, perfume burner and pisspot (from Scappi's *Opera dell'arte del cucinare*).

Titian, *Danae*, 1546 (Naples, Museo di Capodimonte). Cardinal Alessandro Farnese had his mistress portrayed as the nymph Danae, seduced by Jupiter disguised, in a highly appropriate gesture for this wealthy churchman, as a shower of gold.

Vatican, Sala Regia, begun 1540. Designed for the reception of kings and emperors, this great hall functioned as the entrance hall and focal point during papal conclaves, its doors guarded by teams of bishops and squads of soldiers in an attempt to prevent unwelcome visitors.

Vatican, Sistine Chapel, begun 1477. The 1559 conclave would be the last time that this majestic space would be used as a dormitory; after three months, conditions inside had deteriorated to such an extent that it had to be fumigated.

Pietro Perugino, *Christ's Charge to St Peter*, 1481 (Vatican, Sistine Chapel). It was widely believed that the cardinal who was allocated the cell beneath this scene of Christ appointing St Peter as the first pope would be elected at the end of the conclave.

curtains for privacy, and laid out pallets on the floor for himself and the other conclavists. Ippolito owned a collapsible bed which he used when travelling, but his conclave bed was probably a more robust affair set on trestles, which would have had the added advantage of converting into a couch during the day.[9] Strikingly, while he made no effort to replicate the appearance of his palace apartments, he did ensure that his bed was supplied with all the comforts of home, notably his expensive woollen mattresses and feather pillows as well as fine linen sheets and pillowcases.

Meschino was also in charge of ensuring that the candles were all snuffed out each night and that the charcoal embers in the brazier, which had heated Ippolito's dinner, were fully extinguished. Given the quantities of inflammable materials in the conclave, and the open flames that not only burned inside each of the cubicles but also in all the halls and communal areas, where torches burned day and night, it is remarkable that there are so few stories of fires breaking out on these occasions. However, the dangers associated with fire were better understood in the sixteenth century and the conclave manual contained strict instructions regarding this hazard: 'conclavists must above all take care with every diligence to avoid fire', for example.[10]

In the morning it was Meschino's task to refurbish the cubicle for daytime use. He dismantled the beds and stored the bedding in the overhead lockers, which he reached with a ladder – the explanation for the inclusion of this strange item in the list of equipment each cardinal needed to furnish his conclave cell. He also looked after Ippolito's clothes, which were stored in the large chests that took up more precious space in the cubicles. There is a contemporary illustration of a rudimentary coat-hanger inside a conclave cell, for the use of cardinals like Ippolito, who treasured their silk and velvet vestments – unlike the more puritan Ghislieri who favoured rough, utilitarian woollen cloth for both financial and moral reasons. Meschino also cleaned the room, emptying the rubbish that had accumulated in the wooden boxes and, his least pleasant task, carrying Ippolito's pisspot and commode to the washing area at the end of the loggia where he could throw the contents down the drain. Ippolito's commode, a basic wooden structure with a copper basin inside, had also been colour-coded for the conclave with a new green velvet cover to replace the red he normally preferred.[11] What Ippolito's ledgers do not reveal is whether his courtiers brought their own commodes too, which would have taken up even more space in the cramped cubicle – did they share, or did they use the communal latrines?

PARTIES ON 22 SEPTEMBER

- Spanish led by Sforza and Madruzzo   17 votes
- New cardinals led by Carafa and Farnese   14 votes
- French led by Ippolito d'Este and Guise   14 votes

two-thirds majority needed: 30 votes

As the end of September approached, and the sweltering heat started to subside, Ippolito was preoccupied with devising tactics to counter the campaign led by Carafa and Farnese to elect Carpi, which had once again ominously begun to gather pace. The French decided to press for the election of one of their own, the elderly François de Tournon, who was Catherine de' Medici's second choice for the tiara. The difficulty with Tournon's candidacy was that he was foreign and they knew that a direct attempt at election, whether by scrutiny or by homage, was unlikely to succeed. So, they decided to use the feint of honouring this much-respected cardinal in much the same manner as the Spanish had done with Cueva ten days earlier. By the evening of Thursday, 21 September, Ippolito and Guise had obtained promises of twenty-eight secure votes as well as conditional offers of support from four or five other cardinals which would materialize if the vote got close to provide the two-thirds majority. The plan was to have Tournon's name read out from twenty-four ballot papers and then for Bellay, Armagnac, Strozzi and Crispi, who would all have placed their votes elsewhere, to act as if suddenly inspired to change their minds and to offer their votes to the Frenchman, a ploy that they hoped would encourage those who had offered conditional support to join in the acclamation.

Unfortunately, the details of this plot were leaked to Carafa, who scuppered the project by deviously spreading a rumour around the conclave that evening that his party would also be voting for Tournon the next morning, a threat that would make Tournon's election a certainty. Overnight, those who had promised their votes with the intention merely of honouring the Frenchman immediately withdrew their backing and the Spanish countered with a bid to elect the elderly Pacheco at the scrutiny the next day. The Friday morning session was an embarrassing debacle. The voting lists, which Madruzzo leaked out daily to the imperial ambassador so that he, in turn, could forward them on to Emperor Ferdinand, showed that Tournon had only acquired fifteen votes, whereas Pacheco had received nineteen. And when Bellay, Armagnac, Strozzi and Crispi acted out their pre-planned 'inspiration', no one dared to follow them in case the opposition did the same for Pacheco. 'The French were said to have thirty-four votes,' reported the Mantuan ambassador, 'but when it came to the scrutiny they had only twenty-one which has made them absolutely furious.'[12] But the real problem was that Tournon was foreign: 'It is said that if the Italians had stayed faithful we would have a pope,' added the envoy.

Guise expressed his fury in a letter to his brothers in France, the Cardinal of Lorraine and the Duke of Guise: 'We had organized everything so well, and we even had the votes of Farnese himself, as well as those of Sforza, Pacheco, Cueva, Madruzzo and Truchsess and many Italians too.'[13] (Otto Truchsess von Waldburg was Prince-Bishop of Augsburg and a prominent member of the imperial faction.) It was indeed an impressive coup for the French to have garnered the support of so many of the opposition – though it should be remembered that this was, in name at least, a campaign to honour Tournon rather than one to elect him. Still, it says much about Tournon's high standing in the college that the French managed not only to acquire Farnese's vote but also those of all four Habsburg cardinals, as well as Sforza, their party boss, and that these cardinals were prepared to vote for a Frenchman at all, even as a mark of respect.

Despite the failure of the plot, there were lessons to be learned from the experience. 'We now know something of the value that can be placed on the word of several of the cardinals,' Guise informed his brothers, with evident disgust. Moreover, although Ippolito was confident that the conclave could not elect a candidate without the support of the French, he was also uncomfortably aware that the French were equally incapable of electing their own candidate without the assistance of votes from one of the other parties. With the votes so evenly split between the parties, it was becoming increasingly clear that the only way they were going to elect a pope was to find a compromise candidate, and one who could attract cross-party support.

At lunch in Ippolito's cubicle after the failure of the bid for Tournon, he discussed the morning's events with Guise, Bellay and Tournon. The two party bosses summed up the situation in a joint letter to Guise's brothers at the French court: 'Realising that we cannot get a Frenchman elected, and because Farnese, Carafa and the Spanish are insisting continuously on Carpi, whom they have already proposed many times,' they informed them, 'we have been talking the problem over with Tournon and Bellay, and have decided to promote Gonzaga', who was Catherine de' Medici's third candidate for election.[14] Ippolito also wrote to his nephew Alfonso in France to tell him of the plan. 'You will have seen from the letter I wrote to the Cardinal of Lorraine and the Duke of Guise about the present state of this conclave,' Ippolito explained, so 'after having tried every possible way to elect the first two candidates proposed by the king, we are now trying for Gonzaga.'[15] He added, significantly, 'I am certainly motivated by the same enthusiasm as I would have for my own election not only because Gonzaga has been particularly recommended by his majesty and because of the family ties that exist between us, but also for his considerable personal merits which will certainly benefit the papacy, and we are now working on this praiseworthy undertaking.'

PARTY NATIONALITIES ON 24 SEPTEMBER

- Spanish led by Sforza and Madruzzo
  4 foreign 13 Italians   17 votes
- New cardinals led by Carafa and Farnese
  1 foreign 13 Italians   14 votes
- French led by Ippolito d'Este and Guise
  4 foreign 10 Italians   14 votes

two-thirds majority needed: 30 votes

Ippolito was not alone in judging Ercole Gonzaga a suitable candidate for the papal throne and, importantly, one who could expect cross-party support. He was Italian, for a start – and, at fifty-three years of age, far from an old man. Despite his bevy of children, he was a well-respected figure on the progressive wing of the college, and he had had plenty of experience of government while acting as regent for his young nephews in Mantua. He was a prominent member of the Spanish faction, and had been appointed by Philip II as cardinal-protector of Spain. Moreover, he was one of the very few cardinals in the conclave to have been ordained a priest which, the French judged, was a factor that might persuade some of the hardliners in Carafa's party to vote for this more liberal candidate. From Ippolito's point of view, Gonzaga had the added advantage of being family and a favourite of his brother, Duke Ercole. Although he knew that Farnese would never support Gonzaga – the enmity between their families went too deep for that – and that Carafa would probably follow Farnese's lead in this, Ippolito did feel optimistic that Sforza would honour the agreement the two men had made in early September before the conclave opened. If party unity held in the French and Spanish factions, they would have enough to achieve the necessary two-thirds majority.

After several days of discussion with Guise, Bellay, Tournon and other members of his party, Ippolito made contact with Camerlengo Sforza. It is difficult to be certain of the exact date as the documentary evidence is sparse and there were good reasons for ensuring that these delicate negotiations were kept absolutely secret, but it was probably 23 September. What is certain is that Sforza agreed to honour the promise he had made before the conclave and the two parties started to work together, covertly, for the election of Gonzaga. They discussed the hazards they faced: 'Farnese and Carafa will, I freely admit to you, do everything they can to wreck our plans,' he informed his nephew Alfonso in France.[16] They also considered ways by which they could get extra votes from Carafa's cardinals. Both Ippolito and Sforza had connections with the Duke of Florence that they could exploit. Alfonso was son-in-law to the Duke of Florence and Ippolito informed him that he had written to Cosimo I 'asking him to order his cardinals, Rebiba, Gaddi and Innocenzo del Monte to support us'. One of Sforza's conclavists was Francesco Lottino, who was also acting as the agent of Cosimo I in the conclave, and Sforza asked Lottino to back up Ippolito's request and urge the duke to compel the three Florentine cardinals, who were all members of Carafa's party, to abandon party loyalty and vote for Gonzaga.

PARTIES ON 25 SEPTEMBER

- Spanish led by Sforza and Madruzzo   17 votes
- New cardinals led by Carafa and Farnese   14 votes
- French led by Ippolito d'Este and Guise   14 votes

two-thirds majority needed: 30 votes

After days of secret planning, Ippolito convened a more public meeting on 25 September between the four party bosses of the new coalition – himself and Guise with Sforza and his second-in-command, Madruzzo, the Prince-Bishop of Trent, who was, providentially, a close friend of Gonzaga. The men gathered that afternoon – perhaps they all lunched together at Ippolito's dining-table – and drew up a formal agreement to campaign for the election of Gonzaga. They also discussed tactics and, in order to lessen the chances of their plans being leaked to Farnese and Carafa, decided not to waste time by waiting for a reply from Cosimo I but to go ahead immediately without the support of the Florentine cardinals. Once lunch was over, they sent messages to the members of both parties ordering all the cardinals to gather at once in the Cappella Paolina where they intended to elect Gonzaga by homage. By 3 p.m. most of the French party had arrived but only seven of the Spanish cardinals had joined their leaders in the chapel. Leaving Madruzzo in charge, Ippolito, Guise and Sforza hurried out through the Sala Regia in the direction of the different dormitories to work on the absentees who had remained in their cells.

The leaders managed to persuade two more cardinals to go to the Cappella Paolina but were still short of votes when a very undignified row broke out in the Sala Regia. At one end of the great marble hall, Madruzzo could be heard shouting passionately from the Cappella Paolina: 'Mantua! Mantua! Papa! Papa!' At the other end, jeers and taunts issued from the Sistine Chapel where Farnese and Carafa had assembled their supporters, posting Farnese's brother Ranuccio at the door out of the chapel where he was using all his strength to prevent anyone leaving – over a third of the cardinals had cells in the Sistine Chapel, including six of the Spanish party and five of Ippolito's faction. In the noisy uproar it was evident that the plan was not going to succeed, that afternoon at least. The blame game was played out in the letters dispatched by couriers that evening to courts across Europe. Understandably disappointed, the Mantuan ambassador wrote to his duke, who was Gonzaga's nephew, firmly placing the blame on Madruzzo and his wild shouting: 'If it had not been for his excessive haste, the election would have been a success,' he claimed, 'as Este, Guise, Sforza and Sermoneta were all working on those who had not attended to make up the necessary number when Madruzzo began shouting with far too much enthusiasm and excessive optimism.'[17] Madruzzo might have been over-hasty but it was also evident that Sforza's leadership skills had not been as effective as the French had hoped. It was his Spanish cardinals, after all, who had signally failed to join in the election attempt. The camerlengo justified his own shortcomings in a letter to Philip II, in which he claimed that the French had sprung the plan too suddenly and that they had not given him enough time to convince his cardinals to support Gonzaga's candidacy.[18]

In a long letter to his brothers Cardinal Charles and Duke Francis in France, Guise laid all the blame on Carafa and Farnese, but especially on Carafa, whose arrogant disregard for the conventions of deference shocked this French aristocrat. 'Up to this point neither the Spanish nor the Italians have refused to do what Sforza has asked them to do,' he wrote, 'and they would have done so this time had it not been for Farnese and Carafa, who have done all they can to frustrate our plans, especially Carafa. I have never seen even a Burgundian or a Spaniard, nor any other enemy of the French crown, show more contempt for our king than he did,' Guise fumed.[19]

Guise was particularly disgusted by the underhand behaviour of many cardinals – though it was naive, in view of the enormous prize at stake, to be surprised at the political chicanery that had taken place that afternoon. 'I have to confess to you that the longer I am in this place,' he continued to inform Cardinal Charles and Duke Francis, 'the greater I find the hatred and prejudice that exists among a large part of this company, and the less I find I can put trust in their words and promises.' He was particularly incensed by Jean Suau, who was French by birth (he was known as Cardinal Reumano, after his birthplace of Rieumes south-west of Toulouse), and the only foreigner in Carafa's party. 'Worst of all was the malice of Reumano,' he told his brothers. 'At first, when we were assembling our supporters, I noticed that he was reluctant to join us and I assumed this was because he thought I was favouring Gonzaga for my own advantage, so I offered to show him my letter of instruction from the king in order that he would have proof of his sovereign's wishes,' he explained. 'But neither this nor the arguments that Bellay and the others put forward would dissuade him from supporting Carafa in preference to his king, and he excused himself on the grounds of the duty he owed on account of his red hat and with the promise he had made,' Guise raged. 'It is a disgrace that a Frenchman should refuse to obey his true prince and king.'

Despite the fiasco, however, Ippolito and Guise could scent victory; so too could Sforza and Madruzzo. When the four party bosses met that evening to discuss the events of the day, Sforza must have assured the others that he was confident of persuading those Spanish cardinals who had failed to attend the homage in the Cappella Paolina to change their minds. 'We already have twenty-eight or twenty-nine votes,' he informed Philip II, 'and hope with God's help to find the two or three we lack to elect this loyal servant of your majesty.'[20] This was not idle boasting. Gonzaga's standing in the college made this a real possibility. There was also the hope that Cosimo I would respond favourably in the next few days to the letters of Ippolito and Lottino, and order the Florentine cardinals in Carafa's party to vote with the Franco–Spanish coalition. Confident of success, the four cardinals now drew up another pact, more binding than the last one. 'Guise, Este, Madruzzo and Sforza, the leaders of this alliance, have promised and sworn that they will not give their votes to anyone else, and they have all signed the document in their own hands,' the Mantuan ambassador informed his duke; and the broadsheets issued that day in Rome reported that these cardinals 'have given their pledge to Gonzaga, even if it means remaining in the conclave for ten years'.[21] But their mood of optimism was about to be severely dented.

The following day – Tuesday, 26 September – an unforeseen complication materialized without warning in the form of Francisco de Vargas, Philip II's recently appointed ambassador who had finally reached Rome after four weeks on the road from Antwerp. After lunch that day Vargas arrived at the door of the Sala Regia to give a formal address to the cardinals on behalf of Philip II. 'At 3 p.m. the imperial ambassador had an audience with the cardinals at the conclave entrance and he reminded them that their procrastination was inflicting great damage in the Christian world, especially in those parts where heresy is a growing danger,' the master of ceremonies recorded in his diary.[22] The delay was indeed exceptional: this election had already lasted longer than all but one of the thirteen conclaves of the last one hundred years. 'Then the ambassador of the King of Spain, who is called Vargas, gave a very eloquent address on behalf of his master,' Firmano continued. He had not met the ambassador before, nor indeed had Ippolito or many of his colleagues. Vargas may have made a good impression that afternoon but, as both Ippolito and Firmano were soon to find out, he was to cause them both a lot of trouble.

Francisco de Vargas was a very ambitious man. A clever lawyer from a modest bourgeois background, he had worked diligently to carve out a career for himself as a diplomat in the service of the Spanish crown but his progress had been hampered by his lack of influence at court. Thanks to the timely death of his predecessor and the absence of any better candidate to take up the post, it had been a real stroke of luck for Vargas to secure this appointment as ambassador to Rome at such a critical time. It was a rare opportunity: providing he could engineer the election of a pope who was a staunch ally of Spain, he would be able to establish himself among the royal favourites – his wife had retired to a convent giving rise to rumours, reported by the Venetian ambassador, that Vargas coveted a cardinal's hat, for which he needed Philip II's favour.[23] Vargas was determined above all on managing the election without the help of the French – and especially without the help of Ippolito, whom he described as that cardinal 'so hated by God and the Spanish king'.[24] It was a policy that was to have important repercussions inside the Vatican.

Vargas had no scruples about how he achieved his aim and Ippolito was soon informed that the ambassador had made several unofficial, and highly illegal, excursions into the conclave. He made his first visit during the evening of Wednesday, 27 September, the day after his address to the cardinals, and came in almost every night after that. As his correspondence with Philip II reveals, he made no attempt to disguise his presence at these clandestine meetings which were, as the king himself must have known, categorically against the rules. On that first night, for example, he reported that he had a long talk with Sforza; two nights later he was again in the Vatican 'talking privately to Farnese and Carafa'.[25] He gained access into the conclave through various windows that had conveniently been left unlocked, and later through holes that were deliberately chiselled into the walls behind the cubicles, one of which was in Carpi's cell in the Sala Ducale.

'I left Antwerp as soon as news arrived of the pope's death', Vargas informed Philip II after his candle-lit chat with Sforza that Wednesday night, 'and, travelling with all possible speed, I arrived here three days ago to find a very difficult situation.'[26] By 'difficult' he meant, of course, the joint Franco–Spanish campaign to elect Gonzaga. Just how close Ippolito's cousin was to the papal tiara is evident from the same letter. Vargas reported that on 28 September Gonzaga had received twenty-nine votes, lacking just two for election. For the ambitious envoy, the destruction of this coalition was an urgent priority. He was soon at work on the Spanish cardinals, using the political argument that giving the papal tiara to this member of Italy's ruling elite would threaten Spanish interests in the peninsula. He went so far as to hint that he had 'knowledge', entirely fictitious, that a formal alliance existed between France and the dukes of Ferrara, Florence, Mantua and Urbino to undermine the king's authority in Italy. Farnese confirmed the existence of this so-called plot to Philip II and, according to the Venetian ambassador to Spain, 'tried to make the king suspicious of Gonzaga by advising his majesty to be very cautious in his support of [Gonzaga], because a league had been formed between him and all non-Spanish Italy'.[27]

PARTIES ON 28 SEPTEMBER

- Spanish led by Sforza and Madruzzo   17 votes
- New cardinals led by Carafa and Farnese   15 votes
- French led by Ippolito d'Este and Guise   14 votes

two-thirds majority needed: 31 votes

Over the next few days Vargas's schemes to discredit Gonzaga began to pay off. While the French party remained firmly behind Ippolito, Sforza's cardinals were becoming increasing reluctant to follow their leader. On 30 September, the imperial ambassador reported that Gonzaga's vote count had dropped to twenty-four votes, and that five Spanish cardinals had remained neutral. Ippolito and Sforza continued to canvass hard for Gonzaga but the momentum of the campaign began to slip away. On 4 October, the Mantuan ambassador reported that Gonzaga received twenty-three votes that day, with seven cardinals remaining neutral.[28] But Ippolito and Sforza remained optimistic, especially when Capizucchi, one of Carafa's cardinals, left the conclave through illness – one less vote for the opposition, and the added advantage of the two-thirds majority being reduced from thirty-one to thirty votes. Of the neutrals, the Mantuan ambassador reckoned that four could be persuaded to support Gonzaga, including Cueva and Truchsess, while the conservative Franciscan Dolera, who had voted against Gonzaga, had promised to change sides if the vote count got to twenty-eight or twenty-nine. But that still left Ippolito and Sforza short of two votes and, with Vargas working energetically against them, these were proving very difficult to find.

PARTIES ON 4 OCTOBER

- Spanish led by Sforza and Madruzzo   17 votes
- New cardinals led by Carafa and Farnese   14 votes
- French led by Ippolito d'Este and Guise   14 votes

two-thirds majority needed: 30 votes

The principal difficulty facing the coalition was the absence of concrete information regarding Philip II's opinion of Gonzaga, and the unscrupulous Vargas exploited this tiny seed of doubt to the full. If the king could be persuaded to nominate Gonzaga, who was, after all, the cardinal-protector of the Spanish crown, then Ippolito and Sforza would have no difficulty gaining the extra votes for Gonzaga's election. Equally, if Philip II was against his cardinal-protector, then Gonzaga had no chance whatsoever. By the beginning of October, it was evident to the party bosses, and to Vargas in particular, that the conclave needed to know Philip II's views.

In early October an astonishing quantity of letters left the conclave bound for Spain.[29] Sforza and Madruzzo, still committed to their pact with Ippolito and Guise, sent no fewer than five letters to Philip II begging him to order the Spanish cardinals to vote for Gonzaga.[30] They justified their alliance with the French, and their refusal to follow Vargas's instructions, by arguing that Gonzaga was a highly suitable candidate for the papal throne, and a man who had always been loyal to the Spanish crown. They dismissed reports of the existence of a league of Italian princes, saying that Gonzaga would in no way threaten Spanish interests in Italy. Gonzaga himself wrote to Philip II pledging his support for Spain, though unfortunately his courier was arrested in Florence by Cosimo I and sent back to Rome. Vargas, by contrast, begged Philip II for a letter in which the king explicitly excluded Gonzaga, and accusingly listed by name all those Spanish cardinals, including the party leaders, who had voted with the opposition.

Meanwhile, rumours that foreign rulers were interfering in the election was causing fury on the streets of Rome – with good reason since the scale of the interference was unacceptably high. Vargas was not the only ambassador resorting to illicit practices: the imperial envoy, Francis von Thurm, obtained daily voting figures from Madruzzo to forward to Ferdinand I in Vienna. In the city, the unprecedented length of the conclave was blamed on this meddling, and the atmosphere became tense with the threat of violence. On 3 October the cardinals assembled in the Sala Regia to hear an address from a delegation of city magistrates who described an incident the previous night at the palace of Ambassador Angoulême, when an official was shot while trying to confiscate a banned weapon from a member of the embassy staff. The mob had then tried to set fire to the residence, for which the magistrates apologized, but they warned the cardinals that if a pope was not elected very soon, they would be forced to use measures to prevent any more letters being sent out of the conclave.[31]

Inside his cell in the Sala Ducale, Ippolito might have been worried about the slipping vote count for Gonzaga but he must have taken some comfort to see the difficulties that Vargas was facing. The ambassador was not only attempting to discredit Gonzaga: he was also determined to move the Spanish party from its alliance with the French to one with Carafa's party instead. While it was evident that Vargas's scheme worked well on paper – he could do the arithmetic, these two parties did have a two-thirds majority – it was proving a formidable task to put the plan into practice.

For a start, Vargas seems to have underestimated the scale of animosities that existed between the personalities involved. He dismissed the bitter rivalry that had existed between Paul III's two grandsons for the best part of thirty years. 'The discord between Sforza and Farnese is causing great damage,' he wrote to Philip II on 28 September, carefully transcribing the passage into code before adding naively, 'and I am working hard to reconcile them.'[32] There was also a marked lack of trust between Sforza and Carafa that dated back to the camerlengo's imprisonment by Paul IV in Castel Sant'Angelo on charges of spying for Spain. The combination of Sforza and Vargas too was unfortunate, though it had been forced on Philip II after the death of his old ambassador. The king must have been aware of the potential for animosity between the two men, not least because they sided with the opposing factions that divided his court: Sforza with the old guard, the ambitious Vargas with the new men. Sforza objected to the ambassador's arrogance and deeply disliked taking orders from this social inferior, while Vargas could not comprehend how the leader of the Spanish party could even imagine voting with the French – all in all, not a recipe for success.

Even if these two parties could be persuaded into an alliance, Vargas still faced the thorny dilemma of finding a candidate on whom both sides could agree. Vargas himself was determined to force the election of either Carpi or Pacheco – the former who had been on the list Philip II had given Vargas's predecessor, and the latter who was a Spaniard by birth. The ambassador seems to have ignored the fact that neither cardinal could claim broad support in the college. Carpi was a sworn enemy of several powerful figures, not least Ippolito and Sforza, whereas Pacheco was widely judged to be lazy. 'He spends twenty-two hours a day eating and sleeping and [attending to] other personal necessities,' as one cardinal judged.[33]

Vargas's own preference was for Carpi. Shortly after his arrival in Rome he had written enthusiastically to the king that 'I believe it will be possible to elect Carpi', though he did qualify his optimism by adding that he judged 'those who are against him are very resolute in their opposition', a tacit gesture to the strength of Ippolito's party.[34] However, while Carpi and

Pacheco were acceptable as candidates to both Carafa and Farnese, they were entirely unacceptable to Sforza. Vargas might be forgiven for being unaware of the pact that Ippolito and Sforza had made to exclude Carpi, but he must have seen at first hand the animosity that existed between Sforza and Pacheco, who sniped continually to the ambassador about his boss's incompetence. Vargas's predicament was made worse by the fact that Sforza, as leader of a larger number of cardinals than Carafa and Farnese, would need to have an important say in the choice.

Sforza meanwhile had the unenviable position of being obliged to sit on the fence. In public, he continued to uphold his pact with Ippolito and the French to persevere with the campaign for Gonzaga, but he also had to perform his duties as leader of the Spanish party and negotiate the choice of a Spanish candidate with Vargas. Ippolito himself could play a waiting game, knowing that even if Vargas did manage to unite Sforza with Carafa and Farnese, it was still going to be possible for the French to sway the odd vote from the alliance to prevent the election of a candidate unacceptable to France. As he had written to his brother on 20 September, he considered it to be virtually impossible for a pope to be elected without the support of his party.

With his mind preoccupied with these tense negotiations, it must have come as a terrible shock to Ippolito when his brother's ambassador arrived at the conclave door with the tragic news that Ercole had died suddenly in Ferrara on Tuesday, 3 October. There were more details in a letter from their younger brother Francesco, who apologized that it had taken him four days to put pen to paper, but, he wrote, 'I have been so stricken with grief and distress that I was unable to write to you earlier'.[35] The duke had been in bed for a few days, Francesco wrote, 'as you already know' and 'he was fine during all that day [Monday] until about midnight' but 'although his previous good health gave us hope, the doctors were less optimistic... and he was overtaken by a most severe paroxysm which shook him so badly that they had to tie him down and at ten o'clock the following morning he passed on to a better life' – he was only fifty-one years old.

Duke Ercole's death was a serious blow to Ippolito. Quite apart from the personal loss of a much-loved elder brother, with whom he had hunted, jousted, played tennis, gambled and squabbled over the years, he had also lost his most loyal ally and all the political support his brother was so generously providing for his election campaign. He could not expect his nephew – now Alfonso II – to have the same priorities regarding the conclave, not least because the new duke's father-in-law was Cosimo I, who had his own agenda for the next occupant of the papal throne. In a letter to the twenty-five-year-old, Ippolito assured his nephew of his continuing loyalty and wrote of his sadness at Ercole's demise. 'You can imagine how much his unexpected death has distressed me, not only because of our family ties but also because it has happened so suddenly; one day I had news that he was ill and the next that he was dead,' Ippolito grieved.[36] 'I am so very sorry that I am locked up in a place where I can do so little to help you,' he apologized, and attempted to comfort his nephew. 'These things are sent from God and we must come to terms with his will,' he wrote, adding that 'the one thing that comforts me above all others is that the state will fall into your hands.'

Ippolito could offer comfort but he could not be sure that the duchy would fall into his nephew's hands. Alfonso II himself was a long way from Ferrara, thoroughly enjoying life at the French court, much as Ippolito himself had done two decades earlier. With an absent heir, the succession was fraught with danger – the Este princes were notorious for their illegitimate offspring and there were fears that this power vacuum might offer the opportunity for one of them to seize the duchy. Ippolito, who would have been the obvious member of the family to take charge, was forbidden from leaving the conclave. The safety of the succession was in the hands of the dowager duchess, Renée of France, though Cosimo I obligingly sent a detachment of troops to Ferrara to assist her. Ippolito expressed his fears openly, and in his own hand, to his old friend Renée, the grieving widow: 'My greatest wish is to hear that the new duke has come home, and that he has found his duchy in the good state that I know your excellency is trying hard to maintain.'[37]

It must have been a very sad moment when, a few days later, Ippolito received his brother's last letter, written from his sick bed on 30 September, three days before he died. He started by apologizing to Ippolito for not replying sooner 'to the letter you were so kind to write to me on 18 September but I have been confined to my bed for the last week with a slight fever of which I am still not entirely free.'[38] He does not seem to have felt very ill at this stage for he continued with great enthusiasm. 'I am extremely pleased to hear that you and Gonzaga are getting on so well together, although I wish that your letter had not been so brief,' he chided his younger brother. 'When you are sure that you yourself cannot be made pope,' he advised, 'do not lose time' in getting Gonzaga elected. He also warned his brother of the dangers posed by the arrival of Vargas – Ercole had certainly got that right. The duke ended on an optimistic note, and one that must have been unbearably poignant to read: 'I am looking forward to the good news that either one or the other of you has been elected pope and it will make me jump out of bed immediately, more vigorous than a lion.'

5

Banquets

5–26 OCTOBER

With Ippolito preoccupied with his own grief and worries about the succession in Ferrara, it was perhaps fortunate for him that the intensity of the past fortnight suddenly evaporated in early October and the conclave ground to a halt. The daily routine continued in the Cappella Paolina, where the tedium of the lengthy and inconclusive voting sessions must have been considerably enlivened by the anticipation of the food baskets containing lunch and dinner. The French campaign for Gonzaga, which had begun to wilt under pressure from Vargas, was now on hold while everyone waited to hear Philip II's reactions to the letters on their way to the royal court at Toledo. 'There is not much to say about the business here,' Ippolito informed his sister-in-law on 15 October, 'everything hinges on the answer from Spain and once it arrives we will have a better idea of what is going to happen.'[1] The cardinals knew they had a long wait ahead of them. The king's replies could not be expected any time soon, certainly not before the end of the month – in fact, the report sent by Vargas on 3 October took over three weeks to reach Spain, where one of the royal secretaries marked it carefully as 'received on 26 October'.[2]

In early October, the news coming out of the conclave switched abruptly from details of nail-biting scrutiny sessions and anger at the interference of foreign rulers to the growing lack of security in the Vatican, where the regulations regarding secrecy were being openly flouted. Sforza, Carafa and Farnese were having regular nightly conversations with Vargas that sometimes lasted until dawn, while Madruzzo had been sending out the daily voting figures to the imperial ambassador ever since the conclave opened. Certainly the betting touts in Rome were regularly supplied with information, as were the journalists editing the city's newssheets and, of course, Pasquino. There is plenty of evidence that other cardinals were also ignoring the rules. Carpi sent one of his conclavists out of the Vatican 'using the excuse that the man was ill' but, in fact, he had been sent to negotiate with the Spanish ambassador on Carpi's behalf in private, without the intimidating presence of the party bosses.[3] Ambassador Angoulême reported that Giovanni Carafa, the cuckolded Duke of Paliano 'has been in Rome for a night to speak in secret with his brother the cardinal'.[4]

Indeed, reading about the election in letters, diaries and reports, we have so much information about what was going on behind the locked doors that it is sometimes difficult to remember that there were any rules governing its security. So, it is rather reassuring to find that there were people outside the conclave who did try to observe the regulations – Ippolito's brother Francesco for one. 'I had planned to send a courtier to tell you all the details of the duke's death in person,' he explained, 'but, because you are in the conclave and it is widely believed that the *sede vacante* will last for some time yet, my gentleman would not have been able to carry out my instructions at the present time, so I resolved to write to you instead.'[5]

For the harassed master of ceremonies, whose job it was to ensure the smooth running of the papal election, the conclave was rapidly turning into a nightmare. With neither the social status nor the personal clout to enforce his authority inside the Vatican, Firmano was in danger of losing control of the situation and the terse entries in his diary are evidence of the disarray. On 2 October an incident occurred that seems to have been the last straw for the unfortunate official: 'Cardinal Capizucchi, having been taken gravely ill, left the conclave at 3 p.m., and on this occasion the door was left open which allowed the brother of the Cardinal of Guise to come inside', he recorded, scandalized by this flagrant breach of the rules.[6] Guise's twenty-five-year-old brother François, Grand Prior of France, was speedily found and evicted.

Later that afternoon, having seen personally to the relocking of the door, Firmano finally took action, summoning the cardinals to a meeting in the Cappella Paolina where he subjected them to a tirade on their misdeeds, breaking rules that, he reminded his audience, they had solemnly sworn to uphold. Among the infringements he cited were unofficial contacts with the outside world, illegal opening of sealed doors and windows, the presence of far too many unauthorized persons inside the Vatican, improper behaviour on the part of the cardinals themselves, and so on. 'Conclavists have been seen at the windows of the rooms which look out onto the piazza in front of St Peter's and this is shocking behaviour,' he scolded them. One of the conclave doctors had been seen talking at the door in the Sala Regia and the master of ceremonies had heard reports that other people had been observed 'talking at openings which have been made all over the conclave and there have been an infinite number of other examples of rule-breaking'.[7] He must have had his suspicions of Vargas's nightly visits into the conclave, though he chose not to mention them. As his tirade concluded, he told them with rather more force than one might have expected that 'it is essential that all this ceases at once'.

After he had finished berating the cardinals for their unseemly behaviour, Firmano advised them to elect a committee that would be in charge of restoring order in the conclave. Typically, college committees contained representatives of each class of cardinal (bishops, priests and deacons) but it is clear from the names listed by the master of ceremonies in his diary that this particular one also took account of the factional divisions within the conclave – it would, after all, have been pointless to expect delegates chosen largely from one party to take any serious measures that would enforce security across the board. There was no cardinal-bishop on the first committee, which served for the week of 2–8 October: it consisted of two priests, Madruzzo (Spain) and Scotti (Carafa), and two deacons, Ippolito (France) and Carafa himself. The next day the cardinals had 'a long discussion of how to reform the conclave on account of the above-mentioned scandals'.[8]

Firmano's next entry, on 5 October, shows that steps were finally being taken to enforce the regulations limiting the number of unauthorized personnel in the Vatican: 'After voting the cardinals in charge of reforming the conclave met in the cubicle of the dean [Bellay] and it was agreed that each cardinal must have no more than three conclavists, with a fourth if they were ill.' Meanwhile, he observed, 'all agents of foreign princes and businessmen must be expelled.'[9] A few days later the cardinals voted to enforce the physical security of the conclave: 'All openings, however small, that have been made in the cubicles or other parts of the conclave are to be closed' – a clear reference to Vargas's nightly visits and that 'the committee will check all these places again in seven days'.[10] Any breach of the rules was to be severely punished: 'If any conclavist starts hanging around the door of the conclave, for whatever reason, he is to be expelled.'

That day, Firmano finally turned his attention to the behaviour of the cardinals themselves, and the irregularities that he'd observed but had so far failed to correct. Regarding the scrutinies, for example: 'No cardinal is to show his voting paper to another, nor make any kind of sign', which suggests that even the conduct of the papal election was not all it should have been. There was also far too much night-time activity for his taste: 'It was decided that after I had rung my bell, which I ring at 11.30 p.m., no cardinal or conclavist is to move around the conclave.' The master of ceremonies was particularly scandalized by the lavish dinner parties that had become a regular feature of life inside the Vatican during this conclave: 'Many cardinals are eating together, or rather, as I told them, banqueting in groups' – evidently not the behaviour he expected from these heirs-in-waiting to the papal throne, so 'it was ordered that no cardinal was to dine in the cubicle of another, and that I would intervene personally in the provision of food'. We can imagine how irritated the cardinals must have been by the strictures of this over-conscientious jobsworth.

There is plenty of evidence in Ippolito's papers to suggest that he was one of those guilty of 'banqueting in groups' – given his taste for ostentatious display, it would not be surprising to find him among Firmano's leading culprits. Ippolito's ledgers show that the meals served in his cell went far beyond plain and simple fare; moreover, his staff were also providing lunches and dinners for Guise, Strozzi and several other French cardinals (see p. 140). Whatever Firmano's opinion, however, these conclave 'banquets' were far less splendid than those at home. There were no musicians or dancers to entertain his guests, for example, nor the ceremonial procession of squires bearing their great platters of meat – Ippolito had left his personal carver behind in Ferrara for the duration of the conclave.[11] But, although he was also without his costly tapestries and leather wall-hangings, he had equipped his cubicle with the entire paraphernalia associated with fine Renaissance dining. His table was covered with expensive white linen tablecloths and napkins, and it glittered with valuable crystal glasses and quantities of silver. Among the items of silver returned to his wardrobe at the end of conclave were eleven large gilded platters, ten smaller plates, two gilded sweetmeat dishes decorated with figures, four gilded and engraved salts, four gilded cups engraved with leaves and birds, four plainer cups, two gilded silver jugs engraved with his coat-of-arms, two silver carafes and six silver candlesticks.[12]

Almost as astonishing as the large quantity of silver, stored by Meschino under lock and key in the overhead cupboards, was the amount of wine consumed. Ippolito's ledgers show that 157 barrels of wine were carried from the cellars at Palazzo Monte Giordano to the Vatican during this conclave – the porter earned 5 *baiocchi* for each barrel, the price of a pig's head.[13] There were thirty-two jugs in each barrel, which makes forty-five jugs a day! 'Dinner or lunch without a glass of wine is considered not only to be unenjoyable but also unhealthy,' was the judgement of Bartolomeo Platina, a fifteenth-century humanist and author of a treatise on pleasure, 'since wine for one who is thirsty is sweeter and more welcome than a meal for one who is hungry.'[14] Wine was highly valued by the elite of Renaissance society and, as Ippolito's ledgers reveal, it was drunk in substantial quantities – two litres a day was the average consumption in a cardinal's household of the period.[15]

Lunch and dinner in the Vatican took place at set times. In sixteenth-century Europe, unlike today, the habit of regular meal times was one of the prime indicators of social status. It was only the poor who snacked whenever the opportunity arose. Modest shopkeepers and farmers by contrast ate formal meals at fixed hours, like the idle rich nobility, though this class ate significantly later than thrifty burghers. Both lunch and dinner were broadly similar affairs and consisted of three basic components – first course, main course and dessert. The scale of the meal depended largely on the household budget or, for those like Ippolito who was rich enough to ignore this restraint, on the occasion. For him, a proper banquet might involve as many as ten or fifteen main courses, each composed of a similar number of different dishes, and the courses alternated between hot dishes from the kitchen and platters of cold food from the *credenza*.

Although Ippolito did not dine in such an extravagant manner in the Vatican, we can be certain that he was served this minimum of three courses, and that they each consisted of several different dishes, composed of ingredients that were sourced according to season. His first course consisted of a selection of cold salads and other hors d'oeuvres, prepared by the staff of his *credenza* – not unlike those transcribed from a contemporary cook book written by the papal chef Bartolomeo Scappi (see p. 114). This was followed by a main course, which consisted of a selection of meat dishes, or fish on fast days. The Renaissance diet was rich in meat. It has been estimated that the average consumption was over 1 lb a day.[16] Finally came dessert, also prepared by the *credenzieri*, with sweet pastries, candied fruits, fresh fruit, nuts and cheese. Not all of the cardinals in the conclave ate so extravagantly – Ghislieri, for example, emaciated by strict fasting and a modest diet, rarely ate meat and preferred meals of soup, salad and fish.[17]

FIRST COURSE FROM THE *CREDENZA* FOR DINNER IN OCTOBER[18]

Salad of mixed cooked and raw vegetables
Salad of capers and raisins
Salad of calves feet
Cold meat pies
Capon served cold with sliced lemons and sugar
Sweet mustard
Slices of ox tongue and sausages cooked in red wine
Pastries filled with blancmange

A MAIN COURSE FROM THE KITCHEN FOR LUNCH IN OCTOBER[19]

Pan-fried sweetbreads and livers served with Seville orange
    sauce
Spit-roasted skylarks served with a lime sauce
Spit-roasted quails served with sliced Seville oranges
Spit-roasted partridge served with sliced limes
Pasta filled with sweetbreads and ham
Roast chicken served with sliced limes and sugar
Spit-roasted pigeons served with sugar and capers
Spit-roasted rabbit served with pine-nut sauce
Spit-roasted veal meat balls
Roast haunch of kid
Soup of almonds and pigeon
Squares of meat jelly

A DESSERT COURSE FOR LUNCH IN OCTOBER[20]

Pear tarts filled with almond paste
Amber-coloured jelly squares
Quince tarts
Apples and pears of various sorts
Slices of parmesan cheese
Fresh almonds served on a bed of leaves
Roast chestnuts
Fried sweet pastries served with whipped cream and sugar

The cold food for Ippolito's dining-table in the conclave was prepared at Palazzo Monte Giordano by his *credenzieri* and carried by the palace footmen across the river to the Vatican, maybe a half-hour walk. The hot dishes, on the other hand, were cooked in the Vatican kitchens. The ledgers record that he took on three new kitchen boys specifically to work in these kitchens for the duration of the conclave and employed a new French pastry cook, whose dishes must have added French style and flavour to the display of his political loyalties.[21] There are payments to a muleteer for transporting firewood from the stores at Palazzo Monte Giordano to the Vatican to fuel the ovens, and regular deliveries to the Vatican from Antonio da Gallese, who supplied the terracotta pots in which the cooked food would be transported to the cardinals upstairs.[22] The atmosphere in the Vatican kitchens must have been chaotic, as rival chefs, each with their own meat cleavers, vegetable knives, saucepans and leather spice pouches, sweated over the open fires preparing dishes twice a day for over forty cardinals – probably even noisier, dirtier and more argumentative than the negotiations taking place above them, though at least the chefs had a more substantial sense of achievement.

We cannot be sure exactly what Ippolito and his guests ate – no menus have survived. We do know that Benedetto the baker was making bread for Ippolito's table and the ledgers record an unusually large payment of 87 scudi to a spice merchant for sugar and almonds in October but few of the bills sent in by his greengrocer, fruiterer, fishmonger or butcher are itemized, nor was that of the poulterer, who supplied the plump capons that were such a feature of the Renaissance dining-table (see p. 154). We do know, however, that Ippolito's salads were lusciously dressed with the best olive oil. He reimbursed his agent in Tivoli for the cost of thirty jugs of 'olio di oliva vergine' for his own personal use which, at 0.5 scudi a jug, was nearly four times as expensive as the olive oil he bought for his household.[23] We also know a lot about the food on the dining-tables of cardinals in the middle of the sixteenth century thanks to Bartolomeo Scappi, whose magisterial treatise on the art of cooking, *Opera dell'arte del cucinare* (1570), was the result of his thirty years' experience as a chef in Rome, cooking for several cardinals and popes, including Cardinal Carpi.[24] Unquestionably the prime source on food of the period, this Renaissance equivalent to *Mrs Beeton* runs to 890 pages and contains some 1,400 recipes as well as over one hundred menus, filled with dishes that Ippolito and his colleagues could look forward to at the end of the tedious voting sessions.

The arrival of the cardinals' meals at the Vatican twice a day was one of the distinctive sights of a conclave, a curiously formal ritual that served to remind onlookers of the prestige and power of the papal heirs-in-waiting inside the palace. Scappi had gained first-hand experience of cooking for a conclave while serving as chef to various cardinals and he devoted several pages to the minutiae associated with ceremony, which was a very time-consuming ritual, not least for the bishops on duty at the table monitoring access into the Sala Regia. Each cardinal's meal was packed separately, obliging the bishops to check the contents of almost one hundred baskets each day. Twice a day the cardinals' stewards gathered in the courtyard below with two baskets, one containing hot food prepared in the Vatican kitchens, the other with the cold dishes from the *credenza*, together with bread and wine to accompany the meal. Each steward was summoned individually, according to a list drawn by lot and posted both outside and inside the conclave by the busy master of ceremonies the evening before – those cardinals who were ill were automatically placed at the top of the list. When each cardinal's name was called, a formal procession of members of his household duly ascended the staircase in order:[25]

First came the mace-bearer with the mace of his Most Reverend patron, followed by two footmen each with their batons, which were painted the same colour as the food baskets; then came the steward with four or six squires who carried carafes filled with various wines and clear water; between these came the sommelier... then two footmen who carried the basket filled with dishes from the *credenza*, followed by the *credenziero*, and two more footmen carrying the basket of dishes from the kitchen; also with them were several of the cardinal's courtiers to accompany the food.[26]

At the bishops' table, the procession halted while the contents of each container was minutely examined. The stewards 'could not send in sealed pies or whole chickens, which would be cut open in the presence of the said bishops, nor could they send in wine in anything other than glass containers'. Inside the Sala Regia, the conclavists were likewise summoned in turn to the revolving shelves from where they collected the food baskets, returned the containers used for the last meal and gave the steward orders for the next day, before carrying the baskets to their cardinal's cubicle. After the cardinals and conclavists had finished eating, the left-over food was 'distributed to the conclave servants, the barbers, builders, carpenters, apothecaries, sweepers and others', who hopefully enjoyed the luxurious fare on offer, while the terracotta pots and dishes, and the glass containers all went to the master of ceremonies himself, a highly profitable perk of his unenviable job.[27]

Meanwhile Firmano recorded further measures to safeguard the security of the conclave. On 9 October a new committee was appointed with: two bishops, Bellay (France) and Cesi (France); two priests, Corgna (Spain) and Dolera (Carafa); and two deacons, Savelli (Carafa) and Sermoneta (France).[28] The committee, acting on the orders of the master of ceremonies, instructed the episcopal team guarding the conclave entrance to check all the rooms and passages adjoining the conclave and to seal any holes they found in the walls 'which was their job', as the conscientious Firmano reminded them, shifting some of the blame for the chaos onto their negligence. This was a little unfair – the master of ceremonies seems to have been unaware that it was the cardinals themselves, as we shall see, who were keeping the holes open and co-operating in a manner entirely absent from their fractious confrontations in the Cappella Paolina. The bishops were also ordered to stop all conversations between conclavists and outsiders at the revolving shelves, and to make sure that these orders were passed on to all their off-duty colleagues – it is evident that the bishops too were not above passing the buck.

That same day, Monday, 9 October, Firmano and the committee met in private in Bellay's cubicle – we do not know where this was because, rather oddly, in view of his habitual obsession for detail, the master of ceremonies failed to record the location of this cell on his handwritten draft and it is also missing from the version that was later published. At this meeting 'it was decided to expel five noblemen from the conclave who were said to be negotiating on behalf of several princes' – among those sent out were Pacheco's nephew and one of Carafa's secretaries. 'It was also decided to reduce the amounts of food sent in,' though Firmano's diary does not record how this was to be done and, as Ippolito's food bills show no sign of decreasing (see pp. 154–6), there must be some doubt about whether this was in fact enforced. Certainly no one had taken much notice of the request he had made the previous week that everyone was to remain in their cells overnight, because he was obliged to repeat the order that 'no one is to move around the conclave during the night after my bell has been rung'.

The following day, Tuesday, the committee met again in Bellay's cubicle after lunch, this time to reduce the numbers of unauthorized personnel who were posing as conclavists. They decided 'to summon everyone to the Cappella Paolina, and lock them in the chapel', where their names were recorded. All those who were not named on the list of official conclavists submitted by each cardinal were expelled, though 'those cardinals who were ill were allowed four', Firmano recorded.[29] On Wednesday 'four holes were found in the sacristy and were sealed up' – the sacristy was accessible from the Sistine Chapel, through a locked door under Michelangelo's Last Judgement.[30] Later that afternoon the committee ordered shutters to be placed on the windows in several rooms 'so that the cardinals who are in there cannot be seen from the palace courtyard'. After this flurry of activity, Firmano's diary remained silent for two weeks, which suggests that his attempts to restore order were having some impact.

The reinterpretation of the rules regulating the number of conclavists had a long tradition. Gregory X's reform bull of 1274 had stipulated just two for each cardinal, and this had been stretched to three over the centuries – but even this number had been widely ignored for some time. Ippolito brought seven conclavists with him during the 1549–50 conclave, one of whom was a menial servant, and the other six all courtiers from his household, making a total of eight men bedding down in what must have been a very crowded cell.[31] Unfortunately, we are less well-informed about who his conclavists were on this occasion but what his ledgers make clear is that they – and presumably the conclavists of his fellow cardinals – changed frequently, making it very hard for poor old Firmano to keep track of who was allowed in and who was not. The letter Ippolito wrote to his nephew about the death of Ercole in early October was taken to France by one of the dead duke's courtiers, Count Pagano, 'who has been in here with me for many days so he can talk to you in person and give you an up-to-date account of what has been happening in here'.[32] As we shall see, Ippolito's old friend Provosto Trotti also spent some time inside as did his chamber servant Meschino, who probably shared the job of looking after his master's personal needs with a colleague. Ippolito's chief valet, Montino Priorato, and another courtier, Pietro da Sezza, are both recorded inside the Vatican, bringing with them supplies of bedding from Ippolito's wardrobe, while his secretary Ludovico Ricciolo was evidently sleeping in the cubicle in the Sala Ducale, from where he managed to lose the sheets from his bed.[33]

Officially, at least, the role of a conclavist was basically that of a domestic servant. According to the manual of regulations governing a conclave, he was expected 'to serve his cardinal in all ways, spiritual and domestic, in private and in public' – it was assumed that one of the men would be a chaplain, though there is little evidence that Ippolito observed this particular recommendation.[34] The manual outlined the practical tasks expected, such as the responsibility to avoid the risk of fire, all of which were to be carried out with care to avoid 'clattering with feet or hands, or loud shouting'. In reality, though, the conclavists played a far more active role in the conclave: they were there to offer advice, to undertake delicate negotiations with other cardinals or their conclavists on his behalf and to provide the company of a friend in what was becoming an increasingly spiteful environment.

Moreover, many conclavists had their own agendas, which did not always coincide with that of their cardinal, adding yet another layer of complexity to the scheming and plotting that was going on inside the Vatican. Carafa's conclavist, for example, Fabrizio di Sangro, was a loyal subject of Philip II, one reason no doubt behind Carafa's readiness to ally with Vargas. Sforza's conclavist, Francesco Lottino, who had been Sforza's conclavist in the last three conclaves, was also an agent of Cosimo I. Although he had been willing to help the camerlengo and Ippolito obtain the votes of the Florentine cardinals for Gonzaga, he was also campaigning against Sforza's interests, promoting Cosimo I's own candidates, Medici and Ricci. A highly colourful character who had been responsible for the elimination of several of Cosimo's enemies, including the poisoning of a cardinal, he had weathered several scandals, not least accusations of both Protestant sympathies and sodomy. In later life, he used his experiences to write a treatise on papal elections – a political handbook purporting to show a cardinal how to gain election to the papal throne that was quite as devious as anything written by Machiavelli.

Meanwhile, as in the early days of the conclave, the proliferation of names emerging from the voting urns showed that the real business of electing a pope had been firmly put on hold. There were votes for many improbable candidates, even some for the ex-rent boy Innocenzo del Monte.[35] Galvanized by Vargas, the Spanish concentrated on promoting Pacheco and this elderly Spaniard received between eighteen and twenty-two votes every day from 2 October to the end of the month. The campaign for Pacheco, however, was a feint: Vargas was waiting for the right moment to launch a more serious bid for his preferred candidate, Carpi. Carpi himself occasionally reached eight votes during October, as did Gonzaga while Ippolito had a maximum of seven.[36] Inquisitor General Ghislieri surprised many when he received twenty votes on Thursday, 12 October but the fears that this grim Dominican might be elected evaporated at the scrutiny the following morning when Ghislieri's support fell away to just five votes. However, there were twenty-one votes for Alessandro Farnese's younger brother Ranuccio, which must have worried the hardliners until it was remembered that 13 October was the anniversary of the election of Farnese's grandfather Paul III in 1534.

PARTIES ON 13 OCTOBER

- Spanish led by Sforza and Madruzzo   17 votes
- New cardinals led by Carafa and Farnese   14 votes
- French led by Ippolito d'Este and Guise   13 votes

two-thirds majority needed: 30 votes

The morning session might have been relatively dull but that afternoon the atmosphere in the Cappella Paolina became electric when the imperial cardinal Truchsess publicly denounced Medici as a heretic in front of his red-hatted colleagues. The gulf between the hard-line and moderate wings of the college was suddenly in sharp focus. Truchsess had been horrified by a conversation he had had with Medici a few days previously about the problems the Catholic Church faced in the Empire, where a significant proportion of the population had adopted the Protestant faith, even the heir to Ferdinand I himself. Medici, who was firmly on the liberal side of the Church and favoured pragmatic measures to deal with the Protestants, had told Truchsess, 'we should summon a council and consider what concessions could be made to them', such as 'the marriage of priests' or offering 'communion of both kinds', bread and wine, 'to the laity'.[37] Truchsess, who believed that the only solution to the Protestant problem was the total eradication of this heresy, by violent means if necessary, was deeply shocked. So shocked, indeed, that he felt that the rest of the college should be informed of this heretic in their midst.

Carpi promptly added his voice to that of Truchsess condemning Medici as a heretic, and he was joined by Giovanni Ricci, 'both of them hoping to remove him as an obstacle', as Ambassador Angoulême reported.[38] Carpi, another hardliner, lost no opportunity to bolster his own chances; Ricci's intervention, however, was much more cynical. This astute businessman had ambitions for the papal tiara and he seized this chance of discrediting Medici in the hope that he could replace the gouty lawyer as Cosimo I's favourite, a plan he was pursuing with the active support of Sforza's conclavist Lottino. The prospect of Ricci as pope appalled Angoulême: 'It is said that Ricci has a Portuguese woman living with him as his wife, with whom he has had several children and that he has had a young girl with him in the conclave.'[39] The attempt to discredit Medici had an immediate impact in the scrutinies. By the end of the following week, Medici's vote had dropped to just one, while Ricci's had gone up to six, and Carpi's to eight.

The excitement of Truchsess's accusation soon died down and the conclave returned to its torpid state. With so little happening, Ippolito had time for more domestic matters and wrote to Duke Alfonso petitioning his nephew on behalf of one of his own employees who had worked for him for twenty years and wanted a post at the new court.[40] He also wrote to his sister-in-law Renée to express his relief at hearing the news that Alfonso would soon be on his way home and that all was quiet in Ferrara, adding, 'I ask you to believe that whatever happens I have no greater object than to serve the new duke and his state.'[41] Ippolito was beginning to feel the impact of the new regime: Alfonso's father-in-law, Cosimo I, had started to put pressure on Ippolito to vote for Medici, which Ippolito was resisting, though not for the same reasons as Truchsess. Ippolito, like Medici, favoured the pragmatic approach to Protestantism but he insisted on only supporting those candidates who had been recommended by the French crown: himself, Tournon and Gonzaga.

'We have come to a halt with Gonzaga, while waiting for the reply from Spain, and the affairs of the conclave are at present in as bad a state as they were at the beginning and there is no sign of the election of a pope,' Ippolito and Guise reported to France on 18 October.[42] The French campaign for Gonzaga was further threatened by the continuing ill health of Armagnac, who was showing little sign of recovering from the malady which had forced him to leave the conclave on 20 September. On 12 October

Girolamo Simoncelli, another of the French cardinals, had also been obliged to leave the Vatican because of illness. One piece of good news arrived, however, in the form of a letter from Ferdinand I directing all three of his cardinals – Madruzzo, Morone and Truchsess – to vote for Gonzaga. Vargas, however, continued 'to do everything he can to undermine Gonzaga'. As Angoulême reported: 'It is the general opinion that nothing of profit for Gonzaga will come from Spain.'[43] Vargas attempted to order Madruzzo to stop voting for his old friend Gonzaga but the cardinal responded tartly that he was unable to comprehend why the ambassador should be so rude about a man who had always been so loyal to Spain, and followed this up with a letter to Philip II complaining about Vargas's behaviour.[44] Vargas himself made much of his skills at winning over Sforza. The camerlengo, he was confident, was now 'back on our side', he informed Philip II on 13 October.[45]

Meanwhile, behind the green silk curtains of Ippolito's cubicle, a conspiracy was being hatched which, if successful, promised an upheaval of seismic proportions in the conclave. Because of the secrecy involved, it is not easy to chart its precise progress. It was widely believed by allies and enemies alike that Gonzaga would be excluded by Philip II, and Ippolito knew that his cousin's best chance was to force an election before the king's letters arrived. There was little chance of a reply from Spain before the middle of November, which gave the French about a month – the problem, as before, was where to find the extra votes.

Despite Vargas's optimism, Sforza had not abandoned his alliance with Ippolito and the French. Indeed, on 11 October Carafa gave him an ultimatum: to break with the French or Carafa himself would join Ippolito and force the election of a Frenchman. Sforza asked for time to think and successfully negotiated a six-day breathing space before giving his answer to Carafa; and this was extended by another ten days to 27 October on the grounds that nothing could be decided until news arrived from Spain. How realistic was Carafa's threat? Vargas certainly took it seriously and, although he had no firm evidence of Philip II's intentions towards the Carafa family, he made several generous promises to Carafa on behalf of his monarch. He also begged the king to send a letter containing concrete proof of the monarch's desire to support this dubious family – for example, a guarantee that the duchy of Paliano would remain a Carafa fief – which he could show Carafa to keep the cardinal on the side of Spain.

What Vargas probably did not know was that Carafa himself was under serious pressure from his brother Giovanni, Duke of Paliano, to abandon his alliance with Spain. It was with this in mind that Giovanni gained access into the conclave in early October to speak privately to the cardinal, or as Angoulême put it, 'to persuade him to follow the wishes of the [French] king'.[46] The envoy added the significant information that 'the said duke has done much towards this end since the death of the pope and he seems to mean what he says', but he warned Cardinal Charles of Lorraine, 'nevertheless I would not swear to it as I have little trust in this whole tribe'. Giovanni also wrote to his brother, explaining his reasons, in forceful terms, why Carafa was to stop supporting the Spanish bid for Carpi and to favour the French campaign for Gonzaga. 'It really does not matter who is elected, all that is important is that the new pope should understand that he owes his election to the Carafa family,' he wrote in exasperation. 'Our house does not have the favour of either the King of France or the King of Spain, and our future depends on obtaining the support of the next pope, or we are ruined'

– strong words, indeed.[47] Around 15 October, Carafa and Vargas had a serious row in which the cardinal accused the ambassador of fabricating the promises of support his family could really expect from Spain – the cuckolded duke, and Ippolito, had certainly sown the seeds of doubt in Carafa's mind.

The next piece of the jigsaw came that same day, 15 October, in a letter Ippolito wrote to Alfonso II. He asked his nephew to write to Carafa 'celebrating the friendship and intimacy towards him that you have encountered at the [French] court and of its continuation, using whatever words you think suitable as proof of the affection in which he is held there and of the desire they have to be of service to him, ever more so now that this situation has arisen... and that regarding the conclave, to say that you would be most obliged by any gesture that he could make towards me', not forgetting to add the flattering remark that, 'I would submit myself to his judgement in all things.'[48] In a separate letter, he also asked his nephew to show special favour to Fabrizio di Sangro, Carafa's conclavist, who also held a benefice in the Este duchy. 'Besides being very close to the cardinal, he deserves to be favoured for his own merits which are such that I always take the opportunity to work on his behalf, particularly because he is always so very friendly towards me', Ippolito wrote, 'and for all these reasons I ask your Excellency to help his agent in the most productive way possible.'[49]

Ippolito was now in a position to approach Carafa with the offer of an alliance. Carafa agreed but insisted on terms: he refused to break his partnership with Farnese and the Spanish without firm promises of a principality for his family as well as specific support for himself. Ippolito and Guise were jubilant and on 18 October they wrote to Cardinal Charles and Duke François with the dramatic news.[50] First they explained Sforza's dilemma: 'Although he has been doggedly loyal in his support for our campaign for Gonzaga, he is constrained by the need to secure his own position and that of his family'; in their opinion the camerlengo was likely to be forced to leave the alliance in the near future. They then outlined Carafa's position. 'He is well aware that we can prevent any attempt to elect one of his candidates,' they wrote and they were optimistic that 'he might now consider those offers which he refused at the start of the conclave'. They added an important proviso, however: 'It will be essential, gentlemen, for the Queen Mother to write two letters, both in her own hand, one to Carafa himself, to be sent under cover to Guise, with the most gracious and courteous words she can find, and the other to us.' The two bosses needed the second letter as further proof in order to 'assure Carafa that everything has been set in action for him and for the benefit of his family'.

While Ippolito was plotting to tempt Carafa away from Vargas, the Spanish ambassador was working hard to launch a serious attempt at electing Carpi. 'Carpi has not abandoned his ambitions and for the last three days', reported Angoulême on 20 October, 'I have heard rumours that he is becoming the favourite.' But Vargas was facing insurmountable problems in his attempt to negotiate the alliance he so badly wanted between Sforza, Carafa and Farnese that would enable this. Relations between the four men were increasingly strained and Farnese was the single party boss with whom Vargas remained on satisfactory terms. 'You would not believe the malice and lack of trust that there is between them,' he informed Philip II on 18 October, and the party bosses were still firmly divided on the subject of Carpi.[51] 'Carafa insists that Carpi is his preferred candidate among those named by your majesty,' Vargas continued, but 'Sforza has innumerable difficulties with Carpi'.

Ippolito's position, however, received a further boost in late October. On 20 October Simoncelli returned to the Vatican, restored to health after a week in bed at home. There is an intriguing entry regarding this cardinal in Ippolito's ledgers, showing that there were all sorts of ways that Ippolito could ensure the loyalty of his party. Simoncelli seems to have had money worries and on 27 October there was a payment of 300 scudi 'to Signor Antonio Simoncelli, father of the cardinal' which Ippolito 'is kindly loaning to the cardinal'.[52] There was also good news from Armagnac, who had been absent since late September and was now on the mend. Angoulême confirmed that he was expected to rejoin the conclave on 22 October and there were reports that Bertrand, who had missed the royal galley at Marseilles and travelled overland to Rome, had at last arrived in the city.[53] This elderly cardinal, who had been married and had three children, had become a churchman after the death of his wife and was noted for his piety. Despite receiving his hat from Paul IV, however, he would be voting with the French.

The arrival of a new cardinal, rather than one returning after illness, necessitated a considerable degree of ceremonial in the Vatican and Bertrand's entry was recorded by Firmano who noted the minutiae of the etiquette associated with this arcane ritual in his diary.[54]

On 25 October Cardinal Bertrand, known as [the Cardinal of] Sens, who has now arrived from France, entered the conclave and was received at the door by Farnese and Sforza, the senior cardinal-deacons, who escorted the new cardinal into the Cappella Paolina, where all the other cardinals awaited him in their seats. Preceded by the master of ceremonies, the two said cardinal-deacons brought the new cardinal into the chapel and they all genuflected at the altar, and then did reverence to all the other cardinals. Then the two cardinal-deacons went to their own places, leaving the new cardinal with the master of ceremonies, who led him first to the dean [Bellay], and then to each of the other cardinals, who each greeted him with a kiss on the mouth, as is the custom when any cardinal arrives in Rome. When this was done the master of ceremonies led the new cardinal to his place and when everyone was seated the bull of Julius II was read out [by himself of course] and when it had been read the said cardinal swore to abide by it, as is the custom.

After the ceremony was over, Bertrand was escorted to cubicle number 24, which was situated across from Simoncelli's cell in the overcrowded and increasingly malodorous confines of the Sistine Chapel. The next day, 26 October, there was a commotion in the conclave when 'one of the beams in the room behind the Camera dei Paramenti collapsed and the cardinals who had their cubicles there forced open a door' – a reasonable action in the face of falling masonry, you might think, but Firmano continued in evident exasperation, 'but this was done without permission' and 'when asked by the dean Bellay no one would own up to the deed'.[55] After lunch, Firmano assembled the cardinals in the Cappella Paolina, where they were held hostage for four hours until it was finally agreed that the door had been opened without permission and would now be closed. The incident provides a fitting metaphor for the instability and uncertainty that existed between the cardinals themselves as October drew to a close. Sforza was sitting uncomfortably on the fence, waiting to hear definitive news from Spain before abandoning the bid to elect Gonzaga. Carafa was wondering what the French would offer in return for his support, and whether he could extract a better price from Spain. Vargas was struggling to keep his own ambitions on track by uniting the Spanish party with the cardinals of Carafa and Farnese. Carpi and Gonzaga were also waiting impatiently, each hoping that their names would be on Philip II's list of candidates. Ippolito himself had acquired another supporter and was hoping that Catherine de' Medici would send a positive response to his suggestion of an alliance with Carafa. Everything depended on the courier service and the speed with which two royal letters could reach the conclave, one from Spain and the other from France.

6

❧

Letters from Spain

27 OCTOBER–20 NOVEMBER

'I had planned to send Provosto Trotti to greet you,' Ippolito wrote to his nephew Alfonso on 1 November on hearing that the new duke was returning to Italy by sea and expected to land in Tuscany any day, 'but Farnese's courier has arrived from Spain, and shortly afterwards other couriers arrived with replies to the letters that were sent to Spain, so I decided it would be better to keep him in here with me for another day or two so that I could send him to you with more news.'[1] He added an update on the conclave, which had been deadlocked for almost a month: 'Regarding the business in here, there is little to tell beyond what you will have already heard, as everything has been suspended until we see the orders from Philip II.' In fact, the whole conclave was on tenterhooks: four days earlier a letter from Spain had arrived at Vargas's palace but the ambassador was showing an uncharacteristic reluctance to reveal its contents.

Even the most optimistic cardinal knew that this could not possibly be a reply to any of the urgent letters sent from the conclave in early October – indeed, the courier carrying the missive containing Philip II's instructions about Gonzaga had only just started out on his long journey from Spain. However, this letter, which bore the date 8–9 October, did contain some dramatic news: Philip II intended to force the next pope to deprive Giovanni Carafa of the duchy of Paliano and to return the fief to the Colonna family. The news was greeted with joy on the streets of Rome and, despite Vargas's attempts to suppress it, was soon known inside the Vatican where it met with a mixed response. It must have cheered Ippolito, who hoped that it would persuade Carafa to break his alliance with the Spanish. It was a disaster for Vargas, who attempted to deny the truth of the story, even to Carafa's face, but it was too late. Carafa was furious. Vargas resorted to bribery in an attempt to save the situation and, without the king's knowledge, made an offer of a large 'loan' of 7,000 scudi to Carafa on Philip II's behalf. Sforza wrote to the king to complain about the impropriety of Vargas's behaviour, but the ambassador had few scruples about offering the bribe and Carafa had even less in accepting it. Carafa was back in the Spanish fold, with Ippolito and the French again on the defensive.

The excitement soon died down and the conclave was restored to its habitual torpor. On Monday, 30 October the scrutiny lists recorded votes for a total of forty-three of the forty-five cardinals present in the Cappella Paolina.[2] Pacheco was named on nineteen ballot papers; Cueva on eighteen; Gonzaga on eleven; Carpi and Ippolito both on seven; Ghislieri and Tournon on six; Medici, Bertrand and Ranuccio Farnese all on three; Alessandro Farnese, Sforza, Ricci and Guise had two each; there were no votes for the three sick cardinals, Armagnac, Capizucchi and Simoncelli, who were still recuperating in their residences in Rome though there was a vote for the absent Cardinal of Lorraine. Only two cardinals who were in the Vatican received no votes at all: Innocenzo del Monte, Julius III's erstwhile toy boy, and Carlo Carafa.

PARTIES ON 31 OCTOBER

- Spanish led by Sforza and Madruzzo   17 votes
- New cardinals led by Carafa and Farnese   15 votes
- French led by Ippolito d'Este and Guise   16 votes

two-thirds majority needed: 32 votes

That evening Armagnac returned to the Vatican after six weeks in bed and the following day, 31 October, Capizucchi also came back to the palace after an absence of four weeks, although he was still unwell and confined to bed in his cubicle. All forty-eight cardinals attending the conclave were now all resident in the Vatican for the first time since the election began in early September. It was the eve of the feast of All Saints and late that afternoon five priests were admitted into the Vatican to hear confession so that the cardinals and their conclavists could all take communion the following day. At the door into the Sala Regia the priests all had to swear 'not to speak to any cardinal about anything regarding the election, nor to pass on any information with which they are entrusted in the conclave'.[3] Voting was suspended in honour of All Saints' Day: forty-one cardinals took communion at mass in the Cappella Paolina and five, including Capizucchi and Medici, who were too poorly to leave their cubicles, received communion in their beds, while the conclavists, 170 in all, were given communion at a special altar set up in the loggia.

It was now November and the sweltering heat of early September was a very distant memory. The sun now set in the late afternoon: the twenty-four-hour clock of the sixteenth century was measured from sunset, and the master-of-ceremonies' bed-time bell, which he rang 'at four-and-one-half hours' sounded earlier and earlier. The weather had begun to turn cold, and we can assume that Firmano ordered the fires to be lit. The woodcuts illustrating Scappi's treatise show an elegantly moulded copper bedwarmer filled with hot coals among the items furnishing a conclave cubicle, as well as an ingenious device that he described as 'an instrument for keeping the feet warm', a wooden box with a copper-lined attachment into which was inserted an iron plug that had been heated on a fire – this gadget would have been particularly welcome during the long and tedious voting sessions in the Cappella Paolina with its cold marble floor.

Ippolito's ledgers provide ample evidence of how chilly it must have been in those magnificent halls. On 30 October, Meschino's colleague Battista da Gaeta brought supplies of warm clothes into the conclave, including eight coats, many lined with fur, and the following day Meschino himself arrived with seven pairs of understockings.[4] Over the next few days more winter items arrived from Palazzo Monte Giordano for Ippolito and for the French cardinals.[5] There were six woollen blankets, some red and others white, for the beds of Ippolito, his conclavists and for Guise and the others. A packet of squirrel pelts was sent down from Ferrara and given to Guise so that his servant could line his robes with fur. By the middle of November it was cold enough for Ippolito to don a warm red woollen nightshirt in bed – like most men of the period, he normally slept naked but for a fine linen bed cap on his head. He also requested his luxurious sable coat from the wardrobe at Monte Giordano, and the tailor removed the sable lining from another garment in order to lengthen it for added warmth. With his bulky fur coat under a red silk cassock, he must have cut a majestic figure as he swept along the corridor to and from the Sala Regia – a galleon in full sail.

WINTER CLOTHES CONSIGNED TO BATTISTA DA GAETA ON 30 OCTOBER[6]

- 1 coat of purple silk cloth
- 1 coat of dark red satin lined with sable
- 1 coat of purple satin lined with squirrel
- 1 coat of dark red satin lined with sable
- 1 coat of dark red damask lined with sable
- 1 coat of red kermes silk taffeta lined with sable
- 1 coat of black velvet lined with fur
- 1 coat of dark red kermes satin lined with lynx fur

After mass in the chapel on 2 November, All Souls' Day, Ippolito spent several hours dictating letters to his secretary – it is an indication of just how time-consuming the scrutinies were that nearly all the letters he sent from the conclave are dated to days like this one when no voting took place. By our standards, writing paper was expensive: 1 scudo, worth six days' pay for a master builder, bought just 750 sheets of the top-quality paper that Ippolito used, though cheaper rag paper could be found at half the price. His ledgers record the payment of a stationer's bill for 23.64 scudi for the supply of loose sheets of writing paper.[7] He seems to have used an astonishing quantity of the stuff during the conclave. Most of his letters were dictated to one of the conclavists, who drafted them in note form before writing them out neatly in a finished version for Ippolito to sign, using expensive paper for both draft and copy; the sheets would also have been used for ballot papers, private notes to Sforza, for example, or to Carafa, and to others with invitations to dinner.

One of the letters he wrote on 1 November was to his sister-in-law, with general news about the conclave and family issues. The bulk of their correspondence, however, involved her requests for favours to loyal members of her household. As duchess she had been able to grant her own favours but Duke Ercole's death deprived her of status and income – and she was soon to be forced to retire to France (see p. 234). Ippolito gave a very polite refusal to grant a benefice in the archbishopric of Milan which, as he explained, 'it is no longer in my power to do' – he had not been Archbishop of Milan for several years now – and an equally polite prevarication for other requests: 'You can be sure that once a pope is elected I will not forget to organize what you want.'[8] He himself was the petitioner in another letter written that day to Alfonso II on behalf of a faithful servant, who had worked for him in Ferrara and had been a favourite of his daughter.[9]

Ippolito also wrote to Alfonso II on 1 November, congratulating him on his decision to travel home via Tuscany, 'not only for your own comfort but also for the pleasure this visit will bring to the Duke and Duchess of Florence, and to the lady your wife.'[10] In a long letter to Renée he confided his worries about Alfonso's marriage to Lucrezia de' Medici and hoped that the new duke 'would use this occasion to bring her home to Ferrara'. It was a real cause for concern that the duke had shown scant interest in his teenage bride. Although the couple had been married in Florence in July 1558, Alfonso had left for France immediately after the ceremony and the marriage was still unconsummated. Alfonso's agent in Florence also worried about the unhappy bride. 'Can you not express a little love, at least in writing,' he advised the duke.[11]

A week later Ippolito wrote more letters to Alfonso and to Renée, more favours to grant and more to request.[12] He asked his sister-in-law, still in charge in the absence of the new duke, to intervene on behalf of one of his courtiers who had encountered problems with officialdom when he tried to send a barge-load of wine to Venice. He wrote a very polite reply to three more letters he received from Renée: 'I will not fail to deal with your requests as soon as I am out of this place,' he promised. With his hopes of a future alliance with Carafa in mind, he reminded his nephew of the need to show goodwill towards Carafa's conclavist Fabrizio di Sangro – Ippolito was clearly now better informed, no doubt by Sangro himself during one of their conversations in the conclave, and he went into some detail about the problems that Sangro's agent was having with the law courts in Ferrara.

Carafa himself was getting increasingly impatient in the Vatican. 'The arguments between Sforza, Farnese and Carafa have reached a peak of suspicion and enmity,' Vargas informed Philip II on 5 November.[13] The ambassador had also learned of the efforts Ippolito was making to get Carafa to change sides. 'Carafa is in such a state of desperation that some days he sides with the French, and they have despatched a courier to France,' he reported, adding rather sceptically: 'Guise claims to have carte blanche to negotiate with him.' Vargas was still unaware, it seems, of the extent of Carafa's involvement with the French party; he was also unaware of the clout that Guise and Ippolito wielded at the French court.

Sforza too was vacillating: his dilemma was whether or not to abandon the French. Although he continued to support their bid for Gonzaga in the absence of any concrete statement from Philip II, he was well aware that this infuriated Vargas and that the ambassador was determined to discredit his standing with the king. For example, Vargas sent a blacklist of nine cardinals, headed by Sforza, 'who have been and are still voting for

Gonzaga'.[14] In the same letter he stoked anti-French sentiment with the scandalous 'news' that Guise's brother had been inside the Vatican again, and that this time 'the Grand Prior of France entered the conclave and he was given permission to come in and even allowed to be present at the scrutiny, both of which are the most shameful and disgraceful things that you can imagine.' There is no mention of these flagrant breaches of the rules in other sources and indeed it is hardly credible that the officious Firmano would have given permission for an outsider to enter the conclave, let alone to sit in on a voting session – it seems more likely that Vargas was exaggerating the perfidy of the French for political effect.

Ippolito himself must have had good reason to be relieved when the grand prior finally left Rome a few days later, along with the rest of the entourage of French courtiers who had accompanied Guise and his brother on their voyage from France. The French visitors had meant a lot of extra chores for the staff in Palazzo Monte Giordano – meals to cook, rooms to clean, sheets to wash and so on, in addition to their time-consuming task of catering for the needs of Ippolito, Guise and the conclavists in the Vatican. While the grand prior himself was lodged in the guest apartments at the palace, Ippolito had rented two houses nearby for the others, providing some of the furnishings from his wardrobe and hiring the rest from a dealer in second-hand goods.[15] It is evident from Ippolito's inventories that not all his possessions were returned when the French courtiers departed. Listed as missing, or stolen, were four fine linen sheets, one white wool blanket, a cushion, a pillow, five beds, six bedcovers, seven expensive wool mattresses, three cheaper palliasses and five tables, as well as three large and valuable silver platters, these all specified as stolen.[16]

That November the master of Ippolito's wardrobe, Diomede Tridapalle, was particularly busy with the task of organizing new furnishings for the palace and making new outfits for Ippolito that would be needed once the conclave was over – the whole household must have hoped that, at the very least, the new pope would prove well-disposed towards their cardinal and restore his posts, his privileges and his wealth. Although much of the material for these items came from stocks in Ippolito's wardrobe, which had finally arrived from Ferrara at the beginning of October, extra items were needed. Ippolito's agent in Milan spent 70 scudi on large quantities of gold and silver brocade while Diomede ordered some 400 yards of purple velvets and silk cloth from the Capponi warehouse in Florence, a celebrated supplier of quality textiles – we do not know the price of this material, but it came in four bales that cost 12 scudi to transport to Rome.[17] Diomede also commissioned six new walnut chairs upholstered with purple cloth and gold edging and made other purchases in Rome, including a payment of 95 scudi to Camillo *banderaio*, who specialized in the manufacture of fringes and braid made of expensive gold and silver thread – his shop, with its valuable stock, remained open for business despite the anarchy of the *sede vacante*.[18]

The autumn also saw a lot of extra work for Ippolito's tailor – quite a change from the relatively easy time he had spent in Ferrara during his master's exile. In September, Diomede commissioned him to start work on a set of luxurious bed hangings ornamented with gold and red fringes, which required stitching over 200 yards of red damask.[19] This damask was particularly expensive as it was dyed using kermes (It: *cremesino*, from the Arabic, *qirmiz*), a red pigment made from crushed insects and imported to Italy at immense cost from the Middle East. The tailor's next task had been to make a new set of furnishings for Ippolito's coach, using purple cloth with a matching silk lining.[20] In early October he had made new black covers for the coach horses, perhaps to mark the death of Duke Ercole, and started work on the scarlet blanket that Ippolito would need for his mule once the conclave was over and he started attending consistories again.[21] At the end of the month, the tailor began work on a religious cape, which was to be lavishly lined with white ermine, as well as a purple silk *saglio*, a tunic Ippolito would wear with his breeches and hose – evidently he intended to don secular attire again once the conclave was over.[22] In the middle of November the tailor's poor fingers were hard at work sewing a second set of bed hangings, this one made of purple silk decorated with matching fringes; it also included a purple velvet canopy, a counterpane of purple satin and pommels painted with Ippolito's coat-of-arms.[23]

Meanwhile, on 11 November the long-awaited letter from Philip II arrived at Vargas's palace and the election jerked suddenly back into life. Writing on 27 October in answer to the urgent letters from Rome, the king outlined his position with great reluctance. Under pressure from diplomats of all nations to name his candidates, he had prevaricated and asked his councils of state for advice: both had cautioned him against naming a favourite, one on the grounds that it would be dangerous for the king to be seen as responsible for the election of a bad pope and the other that it would be better to name only those cardinals he wished specifically to exclude from election.[24] Eventually, the king's intentions were leaked. The Venetian ambassador reported from Toledo on 14 November that 'in public the king declines to interfere in the conclave, his only desire being that the cardinals should elect an honest man' but, the envoy added in code, 'I am informed that privately the king wishes the election of Carpi, Medici or Morone, and does not want either Gonzaga or Pacheco; he objects to the former because his family is too powerful in Italy and to the latter because he is connected to an illustrious family in Spain', a factor that could affect the delicate balance between the factions at the Spanish court.[25]

In fact, Philip II had written another letter to Vargas a week earlier. In this one, which was dated 20 October, he instructed his ambassador to do everything possible to prevent the election of Gonzaga but Vargas was expressly ordered not to tell anyone of his exclusion of Gonzaga, though he could inform Sforza if absolutely necessary, and he was at all costs to maintain the fiction that the king supported the campaign for Gonzaga. As the Venetian ambassador in Spain explained, 'his majesty is much troubled about this... on the one hand he does not wish Gonzaga to be elected but on the other he worries about upsetting the Gonzaga family', not least the cardinal's brother Ferrante, who was Philip II's governor in Milan.[26] Unfortunately this cautionary missive was inexplicably delayed – letters did go missing, couriers could be held up on the road. So it was the second letter that was delivered to Vargas on 11 November, the one in which the king repeated his specific exclusion of Gonzaga but had not thought it necessary to reiterate the urgent need for secrecy.

Vargas was jubilant. Climbing into the conclave that evening as usual, through one of the open windows or the hole in the wall, the ambassador had a meeting with Sforza at which he informed the camerlengo of the king's decision and ordered him to tell Gonzaga that he had been excluded by the king. Vargas must have relished this moment of triumph over Sforza. Gonzaga dutifully informed Ippolito of his decision to stand down. Neither man was very surprised. 'Because of the very long wait that there has been for the answer from Spain, Gonzaga had foreseen this news,' Ippolito and Guise informed Catherine de' Medici, 'and he has declared that he does not want to draw out the business of this conclave any longer and he is very grateful to all those who have supported his campaign for the papacy.' [27] Everyone in the conclave and courts abroad now knew Philip II's real opinion of Gonzaga, which he had been at such pains to keep secret. And Vargas must have had a shock when the first letter, that of 20 October, arrived a week later: the king's fury at his ambassador's actions would have serious repercussions. In the short term, however, Philip II's letter had considerably strengthened Vargas's position. With royal approval for his destruction of Gonzaga's campaign, Sforza was obliged to break his alliance with the French and now, with Sforza back under his control, Vargas had a very real chance of manoeuvring his own candidate into power. All he needed was to keep Carafa on his side.

While Sforza was telling Gonzaga the bad news, Vargas held a meeting with Carafa. He began by reassuring this irascible and unpredictable ally. He promised, with no basis for such a claim, that the king would be generous in his support of Carafa. 'Half a word from him is worth more than all the promises and guarantees of any other prince,' as he put it.[28] Carafa, however, was not to be satisfied with these vague words and insisted on more concrete proof of the favours that Philip II would grant to his family, especially to his brother Giovanni, soon to be the ex-Duke of Paliano and disinherited on the orders of the king himself. At this point, with the light of victory beckoning, ambition got the better of the ambassador. He overstepped his authority and forged a written note from Philip II promising that Carafa's loyalty would be rewarded with a principality for the cuckolded Giovanni. It was enough – Carafa was hooked. Back home later that night, Vargas could reflect with some satisfaction on his achievements that day: he had broken the alliance between Sforza and Ippolito, and he had restored unity to the Spanish party that had split over the candidacy of Gonzaga. He could now work openly to secure the election of his preferred candidate, Carpi.

As Vargas's campaign for Carpi began to take shape, Ippolito and Guise received the reply to the letter they had sent to France on 18 October, in which they had asked Catherine de' Medici to send tangible proof of what would be on offer to Carafa in return for his support – Carafa must have thoroughly enjoyed being courted in such a fashion by the two superpowers of Europe. The dowager queen did exactly as Ippolito and Guise had requested and they now had letters for Carafa, written in her own hand, outlining the rewards the cardinal could expect from the French crown. The precise terms of the offer do not survive but, according to Cosimo I's ambassador, it included not only the guarantee of all the cardinal's benefices in Italy, as well as the huge sum of 30,000 scudi in cash, but also the marquisate of Saluzzo for Giovanni.[29] This was a very generous offer, and one which rewarded the Duke of Paliano for his loyal and persistent attempts to persuade his brother to abandon the Spanish and join the French. Vargas, who had been unable to extract a guarantee on this scale from his own monarch, paid Ippolito the compliment of describing him as 'the most formidable opponent I have ever seen.'[30]

Unfortunately the impact of the French offer was not all that Ippolito and Guise could have desired. 'We have been much assisted by the dispatch that it has pleased your majesty to send us on the third of this month with the Queen Mother's letters to Carafa,' they replied formally to the king, 'which we gave to him, and he received them with great regard and esteem at the great favour and honour you have shown to him.'[31] But – there was inevitably a 'but' – they cautioned (with understandable frustration) that 'he insists absolutely on this remaining a secret and will not promise anything as long as the campaign for Carpi is underway and he refuses to be diverted from it in any way, and will not support another candidate'. Vargas, they continued 'is doing everything he can, writing to some cardinals and speaking to others, to coax and wheedle them into supporting Carpi'.

PARTIES ON 15 NOVEMBER

- Spanish led by Sforza and Madruzzo   17 votes
- New cardinals led by Carafa and Farnese   15 votes
- French led by Ippolito d'Este and Guise   16 votes

two-thirds majority needed: 32 votes

Vargas's campaign for Carpi's election began in earnest on Wednesday, 15 November. Sforza, Madruzzo, Farnese and Carafa were now all working together, if not in complete amity then at least with a degree of agreement between them, no doubt assisted by Vargas who was regularly in attendance at night-time meetings with all four party bosses. They knew that if they could get all their supporters behind them, then they had exactly the thirty-two votes necessary to secure Carpi's election and the key to success would be to build up momentum in Carpi's favour.

However, Carpi only received a disappointing nine votes in the scrutiny that day and, though he had eleven the next morning, the vote count had only increased to twelve on Friday.[32] Even the stubborn Vargas had to admit that the strength of the opposition to Carpi, spearheaded by Ippolito, made him unelectable and the campaign was abandoned on Sunday. Carpi accepted the decision with good grace and agreed to withdraw from the race.

In the space of a week, the two candidates who had dominated the conclave since it had begun in early September were both out. 'We are still adjusting to the fact', Ippolito and Guise informed their king on Monday, 20 November, 'that Carpi, just like Gonzaga, has declared that he no longer has any pretensions to the papal throne.'[33] With these two favourites out of the race, Ippolito could now start to build up support for his own ambitions for the papal tiara. As he had also been excluded by Philip II, he could not expect to make an alliance with the Spanish cardinals and he knew he needed Carafa's votes to succeed. Ippolito and Guise, who had extracted a promise from Carafa that he would join the French after Carpi's campaign was over, were now waiting for him to honour his word. Carafa, however, continued to prevaricate. 'For our part, we have not been losing time', they continued in their letter to the king of 20 November. 'We are trying to come to some agreement with Carafa, who replies to us with favourable words, that he will do what he promises in good time.' Ippolito and Guise must have been very aware that it would not help to force the unpredictable Carafa into a corner. 'We are both prepared to give him more time' and 'to conduct ourselves with him in the most patient way possible,' they added, judiciously.

Ippolito must also have been buoyed up to hear of the safe landing of his nephew Alfonso on the coast of Tuscany. On 18

November he wrote to Renée: 'Yesterday evening there was news here that the duke landed at Livorno on 14 November, which is an enormous relief to me... and if this is true your excellency will have been informed earlier than me, though I have heard nothing from him.'[34] The new duke was to spend a few days as the guest of his father-in-law, Cosimo I, and the business of the election would certainly feature prominently in their conversations.

Over the past few weeks, Ippolito had tried to negotiate with Cosimo, asking him to order the Florentine cardinals to support his own campaign for election, which he intended to launch as soon as Carafa was on board. In return, Ippolito promised the votes of the entire French party to elect Cosimo's own candidate Medici, but not until his own campaign had failed. Cosimo, however, remained unenthusiastic. He explained to Alfonso, with some impatience, that Ippolito would never be elected as he had been specifically excluded by Philip II, and that he should 'stop wasting time and nominate Medici'.[35] He also asked his son-in-law to persuade Ippolito to back down. Lottino – Sforza's conclavist as well as Cosimo I's agent – confided his worries to Cosimo that a campaign for Medici was as likely to fail as Gonzaga's had done, but he added that Medici's gout and generally poor health would make him an attractive candidate to Ippolito, who would recognize that a sickly pope likely meant another conclave in the near future.[36]

Alfonso II finally arrived back safely in Ferrara on 20 November, where he attended the solemn funeral ceremonies for his father and then his own formal investiture as duke. A magnificent procession of courtiers, nobles, clerics, lawyers, government officials and musicians celebrated his accession, winding its way through the streets of Alfonso's new capital that had been lavishly decorated with festoons of greenery, the family coat-of-arms, and statues of Peace and Abundance. What a contrast to Rome where the power vacuum dragged on and on, with no end in sight.

The conclave had now lasted nearly three months and the mood on the streets of Rome was verging on desperation. Large crowds gathered each day in the piazza in front of St Peter's but they waited in vain for the ornamental papal cross to appear in the great window of the Cappella Paolina. Ambassador Angoulême was at the conclave door on 14 November to urge the cardinals to come to a decision, followed a few days later by his imperial counterpart. It was clear the long duration of the conclave was causing major problems for the Catholic Church as well as for the Romans, who had been without a government or law courts since the middle of August. The city magistrates sent a deputation to the Vatican to complain that they were running out of funds and could no longer pay the large numbers of the soldiers keeping order on the streets. There were worries too about how to cope with the numbers of German Protestants who were apparently arriving in the city disguised as monks and openly preaching their heretical beliefs.[37] And rumours that food stocks were running low were fuelling the chaos.

Ippolito's ledgers, however, do not confirm these reports of violence on the streets and suggest that rumours of famine were scaremongering. There is some evidence that firewood was scarce – Ippolito bought a large load of logs from Cardinal Sermoneta, one of the Italians in his party, rather than from his usual suppliers, though the carter does not seem to have had any problems delivering to Palazzo Monte Giordano.[38] It is also possible that the Neapolitan wine merchants had ceased trading in Rome because Ippolito sent one of his courtiers to Naples carrying over 1,200 scudi in letters of credit to buy wine in the kingdom – given the amount that was being consumed inside the Vatican, we know that wine was certainly a major priority.[39] Nor does it seem that there were any difficulties when the first delivery of 192 barrels of *vino greco* from Ischia arrived at the port of Rome, where the customs officials duly collected their tax before they were loaded onto carts for the journey through the streets to the palace cellars.[40] Moreover, Antonio the butcher, Jacomo the greengrocer, Gianino the fruit seller and all the other shopkeepers continued to make their regular deliveries of food, while the large carts bringing hay, straw and fodder for Ippolito's stables rumbled regularly along the city streets.

MEAT PRICES (per lb)[41]

December 1559		June 1560
• 6 baiocchi	veal	5 baiocchi
• 4 *ditto*	stewing steak	4
• 3 *ditto*	mutton	3
• 2.4 *ditto*	cheap beef	2.5

There is little evidence in the ledgers of a dramatic rise in food prices. One of the few itemized bills in Ippolito's ledgers are those sent in by the butcher for the deliveries made to Palazzo Monte Giordano in December and June the following year, and the price differences are minimal. Moreover, there was no significant rise in the price of grain, a sure sign of an approaching famine. Ippolito had paid just over 3 scudi for a *rubbia* of wheat in September and though the price had risen, which was normal during a *sede vacante*, it had only reached

4 scudi by the beginning of January, nowhere near the 8 or 9 scudi that would have brought real hardship.[42] However, the long duration of the conclave was beginning to be felt by all the cardinals, not just Ippolito, in their purses.

Fraying Tempers

21 November–16 December

The conclave was now nearing the end of its third month and it is evident from Ippolito's ledgers that it was imposing a strain on his finances. By the middle of November, his treasurer Francesco Novello faced a serious cash-flow problem. Since the opening of the conclave, he had received a total of 6,745 scudi – 3,245 scudi in income from Ippolito's French benefices, forwarded in letters of credit from Lyon and Paris, and 3,500 scudi, a loan from Duke Ercole – but the bills paid over the same period, meticulously recorded by the bookkeeper, amounted to over 9,000 scudi.[1] Having been sacked by Paul IV as cardinal-protector of France and governor of Tivoli, there was no income from either of these two lucrative posts – nor would there be in the future, Novello knew, unless the conclave elected a pope inclined to grant favours to Ippolito. Moreover, although it had been relatively easy to economize while in exile in Ferrara, this was not an option now. Promoting the image of Ippolito as one of most prestigious cardinals in the college was of primary importance – he could not afford to stint.

The conclave routinely involved additional expenses. Among the more minor ones were the cost of transporting firewood to the Vatican kitchens and paying the wages of the extra staff working there for the duration of the conclave (see p. 115). Much more costly were the expenses he incurred as leader of a party that included several cardinals without residences in Rome, obliging Ippolito to play host. He had furnished the conclave cubicles for his French colleagues at his own expense, and paid the bills for accommodation for the French courtiers who had come to Rome with Guise and Strozzi, which included the rent of rooms (57.64 scudi) and the hire of bedding and furniture (103.09 scudi) from Francesco, a dealer in second-hand goods who had a shop near the church of Santa Maria della Pace, not far from the Piazza Navona and the 'talking statue' of Pasquino.[2]

By far the greatest expense, however, were the supplies needed for Ippolito's cooks and *credenzieri* to create the lavish spread of dishes that they provided for the dining tables of Ippolito and his colleagues in the Vatican. Food was far more expensive in Rome than it had been in Ferrara – chickens, for example, were twice the price.[3] Under normal circumstances, Novello would have settled the bills of the regular tradesmen at the end of each month but by November many invoices were still unpaid and the treasurer negotiated terms with several shopkeepers. Silvestro, who supplied poultry and the game birds of which Ippolito was particularly fond, agreed to accept 170 scudi on account for the 635.45 scudi he was owed on the supplies he had delivered to Palazzo Monte Giordano during October.[4] Battista Facianis, the grocer, proved even more accommodating: his September and October bills for the cheese, cured ham, raisins, almonds and other dry goods Ippolito had consumed were both outstanding but he accepted an interim payment of 150 scudi from Novello, and the bills themselves, which amounted to 503.85 scudi, were not settled until December.[5]

THE COST OF THE CONCLAVE[6]

Average (in scudi)

Item	Sep.	Oct.	Nov.	Dec.	Feb.–May 1560
meat	300.55	378.34	362.78	451.50	121.44
poultry & game	541.24	635.45	503.70	476.81	110.03
fish	320.99	157.03	190.58	182.52	59.39
vegetables	40.74	60.57	63.74	64.53	7.18
fruit	143.95	116.86	94.13	89.93	12.74
groceries	253.54	250.31	273.41	165.29	143.38
sugar & spices	87.45	n/a	101.79	n/a	27.45
firewood	116.75	96.25	77.55	295.50	63.43
pottery	214.68	104.39	88.95	n/a	16.95
glass	31.39	48.50	14.41	9.07	2.88
wine	1413.77	1108.22	1335.50	640.39	311.20
misc household	113.97	258.51	265.34	340.66	245.57
brooms	3.34	n/a	3.73	n/a	3.30
tallow candles	14.32	20.45	58.18	n/a	19.27
TOTALS	**3596.68**	**3234.88**	**3433.79**	**2716.20**	**1144.21**

Turning the pages of Ippolito's ledgers for 1559 and 1560, we can see just how much the conclave banquets were costing him. Comparing the total sums spent on food and other supplies during the months of September to December 1559 with an average figure for the bills for the same items bought in the early months of 1560 after the conclave was over, it is evident that his expenditure was strikingly higher during the conclave. As there is no evidence to suggest that these marked differences were caused by price rises – the price of meat, as we have seen, remained largely unchanged (see p. 150) – we have to conclude that Ippolito's staff needed significantly more supplies.

During the conclave Ippolito's ledgers record the purchase of twice as much meat from the butcher and twice the quantity of goods from Battista Facianis's grocery shop; some months he bought over five times the amounts of poultry, game and fish. The bills for fruit and vegetables were higher still but it is likely that by the spring of 1560 Ippolito's cooks and *credenza* staff were able to take advantage of the plants that were sown during the autumn in the kitchen garden at his villa on the Quirinal (see p. 8). The pattern becomes even clearer when you look at the last three items in the table, none of which concerned the conclave: the bills for miscellaneous expenses of the household at Palazzo Monte Giordano and those for the brooms used to sweep the palace floors hardly change at all, while the rise in the candle-maker's bill for November surely reflected the decreasing hours of daylight as winter approached.

The largest changes occurred in the bills for pottery and glass – the terracotta pots in which Ippolito's dishes were transported to the conclave, and the carafes and glasses for his wine. The quantities involved here were immense: the October bill for glass, which came to 48.50 scudi, looks modest enough when set against 635.45 scudi for poultry and game, for example, but this sum would have paid for the huge number of 533 crystal glasses, the most expensive item supplied by Gaudenzio the beaker-maker (It: *bichiraro*), or over 1,000 carafes.[7] Ippolito and his guests had brand new pottery and glass at every meal, after which these containers were given to Firmano as one of the perks of his job – intriguingly, we can now put a financial value (511.39 scudi, to be precise) on what was effectively the tip that Ippolito was obliged to give this official for his services, a sum which suggests that, although the post of papal master of ceremonies might have had its disadvantages, it was certainly a lucrative appointment.

It is unlikely that Ippolito himself lost any sleep over how he was going to pay his bills. He had enough clout at the papal court to borrow, and he would have considerably more if he managed to engineer his own election – as we know from the activities of Diomede in his wardrobe (see p. 141–2), he was certainly making no effort to stint on display, and when he sent Novello to Naples on business in November, the treasurer spent 236.36 scudi on twelve elegantly decorated gilded cups to add to Ippolito's already impressive collection of silver.[8] Splendidly wined and dined in his luxurious cubicle in the Sala Ducale, Ippolito would have been fully preoccupied those dark evenings in mid-November with his own campaign for the papal tiara and, above all, how he was to secure the votes of the Carafa party to achieve his ambition. As he had informed Catherine de' Medici on Monday, 20 November, he did not intend to rush this unpredictable ally but rather to be patient and give Carafa time to make up his own mind when to join the French.

Carafa took the best part of a week to consider his position and it was an astute move on Ippolito's part to give him space. On Sunday, 26 November, Carafa met with Sforza, Madruzzo and Farnese to inform them of his intention to join Ippolito and Guise, and the following day he held a similar conversation with Vargas. These meetings must have been stormy. The news of Carafa's desertion was a disaster for the Spanish and Pacheco, in particular, must have been apoplectic with fury. The week before, the Roman newssheets had reported a blazing row between Pacheco and Carafa in which the Spanish grandee had accused Paul IV's nephew of delaying the election by his 'improper dealings', adding angrily that 'this was not suitable behaviour for a conclave, nor the way that cardinals should deal with one another and that he was astonished by [Carafa's] presumption and audacity and the lack of respect he was displaying to the sacred college'.[9]

With Carafa on his side, Ippolito could now begin to plan his own campaign in earnest – and he knew that it was essential to act at once as two members of his party, Capodiferro and Dandino, were both seriously ill. However, before he was able to put his plans into action, the officious master of ceremonies interrupted proceedings with another spate of measures to reform the conclave. On the Monday afternoon the cardinals were summoned to the door of the Sala Regia to hear a delegation of city magistrates complain yet again about the delay, and about the excessive interference from outside. The efforts that Firmano had made to reform the conclave six weeks earlier had proved largely ineffectual and, once again, the Vatican halls were swarming with men, none of whom had the right to be there but who all had personal or political reasons for wanting to influence the election.

The following day, Tuesday, 28 November, Firmano summoned the cardinals to a meeting in the Cappella Paolina at which new measures to improve security were discussed, notably that all the unauthorized personnel were to be promptly expelled. The cardinals elected another committee to take charge of the reforms – a bishop, Cesi (France), a priest, Madruzzo (Spain), and a deacon, Carafa – and on the Wednesday the committee locked all the registered conclavists into the Cappella Paolina while another search was made of all the cells and other spaces for intruders. Amazingly, they discovered over eighty people – some reports claim that there were over a hundred – all of whom were summarily evicted, as were 'many nobles who are listed as conclavists of various cardinals but who have been interfering in the election', as an outraged Firmano recorded in his diary, though, unfortunately for us, he gave no names.[10]

Reading between the lines of Firmano's terse diary entries, it is evident that he, and the city officials too, laid the blame for the lack of security on the team of bishops, whose job it was not only to monitor the door into the Sala Regia but also, significantly, to check the adjoining rooms to ensure the conclave remained sealed. Despite attempts to cajole the bishops in early October, they had clearly not been doing their job properly and Firmano now made other arrangements. A lawyer was appointed to supervise the bishops in their inspection of food baskets, and government officials took over responsibility for security in the Vatican. The new team adopted far stricter measures, patrolling all the rooms that adjoined the conclave – 'above, below and beside' – to ensure that windows and communicating doors remained closed so that the cardinals were completely cut off from the world outside.[11] Unfortunately, the naive Firmano seems not to have realized that it was the cardinals themselves, working together with a degree of solidarity that was entirely absent from their venomous negotiations in the Cappella Paolina, who were conspiring to ensure that these holes remained open.

The following day, 30 November, the master of ceremonies announced what must have been a universally welcome measure. Having cancelled the morning scrutiny, he unlocked the door in the Sala Regia to allow a team of twelve cleaners into the Vatican to fumigate the rooms 'where the smell has become insupportable'.[12] The conclave had lasted twelve long weeks and conditions inside must have been appalling. Over 200 men – well over that number, if you include all the unauthorized visitors – had been confined in these magnificent but airless marble halls for eighty-seven days, the windows sealed for most of the time at least, and the doors out onto the loggia firmly closed against the winter chill. With the rancid smell of tallow candles now enriched with the odours of unwashed bodies, stale sweat, soiled clothes and bed linen, dirty commodes and rotting food, the stench must indeed have been truly dreadful.

Ippolito and his aristocratic colleagues were accustomed to the luxury of their own bathrooms, which were high fashion in Italy and France among the rich at that time, though more for the pleasure of bathing or sweating than for reasons of hygiene. The supplies of towels and water pots in his cubicle suggest that Ippolito did wash regularly, but he would have believed, as did most of his contemporaries, that it was the regular changing of his undergarments, which absorbed dirt, that kept him clean. Ippolito wore a clean white shirt every day – made of expensive fine linen, of course, and elaborately embroidered with coloured thread. We do not know who laundered these shirts in 1559 but during the 1549–50 conclave they had been washed along with his towels, sheets and pillowcases by the nuns at the convent of Campo Marzio.[13] However, not all the cardinals and conclavists had the same standards of personal hygiene: some would have been unable to afford the expense of daily laundry; and the more ascetic cardinals despised the obsession with cleanliness as a decadent luxury – we know, for example, that the Dominican Ghislieri wore his hair shirt day and night under his cardinal's robes.

A lot of the cardinals were sick, adding the stench of illness to the general squalor; and a sense of panic heightened the already tense atmosphere of the conclave. 'Many desired to leave because they were terrified that those who were ill might be contagious,' Firmano recorded, in more graphic terms than usual.[14] Particularly frightening was the state of the two French cardinals: Dandino lay in his cubicle in the Sala Ducale, his body covered with ominous purple blotches, the symptoms of 'purple fever', while Capodiferro, next door in the Sala del Concistoro, had become far too weak to be moved.[15] Bellay, Saraceni and Ghislieri were also all in bed, the latter probably suffering from the kidney stones which were to plague him for many more years, and which he treated with asses milk, much to the horror of his doctors. Medici had spent most of the past three months confined to his cubicle with gout and Madruzzo was also in agony with this painful affliction – Ippolito, as well as his enemy Carpi and Cueva, all fellow sufferers, were fortunate to avoid attacks of this upper-class malady during the lengthy conclave. There were rumours too that Sforza was also ill: according to Vargas he was confined to his cubicle that day, 30 November, not well enough to attend a meeting with the ambassador, though this could just as easily have been a bout of political flu.[16]

PARTIES ON 30 NOVEMBER

- Spanish led by Sforza and Madruzzo   17 votes
- New cardinals led by Carafa and Farnese   15 votes
- French led by Ippolito d'Este and Guise   16 votes

two-thirds majority needed: 32 votes

Ippolito himself seems to have remained in robust health and after lunch on 30 November, with the sulphurous fumes left by the cleaners that morning disguising the foetid stench of illness and filth, he opened his bid for the papal tiara. The French had decided to attempt to elect their party boss by homage and had managed to secure the votes of twenty-eight cardinals, as well as promises from four or five more if an election looked imminent. For the past few days the rumour mill had been unusually busy and the cardinals anticipated a dramatic voting session – some, it has to be said, more enthusiastically than others. One by one, the French cardinals each knelt before Ippolito; then came Carafa, who was making the first public display of his new allegiance, followed by members of his party, and even some of the Spanish faction. Sforza made no move but it was widely believed that he was one of those who had agreed to change sides if the vote got really close.

Farnese and Carpi, however, remained seated obstinately in their pews, watching in horror as the number of votes rose to twenty, then twenty-five. These two men detested Ippolito but how long would their colleagues hold out for loyalty; would they be prepared to jeopardize their own careers if Ippolito were to be elected? According to the ambassador of Philip II's sister, regent in the Netherlands, many of them 'were so terrified that they almost joined in the homage themselves after seeing Carafa and a large number of Sforza's cardinals doing so, because they assumed that all Carafa's supporters would follow'.[17] In the end, the bid failed but only just. Ippolito had received twenty-seven votes, five short of the thirty-two he needed, largely thanks to Madruzzo, who had persuaded a number of Carafa's party to go over to the opposition at the last minute. The arrogant Vargas would later claim in a letter to Philip II that it was he personally who had prevented Ippolito from becoming pope, and had thus averted a great catastrophe.[18]

Nevertheless, Ippolito must have been delighted with the first session of his campaign: fifty-six per cent of the vote was a very satisfactory figure for the first round, and a good basis on which to build momentum on the following day. He must also have been relieved to see how many of those who had promised their votes had indeed honoured their word – this had been a bid for election, after all, not a show of respect. In a letter to Alfonso II describing the event, he blamed Carafa rather than Madruzzo: 'If Carafa had not been so busy with the reforms' – he had been elected to the committee in charge of enforcing the security measures two days earlier – 'he would have had the time to persuade all his cardinals to agree to his plans and things would have been very different.'[19] And Ippolito was not entirely optimistic that Carafa would even now be able to convince those who had failed to vote according to the wishes of their boss: 'The majority of his party are of such hard minds and so lacking in moderation that it is almost incredible.'[20] It was a perceptive assessment of the reformist cardinals created by Paul IV – it is difficult to imagine either Ghislieri or Dolera voting for Ippolito, especially doing homage to this princely figure, wrapped in his luxurious sable-lined coat.

Ambassador Angoulême, by contrast, was far more enthusiastic about the afternoon's events and immediately dispatched an express letter to France describing what had happened. When the letter arrived, it was headline news: 'The Cardinal of Lorraine has announced', ran one report, 'that the candidacy of the Cardinal of Ferrara was proceeding so well that it was expected he would be elected by the end of the week.'[21] As the cardinals returned to their cells that evening of 30 November to await the arrival of their food baskets and dinner, rumours started to spread throughout the conclave that the French had started to redouble their efforts to gain the extra votes needed for Ippolito and that they intended to make another bid for him at the morning scrutiny. However, as the ambassador of the Netherlands reported in astonishment: 'Around 7 p.m. this evening there was news not only that [the French] were doing little about this but actually doing nothing at all.'[22] What had happened was that Ippolito had lost the votes of two of his party. Dandino's condition had deteriorated to such an extent that the doctors insisted that he must leave the conclave the following morning. And it was clear to all that Capodiferro was on his death bed – perhaps he was in a coma. The fifty-seven-year-old cardinal died in his cubicle in the Sala del Concistoro the following day.

When he arrived in the Vatican that night for his regular meetings with his allies, Vargas was unaware that Ippolito had halted his campaign. 'I have spent more than five hours tonight in the conclave speaking with several cardinals about what has happened and trying to find a solution,' the ambassador added in a postscript to a very long letter he wrote to Philip II that afternoon.[23] If we are correct in assuming that the hole in the wall through which Vargas communicated with his cardinals was behind Carpi's cell, then Ippolito was unlikely to have had much sleep that night because of the noise from across the passageway of the Sala Ducale. Long after the master of ceremonies rang his irritating bed-time bell, the Spanish ambassador could be heard loudly haranguing his cardinals: they had not used sufficient force and guile to oppose Ippolito's bid, and the election of this cardinal, the ambassador threatened in dramatic terms, would inevitably bring war as well as schism – he even had the cheek to accuse Ippolito of using bribery to buy the papal tiara.

Meanwhile, Ippolito was coming under increasing pressure

from Cosimo I to drop all the French candidates in favour of Medici, the duke's own choice. On 3 December, which was a Sunday so there was no voting, Ippolito replied to two letters he had received that week from Alfonso II, who was conscientiously following the advice of his father-in-law and doing all he could to urge Ippolito to follow the wishes of the Duke of Florence. It was evident that the new regime in Ferrara would be based on an entirely different network of loyalties from that of his dead brother, Ercole, who had made a priority of Ferrara's alliance with France. Ippolito had a tricky letter to write: 'I want to assure you', he insisted to his nephew, 'that, out of respect to you and your state, I will not fail to do all I can to elect a friend of our house'; he added, in very bland terms, 'regarding Medici in particular, I want only to serve and obey you'.[24]

Ippolito had no intention of complying with his nephew's request, for the present at least. He did, however, have plans to elect 'a friend of our house' – he had decided, somewhat surprisingly, to revive the candidacy of Gonzaga, this time with the support of Carafa's cardinals. A few days later he asked his nephew for persuasive words to keep Carafa on side. 'If it is not too much trouble', he requested Alfonso 'to write a letter to Carafa in your own hand to show that you know of his efforts to help my campaign and how hard he has worked and how grateful you are.'[25] It was the second time Ippolito had made this request. The letter Alfonso II wrote on the previous occasion apparently did not display the right level of enthusiasm: 'The last letter was too general and I did not give it to him because I feared it would have the opposite effect.'

SCRUTINY VOTES 1–6 DECEMBER[26]

	Este	Gonzaga	Cueva	Pacheco
• Fri 1 Dec	12	10	11	18
• Sat 2 Dec	11	12	10	18
• Sun 3 Dec	*no voting*			
• Mon 4 Dec	12	11	16	15
• Tues 5 Dec	10	8	16	17
• Wed 6 Dec	11	10	14	15

The week following Ippolito's failed campaign saw the conclave once again in deadlock. The French and the Spanish each marshalled their votes behind their party candidates: Ippolito and Gonzaga for the French, Pacheco and Cueva for Spain. It is not clear from the information that Madruzzo passed to the imperial ambassador where Carafa's party voted, nor how many candidates were named by each cardinal, but it is evident that Pacheco consistently received the most votes. Despite being assiduously promoted by Vargas, this Spanish reformer never received anywhere near enough for election and his vote count began to fall at the end of the week. Any residual hope that Ippolito might have had that Dandino might recover from 'purple fever' vanished on Monday 4, December when news arrived in the conclave that the fifty-year-old cardinal had died in his palace in Rome.

The cardinals had now been in the Vatican for three months and Firmano decided to play his final card and impose drastic cuts on the amounts of food coming into the Vatican. The cardinals, he announced on 5 December, were now restricted to meals of 'one course only'.[27] This was not a real hardship – they were still allowed to eat two meals a day – but it must have been an unwelcome constraint for those like Ippolito who were accustomed to a wide degree of choice at their dining-tables. Exactly how closely the regulation was observed is open to doubt: it made very little difference to the size of Ippolito's food bills – he seems to have eaten less poultry and game than he had in November, but he bought considerably more veal and beef.

There were no scrutinies on Friday, 8 December, the feast of the Immaculate Conception of the Virgin. Instead, Ippolito and his colleagues were summoned to the door of the Sala Regia for an audience with Vargas. Standing by the bishops' table on the other side of the threshold, the ambassador read out a letter he had received a few days earlier from Philip II in which the king urged them – in terms that barely concealed his disapproval of their behaviour – to elect a pope as soon as possible. It was customary on these occasions for the dean of the college to give a speech of thanks, one couched in emollient words and decorous phrases, but today Bellay lost his temper. With a marked, if understandable, lack of respect to both king and ambassador, he replied sharply to the envoy that one of the main reasons that the conclave had dragged on for so long was the excessive and unacceptable interference of Vargas himself. It was hypocrisy, Bellay fumed, for Vargas to urge them in public to hasten the election while doing everything possible behind the scenes to delay it. If the cardinals were left alone then the election would be easily accomplished. 'There are no disagreements inside the walls of this conclave that have not been brought in from outside,' he retorted.[28]

The row escalated dramatically. Unsurprisingly, Vargas took offence at the tone of Bellay's remarks, especially at the dean's implied criticism of Philip II, and retaliated by insisting that neither he nor his king were to blame for the lengthy delay. Bellay then accused Vargas of threatening several Spanish cardinals with the loss of revenues from their benefices if they refused to obey his orders. At this point the cardinals joined in. Pacheco shouted out that this was a lie, while Farnese added his voice in defence of Philip II and the crowd of red hats assembled in the Sala Regia erupted into unseemly bickering.

PARTIES ON 8 DECEMBER

- Spanish led by Sforza and Madruzzo   17 votes
- New cardinals led by Carafa and Farnese   15 votes
- French led by Ippolito d'Este and Guise   14 votes

two-thirds majority needed: 31 votes

The following day, Carafa and his party made an attempt for the election of one of their number, the Frenchman Jean Suau, an eminent lawyer made a cardinal by Paul IV and known as Cardinal Reumano. As Ippolito explained to his nephew, this had been part of the deal with Carafa: 'We were content to grant Carafa's request to see if he could elect one of his own party and he chose Reumano who, although he did not want to vote for me, as I have told you, is nevertheless French-born.'[29] The attempt failed, as everyone knew it would, but a rumour got out into the city that evening that Suau had actually been elected. The news was greeted in horror and an angry mob gathered at the Capitol in violent protest. It is not clear whether the Romans disliked Suau because he was French, or because he was one of the cardinals of the hated Paul IV, but the mood turned very ugly and the mob refused to disperse until the magistrates, having checked with the Vatican, reassured them that the rumour was untrue.

By agreeing, albeit with some reluctance, to support Carafa's bid for Suau, Ippolito hoped to secure a reciprocal promise from his new ally for the election of Gonzaga. Madruzzo may have opposed Ippolito's own campaign but the French had little difficulty persuading him to support the candidacy of his old friend. Although this directly contravened Philip II's orders for Gonzaga's exclusion, Madruzzo's loyalty was to the Emperor not to the King of Spain; and he could justify his support for Gonzaga because it followed the orders Ferdinand I had sent to Rome in the middle of October. Carafa, however, proved as tricky as ever. First he asked for time to make up his mind, determined yet again to extract maximum profit from the situation. During the past fortnight he had held meetings with Ippolito, Guise and Madruzzo and on each occasion had 'promised in the greatest possible words', as the Mantuan ambassador explained to his duke, that he would 'bring seven votes with him to make [Gonzaga] pope and that any more would be excessive'.[30] But the attempt to elect Gonzaga 'was delayed so that Carafa could have the opportunity he wanted to satisfy the cardinals of his own party which he did with the Reumano fiasco'.

In the days following the failed attempt to elect Suau, Ippolito was faced with a raft of new problems. Bellay's health had deteriorated to such an extent that he'd been carried out from the conclave and was replaced as dean by another Frenchman, François de Tournon, who was Cardinal-Bishop of Sabina, the second most senior member of the college. Moreover, Ippolito had noticed worrying signs across the passageway from his own cubicle, where he had seen Carafa being warmly welcomed into Carpi's cell. There were also troubling reports that Carafa had held night-time meetings with Vargas. Ippolito would not have been surprised to hear that the Spanish ambassador was trying to persuade Carafa to abandon his alliance with the French and return to the Spanish fold – this political chicanery was par for the course. What Ippolito did not know, although he must have suspected, was that the Spanish ambassador had made an offer to Carafa that the cardinal could not refuse.

Despite his urgent pleas, Vargas had waited in vain for a letter from Philip II with a concrete offer from the king for Carafa. Indeed, Vargas had become so desperate to secure Carafa's support that he took the astonishingly rash step of actually forging a document in Philip II's name – and not just the general offer of vague promises, such as he had made before, but the precise details of a generous cash offer and a principality for Carafa's brother. A triumphant Vargas watched as Carafa added his signature to a formal and binding alliance that committed him to rejecting any candidate excluded by Philip II – notably, in the context of early December, Gonzaga – though the unscrupulous cardinal had also insisted to Vargas that the ambassador must wait for an appropriate moment for him to change sides!

Finally, on 13 December, 'the French decided that [Carafa] had prevaricated long enough', the Mantuan ambassador reported, 'and they asked him for a date' to launch the bid for Gonzaga's election, 'so that they would know how much longer they would have to wait'; much to their surprise, 'he said the following day'.[31] That evening there was much excitement in Ippolito's cell, where the party bosses met to discuss tactics for the morning. Madruzzo was so confident of success that he had sent their silver and other precious possessions back to his palace in the city, so that he could avoid the widespread theft of valuables from the conclave cells that invariably accompanied a papal election.[32] But the warning lights came on when Carafa informed Ippolito and the others that he intended to perform a bizarre feint the next morning: at the beginning of the session he would appear to support Carpi in order, so he said, to mislead the opposition, before changing sides at the critical moment. Ippolito, Guise and Madruzzo were immediately suspicious. Carafa was not trustworthy at the best of times, and his behaviour over the last few days had been far from reassuring. After he left, the French made their own plans for the next day.

PARTIES ON 14 DECEMBER

- Spanish led by Sforza and Madruzzo   17 votes
- New cardinals led by Carafa and Farnese   15 votes
- French led by Ippolito d'Este and Guise   13 votes

two-thirds majority needed: 30 votes

It came as no surprise in the morning when Carafa told the French that they would have to delay the bid for Gonzaga because he needed more time. The Mantuan ambassador now takes up the story: 'When the day and the prearranged hour came, the excellent Carafa' – heavy irony here – 'went to find Guise and Ferrara and told them it would be better to delay everything until after lunch so that Farnese would not disturb anything.'[33] Exactly where this conversation took place is unclear, but it is certain that Carafa must have lured them away from Ippolito's cell in the Sala Ducale. Suddenly, Ippolito and Guise could hear shouts of 'Carpi! Carpi! ringing through the conclave as crowds of Farnese's and Carafa's cardinals gathered at Carpi's cubicle, where the excellent Carafa joined them and he was exposed as the traitor when he himself led Carpi to the Cappella Paolina' – where Farnese and Carafa, in a plot masterminded by Vargas, hoped to elect this pro-Spanish reformist by homage. Ippolito and Guise gathered their party together to resist the momentum that was building, just as it had for Ippolito a fortnight earlier, in the Cappella Paolina.

The French were soon joined by two young cardinals from Carafa's party, Taddeo Gaddi and Vitellozzo Vitelli, aged thirty-nine and twenty-eight respectively, who had both promised their votes for Gonzaga. To the French party's surprise, and no doubt relief, they now 'pledged their loyalty to Guise and Ferrara', the Mantuan envoy continued.[34] Gaddi, in particular, was furious at this latest example of Carafa's duplicitous behaviour, and the two men refused point blank to join their leader in the chapel 'so that Carafa came out to look for them in their cells', both of which were in the Sistine Chapel, and 'got down on his knees and began to entreat them not to forget the duty which they had promised and the loyalty that they were obliged to show him, and then he pleaded with them and implored them but they still refused' to take any part in the election of Carpi. The argument quickly lost any semblance of propriety: 'You are condemning me to death,' Carafa was heard to say. 'You have lied to us,' retorted Vitelli. Much to Ippolito's relief, the bid for Carpi failed and the French, together with their new allies – 'twenty-six cardinals in all, mocking and jeering' as the Mantuan ambassador put it – triumphantly celebrated their victory.[35] Ippolito might well have gloated at the fact that Carpi's vote count had reached only twenty, several fewer than he himself had acquired during his own bid for the papal tiara.

That evening, according to the Mantuan ambassador, yet another angry shouting match could be heard echoing through the marble halls, this time between Carafa and Guise. 'They say that Guise spoke many ugly words to Carafa, accusing him of being unworthy of his family name' – which really was an insult, given the scandals associated with the Carafa brothers. Guise accused Carafa 'of being a traitor, and he spoke many more injurious words but Carafa said nothing more than "Sir, do not offend my honour"; it is true that there are many versions about what really happened, and no one really knows, but you can be sure that all I say is true', as the envoy concluded his account of the events of the past few days. Rome's newssheets reported that the insults were 'so bad that even the street porters would find it hard to say anything worse', and the row was 'in truth, shameful and unworthy of this assembly'.[36] For Vargas, the run-in was proof that Carafa was again back in the Spanish fold: it was 'no small confirmation of our alliance and of the total estrangement between Carafa and [Ippolito] and the French, as well as the end of their campaign for Gonzaga, which has been wearing me out as it was always what I feared most.'[37]

Back in Ippolito's cell, the French discussed their options. 'Seeing the problems we have had with Gonzaga's bid and with mine, we have decided to change course and try for the other candidates named by his majesty,' Ippolito wrote to Alfonso II on 16 December. 'The first of these is Pisani and we have begun to canvass for him but we will only be successful if we can get support from others.'[38] But the canvassing stopped almost immediately when another set of instructions arrived from France a day or so later. 'I wish and desire that you accommodate and agree terms with one or other of the three cardinals named on the list I am sending you, signed by my own hand and herewith enclosed,' ordered François II – in the margin of the printed version of this letter the transcriber has added the names Cesi, Dolera and Medici.[39] The new instructions were not secret, nor did they carry complex diplomatic overtones: 'If you think it necessary you may communicate this list to the other cardinals of your party.' Moreover, as the letter makes clear, Catherine de' Medici did understand that compromise was essential if a pope were ever to be elected. 'Seeing that these three are judged more likely to be elected than any of the others,' the royal brief continued, so 'I am sending three letters of credence to you addressed to each of the said cardinals in order to assist the campaign of the one you choose for pope, so that he will understand my wishes and intentions', and, significantly, 'the great obligation he will have towards me when he is elected pope'.

Ippolito too was determined to elect 'a pope who recognizes that he owes his election principally to us', as he informed Alfonso II, but the difficulty was, in the wake of the irrevocable collapse of the alliance with Carafa, where to find the votes.[40] 'We are trying as hard as we can to get them,' he explained, but the French had been decimated by illness and could now only count on thirteen votes. Worse still, the unity of the French party itself, which had so far proved remarkably enduring, had begun to crack under the strain of this never-ending conclave. Tournon wrote privately to the Cardinal of Lorraine and the Duke of Guise of his discouragement and annoyance: 'We have been trying for a hundred and I don't know how many days and nothing of value has been achieved.'[41] He continued: 'We have been spending our time thinking as much about defeating a pope as about making one, and all this evil comes from one who desires what he cannot have, and the harder he tries the further away it goes' – Tournon was clearly venting his dissatisfaction with Ippolito's leadership.

Addressing Lorraine, Tournon continued, 'you were an eye witness to what happened in the conclave of Pope Julius where we stayed seventy-two days on the same business and passion and we were compelled, as you know, to create the masterpiece we did'. As party leader in the 1549–50 conclave, Ippolito had been responsible for the election of Julius III, 'the masterpiece', who had treated him with great favour but had not shown much gratitude to the French crown and declared war on Henri II.

'God knows,' continued the angry Tournon, 'we could not have done worse.' Tournon and Ippolito did not get on: 'I have told your brother Guise what I think many times and he is greatly troubled and I frequently pity him.' As Tournon concluded in frustration: 'The good Lord will do all he can, and it would be a lot better if [the election] was left up to him.'

8

❦

Election

The weakness of Ippolito's position was abundantly clear on Monday, 18 December when Sforza, Farnese and Carafa, operating at last as an effective coalition under the relentless pressure of the vigilant Vargas, launched their campaign to elect Pacheco. It is evident that the ambassador was unaware that his king had serious doubts about this candidate, who had such close ties to one of the rival factions at his own court (see p. 101). Inside the Cappella Paolina, the morning scrutiny started with a squabble about procedure. The cardinals had taken their usual seats on the hard pews of the chapel but, before they had had a chance to complete their ballot papers, Carafa made the highly irregular suggestion that these should be open to public view after the scrutiny. On the face of it, this appeared to be nothing more than a ploy designed to make it difficult for any of the coalition cardinals to vote against Pacheco, and to identify those who did. Tournon, who was acting as dean while Bellay was ill, rejected the proposal outright arguing, with some force, that this was against the rules and would invalidate an election – it was certainly against the spirit of the private vote. Farnese then retorted that all that was required was the two-thirds majority however it was achieved. As had happened so often over the past three months, another unseemly row erupted among the red hats in the chapel.

PARTIES ON 18 DECEMBER

- Spanish led by Sforza and Madruzzo   17 votes
- New cardinals led by Carafa and Farnese   15 votes
- French led by Ippolito d'Este and Guise   13 votes

two-thirds majority needed: 30 votes

Interestingly, it seems likely that this row had been carefully choreographed. Inevitably, the suggestion of making the ballot papers public would generate much animated discussion but the ensuing furore acted as a smokescreen that enabled the anti-French coalition to achieve an element of surprise with its next move. Suddenly, the bickering was interrupted by the forceful voice of Carpi and the red hats respectfully fell silent as he started on what promised to be a lengthy eulogy on the merits of Pacheco and his suitability for the papal tiara. Then, in a highly theatrical gesture, Carpi stood up and kicked over the voting desk in front of him that now clattered to the ground, spilling his voting papers, quills and ink over the marble floor, and walked over to Pacheco and kissed the elderly cardinal's foot in the traditional act of homage. Many others followed, including all three party bosses – Sforza, Farnese and Carafa – and even Ghislieri and Saraceni, who were both ill, were forced to leave their cubicle beds for the occasion.

The moment the homage started, Ippolito led his cardinals out of the chapel. As they were leaving, one of the Frenchmen asked Suau why he was voting for a man who had refused to support his own candidacy six days earlier. 'Pacheco was right not to vote for an unworthy cardinal,' he replied, 'and I am right to vote for a worthy one.'[1] As the process of acclamation continued in the chapel, loud knocking was heard from the door into the conclave and someone shouted that Bellay had left his sick bed in his palace in Rome and now wanted to be readmitted. But it soon became clear that this was just a rather lame ruse on the part of the French to interrupt the election. They were desperate – on paper the coalition had more than enough votes to elect Pacheco.

Waiting anxiously in the Sala Regia, Ippolito must have been relieved when the door to the Cappella Paolina opened and four more cardinals left the chapel to join him: Savelli, who was one of Carafa's cardinals, together with Corgna, Mercurio and Corner, all from the Spanish party. Significantly, all four were Italians by birth. As he left the chapel Savelli shouted that there were plenty of worthy Italians in the college and that he, as a Roman, could not vote for a foreigner.[2] When the red hats were counted it was found that only twenty-seven had done homage to Pacheco, three short of the thirty votes he needed. 'We came very close to disaster,' Ippolito informed his nephew – they had indeed.[3]

The cardinals retired to their cubicles for lunch and discussed the morning's events over their plates of food and a glass or two of wine. There was relief in the French corner and frustration among the opposition and no doubt some very harsh words for the four Italian deserters. That afternoon the coalition made a second attempt to elect Pacheco but his vote count was found to have dropped since the morning. According to the imperial ambassador, Sforza, Carafa and Farnese had not really wanted to elect Pacheco but had made the attempt to satisfy Vargas and to assure him of their loyalty.[4] The general view in the conclave was that Pacheco's bid for the tiara was over; Vargas, however, did not agree and that night he again took advantage of the hole in the wall to galvanize support for the Spanish grandee, whom he intended to have elected the following morning.

Vargas was furious with the four Italian cardinals who had sabotaged his plans, particularly with Corgna whom he considered the ringleader of the deserters. Corgna, however, was unrepentant and justified his actions in a letter to Philip II. He'd refused, he told the king, to follow the orders of his party leader because he did not consider that Pacheco was capable of a post of this magnitude. 'I would have voted for him if I had not judged him to be both lazy and old': at the age of seventy-one, Pacheco was undoubtedly old but Corgna also had other objections, noting 'he is in poor health and there are several other reasons which I will tell your majesty that make him unfit to rule'.[5] Corgna had first-hand experience of Pacheco's incompetence when the Spaniard had served as viceroy in Naples. Among the 'other reasons' he gave was Pacheco's laziness, his habit of spending too much time at the dining-table and in bed.

Corgna also complained bitterly to the king about the unprincipled methods Vargas had employed that Monday night to make him vote for Pacheco. When Corgna and the others refused to obey, the envoy resorted to ultimatums. 'Vargas, who is your majesty's ambassador,' Corgna reminded Philip II, 'could not persuade us to return so he issued threats against my brother and then tried to blackmail Mercurio, warning him that he would lose all the benefices he has from your majesty.' As the outraged Corgna underlined, the ambassador had attempted to force 'Mercurio, who is poor but a truly good man, to vote against his conscience out of fear of losing all his worldly goods' – this was certainly not Philip II's way of doing business.

While this unpleasant argument was taking place between Vargas and Mercurio at the hole in the conclave wall, the two men were unexpectedly interrupted by the appearance of Guise, who vented his anger at the ambassador in forceful terms – it is likely that Mercurio made a tactical retreat at this point. The French aristocrat reminded Vargas that Philip II had made it abundantly clear in the letters, which the ambassador himself had read out in public audience with the cardinals at the conclave door, that all he wanted was a good pope and one elected according to canon law, and that Vargas must stop interfering in the election immediately. What started as a noisy quarrel soon degenerated into a fistfight when Guise attempted to push Vargas out of the hole and the ambassador responded by punching the cardinal in the face. Not surprisingly, Vargas glossed over the violent altercation in his report to his king, laying all the blame for the argument on 'Guise's insolence when he came to interrupt the talk I was having with Mercurio.'[6] As he explained: 'I have never impeded his conversations nor interfered with any of his cardinals, so why should he decide to hinder my discussions with one of your majesty's most faithful servants.'

Guise had evidently drawn comparisons between Vargas's behaviour and that of his French counterpart, Angoulême. 'If the French ambassador does not choose to come into the conclave,' Vargas continued, 'it is because he has all the cardinals of his faction on his side in such an effective way that they do not dare talk about or even do anything other than what he wants.' It reveals much about Vargas's attitudes to the business of the papal election that he considered that it was the diplomats who were in charge of the national parties, not the party bosses like Ippolito or Sforza. Vargas also reported that Guise had threatened to write to Philip II about his ambassador's behaviour. 'He has decided, as far as I understand, to write to your majesty in order to complain about me, a person who could not be more honourable in the whole world,' he asserted, with a considerable degree of self-righteousness, 'to say that I talk to the cardinals and threaten them and that I am to blame for prolonging the election.' For Vargas, of course, everything was the fault of the French. 'It was they who have tyrannized the conclave ever since the first hour, insisting continuously on the election of Gonzaga and Ferrara, and being so stubborn and using every possible artifice and all the bad manners imaginable,' he explained, and recommended that Philip II should write to the King of France, 'since it is them who are to blame for the delay', he repeated.

According to imperial ambassador Thurm, Guise ended his string of insults with the colourful suggestion that Vargas deserved to be thrown into the Tiber for exceeding his authority.[7] The Frenchman then sent one of his servants to the master of ceremonies with a request for a builder to brick up the hole. His anger had one salutary result: it did, in effect, seal up the conclave at long last. As Ippolito informed his cousin a few days later: 'I am sorry not to have been able to speak with you in person but, due to the excessive licence with which Signor Vargas uses these holes, and by coming in every day, it has become necessary to block them up.'[8] He added, ever the optimist, that 'it might be possible to see you soon either because we have agreed on a pope or, at least, because some of these holes will have been re-opened'. Evidently, it was not just Vargas who was entering illegally: all three parties had been making use of the holes to communicate with the outside world and, moreover, the cardinals had been co-operating very effectively to keep them open. If the cardinals were ever to elect a pope they would need to start co-operating in a similar manner in the Cappella Paolina.

By the middle of December, the cardinals were utterly exhausted, both physically and mentally. They had been fighting for over three months in conditions of extreme discomfort – on 20 December it would be 107 days since they had entered the conclave. They had endured weeks of stress: the unremitting strain of nerve-wracking battles in the Cappella Paolina, the excitement of planning plots and counter-plots, the disappointment of broken promises and of failure, the tedium of the daily routine, lack of exercise and fresh air, and all this living in the confined spaces of their cramped cages, however luxuriously they were furnished, amid the general squalor of the Vatican. Few were optimistic of success any time soon and it was widely predicted that the conclave would last another six months. They even discussed the possibility of closing the conclave for the twelve days of the traditional Christmas–New Year holiday and starting again after Epiphany. For cardinals and conclavists alike, the feasting associated with this festive celebration, fun and laughter with friends and family, and reunions with mistresses, must have been a very enticing prospect to these men, who had been locked up for so long in the dank, gloomy and increasingly poisonous marble halls.

In the days following the failed bid for Pacheco, it must have become all the more evident to Sforza, Carafa and Farnese that, despite the arithmetic that was firmly in their favour, Vargas's stubborn insistence not only on electing a pro-Spanish pope but also doing so without the help of the French, was doomed to failure. There would have to be some form of compromise. Ippolito, by contrast, having been so close to disaster with the bids first to elect Carpi on 14 December and then Pacheco four days later, had been able to re-establish his pivotal position in the conclave. As he had predicted to his brother so long ago, in the sweltering heat of September before Ercole's fatal illness, it was proving to be impossible to elect a pope without some of the French votes – all Ippolito had to do was to make sure that his vote was prominent amongst them.

Behind the green silk curtains of Ippolito's cubicle, the French argued over the merits of the three candidates, Cesi, Dolera and Medici, who had been named in the letter from François II and Catherine de' Medici, and which of them had the best chance of election. The two issues, as they were fully aware, were far from identical. Federigo Cesi, aged fifty-nine, came from an ancient Roman baronial family. He would be a popular choice in the city but it would be hard to swing the Spanish behind him, though the fact that he was one of the few cardinals who had been ordained might be a factor in his favour with Carafa's hard-line reformists. Dolera, who was a year younger than Cesi, would have the votes of these reformists but it would be difficult for this ex-minister general of the Franciscans and prominent theologian to gain broad acceptance in the conclave that had already shown reluctance to stand behind any of the cardinals who had been close to Paul IV. That left the Milanese lawyer, Medici.

Although Medici's pragmatic views on the Protestant issue were regarded as verging on heresy by the hardliners and he had spent most of the conclave confined to his bed with gout, he did have possibilities. A convivial companion with an astute mind, this sixty-year-old enjoyed wide respect in the college. He had a proven record of administration, having served as governor and legate in various cities of the Papal States, and had been an outspoken opponent of Paul IV and his regime. He was also the preferred candidate of Cosimo I, Duke of Florence. But how would this play out on the ballot papers? Medici, who had been given his red hat by Paul III, had a good relationship with Sforza, and there were reasonable grounds to hope that the camerlengo would support Medici as a compromise candidate as he had promised Ippolito before the start of the conclave (see p. 52).

Crunching the numbers Ippolito, Guise and their advisers considered it likely that many of the Spanish party would vote with Sforza thanks to the rumours, which had leaked into the conclave, that Philip II, although uncommitted in public, was privately in favour of Medici's candidacy (see p. 143). However, the combined strength of the sixteen Spanish votes and the thirteen French votes made only twenty-nine, one short of the thirty needed for Medici's election. Moreover, there were several members of the Spanish party who would certainly not support Medici: Carpi, for one, was against him; and Truchsess, as we know, had voiced serious doubts about his religious orthodoxy after Medici had declared himself in favour of negotiation with the Protestants in Germany (see p. 123). There was also the question of how far Vargas would go in order to obstruct a coalition between the French and the Spanish, the very idea of which was anathema to him – however, Vargas had been strangely silent since the hole in the wall had been sealed.

It was trickier to assess how many of the fifteen cardinals in Carafa's party could be persuaded to vote for Medici. Ippolito could count on the votes of the three cardinals who held benefices in Tuscany and owed their loyalty to Cosimo I; also it was likely that Farnese would accept Medici as a compromise candidate. Carafa himself was also not a problem. As Ippolito knew from experience – indeed the whole conclave must have been aware of this fact by now – Carafa's vote was entirely dependent on the strength of the guarantee given by the new pope that he would favour the Carafa family. But there were very serious doubts about whether Carafa's cardinals would follow his lead. He had alienated many of his party on 14 December by the manner in which he had summarily ditched the French bid for Gonzaga and, despite giving his word, treacherously turned his support to Carpi. Many had been so shocked by this duplicitous and opportunistic behaviour that they had transferred their loyalty to Paul IV's great nephew, the nineteen-year-old Alfonso Carafa, who was known to be implacably opposed to Medici, his dislike based largely on Paul IV's distrust of this clever Milanese lawyer.

So Ippolito could rely on five votes, and a sixth had also materialized since the Gonzaga-Carpi fiasco. Vitelli, who had accused Carafa of lying and deserted him during the unsuccessful attempt to elect Carpi a week earlier, now secretly pledged his loyalty to the French campaign for Medici. Aged twenty-eight, Vitelli belonged to a noble family that ruled the papal fief of Città di Castello in the upper Tiber valley, and his ancestors had a long, illustrious tradition of service in the papal armies. He also had close ties with Cosimo I, for whom his father had won the famous victory at Montemurlo in 1537, which had secured the duke's position in Florence when Vitelli was just six years old. It might also prove useful that Vitelli was a close friend of Carafa and of another of his cardinals, Ranuccio Farnese – during the pontificate of Paul IV, these three men, along with Sermoneta who was in the French party, had spent much time hunting together on Carafa's estates and finishing their day with an evening of riotous feasting and high-stakes gambling.[9]

The French now turned their attention to the two Carafa cardinals, agreeing that the best route to securing Alfonso's vote would be an appeal to family loyalty, a decision that would turn out to be significant. Vitelli soon proved his value by acquiring the necessary letters of support from Cosimo I that were to be used to turn Carafa in their favour. The duke duly promised that if Medici were elected then he, Cosimo, would personally guarantee the new pope's support for the Carafa family – it should be heavily underlined at this point that Medici himself knew little, if anything, about these promises being made in his name. Ippolito too played his part. The letter he had asked his nephew to write to Carafa in early December had now arrived: Alfonso II's fulsome praise of the cardinal, the French all hoped, would provide a persuasive backup to the promises made by Cosimo I.

Working together at last, Ippolito and Cosimo I now started to put pressure on Carafa's brothers: the cuckolded Duke Giovanni of Paliano and Marquis Antonio of Montebello, who was the father of Cardinal Alfonso. The two men were staying at Giovanni's castle at Gallese, where the duchess had been murdered the previous August, some 40 miles north of Rome and a four-hour ride up the Via Flaminia. Cosimo I sent his agents to Gallese to put pressure on the brothers while Ippolito sent letters from the Vatican. In mid-December his ledgers record travel expenses for one of his footmen to ride to Gallese with letters and, a few days later, another courier was dispatched carrying further correspondence.[10]

After dinner on Friday, 22 December, the French plan began to take shape. That evening Vitelli took a post-prandial stroll with his party boss and hunting companion Carafa, and the two men left their cubicles in the crowded Sistine Chapel for a less congested space, perhaps the Sala Regia.[11] Here, with all the appearance of a chance encounter, they met Guise and the three held an impromptu conversation – one which had almost certainly been choreographed in careful detail in Ippolito's cell. Guise queried the wisdom of closing the conclave for the Christmas–New Year holiday. He was firmly against this course of action, he said, and wanted to get the election over as quickly as possible so that he could return home to France. Carafa, touchy as ever, retorted rudely that the delay was not his fault but Guise was not to be deterred. The difficulty, Guise continued, is that all the French candidates have been rejected by Spain and nobody could expect a Frenchman would vote for a Spaniard, so they would have to find a compromise candidate, and one who was Italian. Vitelli voiced the opinion that it did not matter who was elected, so long as he was worthy of the papal tiara. Carafa made no comment – as we know, his overwhelming priority was for a pope who would favour his family, worthy or not.

Guise then mentioned the names of two possible compromise candidates: Cesi, who was a member of the French party, or Medici, who was voting with the Spanish. We know that they had both been named by François II but it is not certain that Carafa was aware of this. Guise now made a significant offer on behalf of the French. Keeping up the fiction that Vitelli was still loyal to Carafa, Guise suggested that the two cardinals should choose which candidate they preferred; the French would be happy with either, he promised, and his party would support their choice. Carafa was being steered firmly in the direction of Medici. A bid for Cesi would be automatically opposed by the Spanish whereas Medici could easily prevail, on paper at least, assuming Vargas did not intervene. But Guise added an important proviso: it was essential that Carafa's nephew Alfonso was on board – this was a devious move designed to encourage some of the hardliners in Carafa's party to vote for the progressive Medici.

Vitelli now gave Carafa the letter from Cosimo I, written specifically for this occasion, in which the duke made extensive promises on behalf of Medici – and certainly made without that cardinal's permission. Among other things, Cosimo guaranteed financial compensation for the loss of Paliano, which he would pay from his own pocket if necessary, and all the weight of his personal influence, which would be great if Medici were to be elected, in support of the Carafa family. Carafa, just as the French had expected, agreed to the deal and returned to the Sistine Chapel to start work on his young nephew. His efforts to force Alfonso into submission by ordering him to vote for Medici proved ineffectual; so too did the threat that failing to vote for Medici would result in the ruin of the Carafa family. Finally, Carafa begged him to change his mind but the teenager refused again and again – it was proof at least that Alfonso had inherited the obstinacy that ran in the family.

It was now Sunday, Christmas Eve. In Gallese, the persuasive arguments made by Ippolito and Cosimo I had finally worn down the Carafa brothers into accepting the offer made by Duke Cosimo. Alfonso's father had been cajoled into putting pen to paper to send orders to his son Alfonso to vote for Medici. One can almost hear the thunder of the hooves of the courier's horse as it sped down the Via Flaminia to Rome. In the Vatican, however, the election was on hold while the conclave prepared for the solemn observance of the feast of Christ's birth. On the Sunday, a team of priests were admitted into the conclave in order to hear confession from all the cardinals and conclavists, so that they could receive communion the following day. Late in the evening the cardinals gathered in the Cappella Paolina for the exceptionally long Christmas mass. 'At 11.30 p.m. the cardinals began to celebrate mass and it lasted until 11.30 in the morning,' Firmano concisely recorded in his diary – there were no comforting sheets and blankets for the cardinals that night.[12]

On the morning of Christmas Day, after the long mass was over, Vitelli seized his chance to talk to the stubborn young Alfonso and persuade him to follow his father's wishes. The weapon with which he hoped to change the cardinal's mind was a four-page letter written by the Florentine ambassador in the name of Cosimo I – the same tactic that Vargas had used on Alfonso's uncle, but at least this missive had been drawn up with the approval of its 'author'. In the letter, Cosimo I made major concessions to the Carafa family: he promised to ensure that the duchy of Paliano would remain under papal administration until Philip II granted Giovanni Carafa a new principality and that Carafa's conclavist, Fabrizio di Sangro, would be appointed as legate to Spain in order to negotiate the issue. Alfonso, no doubt influenced by his father's request, finally agreed to the terms and a triumphant Vitelli returned to the French with the news. Ippolito's own role in these negotiations is unclear but he did give a handsome tip of 12 scudi to one of Alfonso's pages the next day, perhaps for carrying the letter from Gallese.[13]

After lunch on Christmas Day, Ippolito and Guise summoned Sforza, Carafa and Farnese to a summit meeting and the party bosses agreed to make their attempt to elect Medici the following morning. In the end, after 112 days of almost constant wrangling – about everything except the holes in the walls – the issue was resolved with an astonishing degree of ease and amity. Late in the afternoon, Vitelli and Alfonso Carafa went to Medici's cubicle, which was next door to Carafa's in the Sistine Chapel, to inform him of the decision. Medici's reaction to this momentous news has not survived but he must have been aware that the French and Cosimo I were canvassing on his behalf. He was also aware that the campaign might well be successful and that he was facing the very real prospect of becoming pope – two days earlier he had mentioned this in a letter to the Duchess of Urbino, voicing his fears about how he would cope with the immense burdens of a job of such magnitude.[14]

Rumours of what the French were planning leaked at speed around the marble halls and generated much excitement. One of the Spanish cardinals, Saraceni, who was far from well, was so certain that the election was settled that he decided to go home immediately. With all the party leaders backing the bid, it was Carpi who attempted to galvanize the opposition into stalling the election. He accused Medici of being guilty of simony and of trying to buy the papal tiara by offering a large sum of money to Alfonso Carafa – certainly promises had been made to the teenage cardinal, but not by Medici, nor with his knowledge. The excitement in the Vatican that evening was palpable – even the habitually dry diary entries of master of ceremonies Firmano record a slight hint of the thrill that must have been echoing around the marble halls: 'At a late hour [the cardinals] began the business of creating Medici pope.'[15]

By the time the conclavists started to collect their dinner baskets from the revolving shelves in the Sala Regia, most of the cardinals had joined the queue that snaked out of the Sistine Chapel as they waited their turn to enter Medici's cell to congratulate him. Even Firmano cannot have expected any of them to obey his bedtime bell, which he rang that evening around 9 p.m. Carafa stood on guard at the door of Medici's cell, checking the voting intentions of each of the visitors – conducting an early exit poll, as it were. When Morone left Medici's cubicle some two hours later, he had a brief chat with Carafa and some of the conclavists who were also still up. Why did the election need to be delayed until the following morning, Morone queried, why not now? Carafa, in a rare display of consideration for the welfare of his colleagues, pointed out that many of the cardinals were already in bed but one of the conclavists offered to wake everyone up so that they could all assemble in the Cappella Paolina.

It was nearly midnight by the time the forty-four weary cardinals, their fur coats and red robes pulled on in haste, collected in the freezing chapel and all knew that the plan was to elect Medici by homage. Madruzzo, who was in too much pain from his gout to walk, was carried there on a chair. The last to arrive was Medici himself, formally escorted by Ippolito and Alfonso Carafa, the architects of the campaign. Even the officious Firmano relented from his habitually conscientious observance of the rules and allowed all the conclavists to crowd into the chapel to witness the momentous event. Tournon, the acting dean, was the first to declare his vote for Medici and, one by one, the others followed. Finally, in the chilly early hours of 26 December, after nearly four months of tortuous negotiations, Medici achieved the two-thirds majority required for election. After the litany of failed attempts – Carpi, Cueva, Tournon, Gonzaga, Gonzaga again, Carpi again, Pacheco, Carpi again, Ippolito, Gonzaga again, Carpi again, Pacheco again – it must have been quite a moment. When the homage was over Ippolito asked Medici what name he would choose? 'Pius, because I intend to be a pious pope', he replied.[16]

As it was so late, the cardinals decided to delay the formal scrutiny, which was needed to complete the election, until the morning. They walked back to their cubicles, confident that this would be a mere formality. The new pope himself was unable to return to his own bed, where he had spent most of the conclave. 'His cell had been pillaged, as is the custom' by the more opportunistic conclavists and conclave staff, and he was obliged to spend the night 'in the cubicle of Alfonso Carafa'

– there is no mention of where the teenager himself slept that night.[17] For many cardinals, there were letters to write before they could get some much-needed sleep. Ippolito and Guise wrote to the Cardinal of Lorraine and the Duke of Guise: 'My lords, this note is to advise you of the creation and election of the new pope, who was Cardinal Medici and is now named Pius IV, who is most obliged to the king and to the Queen Mother to whom he understands he owes his assumption to this dignity.' They signed it 'from the conclave in Rome, 25 December 1559 at eight hours of the night', around 12.30 a.m.[18] Two hours later, Ippolito signed a short letter to his nephew containing the same news: 'This evening with God's help we have agreed on Medici's elevation in which, seeing that we played the principal role', the new pope 'has shown himself to be very grateful to us.'[19]

The following morning, 26 December, the cardinals assembled in the Cappella Paolina for the last act of the conclave ritual. After Pius IV's election had been confirmed by scrutiny, recorded Firmano, 'Farnese, the senior deacon, went to the window and raised the cross to announce to the people that a pope had been chosen.'[20] For the crowds outside there must have been relief that the election was finally over, though no doubt there was some apprehension among the Romans about the nature of their Milanese ruler. Firmano described how the new pope, now dressed in his new white vestments, 'went to the altar in the chapel where he received the homage of all the cardinals who each kissed him on his foot, his hand and his mouth'. As the cannons of Castel Sant'Angelo thundered and roared, their loud booms audible inside the Vatican, the cardinals gathered in the Sala Regia where Firmano solemnly unlocked the door to the staircase leading down to the courtyard of the palace – what a relief it must have been to leave the marble halls behind, with all their squalor and filth, at long last. Preceded by the great papal cross, the cardinals walked in procession across the courtyard and into St Peter's for the formal enthronement of the new pope.

Ippolito's household now began the business of settling conclave business, packing up the contents of Ippolito's cubicle and moving his possessions back to Palazzo Monte Giordano. Provosto Trotti tipped 4 scudi to the conclave barbers while Meschino handed out 25 scudi in tips to various conclavists – sadly the ledgers do not reveal the identities of the recipients, as they are likely to have played important roles in the election.[21] The men dismantled the luxurious cell, stacking the contents onto carts for the trip across the Tiber. It seems that it was not just the custom to pillage the cubicle of the new pope but also those of all the cardinals. According to the lists compiled by Diomede Tridapalle of the individual items of furniture, textiles, linen and silver hangings and silver other items that were returned to the wardrobe, the scale of the thievery revealed was astonishing.

IPPOLITO'S POSSESSIONS 'LOST' IN THE CONCLAVE[22]

- 4 green silk curtains
- 6 woollen blankets
- 23 lengths of green silk
- 2 fine linen sheets
- 2 sheets brought in by Ludovico Ricciolo
- 1 silver fork lost at the Vatican on 13 September
- 1 small silver platter lost at the Vatican on 14 September
- 1 gilded serving dish lost at the Vatican on 17 September
- 10 fine linen napkins lost
- 502 fine linen napkins lost

- 2 linen tablecloths lost in the conclave by Pietro da Sezza
- 2 fine linen sheets lost in the conclave by the Cardinal of Guise
- 2 woollen blankets lost by the Cardinal of Guise
- 1 linen sheet stolen from the cubicle of Cardinal Bertrand

Surprisingly little of Ippolito's valuable silver was missing. Three items – a fork, a plate and a serving dish – were all detailed in the inventory as 'lost' in September and from then on it seems likely that the other thirty-two pieces had been carefully stored in the cubicle cupboards under lock and key. However, the green silk wall-hangings that had added such luxury to Ippolito's cell were gone, though nobody had bothered to remove the lengths of cheaper serge that decorated the exterior of the cubicle. Ippolito's bed was stripped of its green silk curtains, linen sheets and woollen blankets, and there was also a lot of bedding missing from the cubicles of the French cardinals. Above all, a staggering 512 fine linen napkins had been 'lost': this amounts to over four napkins for every day that the conclave lasted, and they were presumably removed from his food baskets after each meal had been consumed. Had Firmano added them to his not inconsiderable pile of perks, or had his staff indulged in some opportunistic pilfering – the napkin haul alone can be valued at about 200 scudi.[23]

That night Rome was ablaze with the bonfires and noisy fireworks that were traditionally lit across the city to celebrate the election of a new pope. Ippolito's ledgers are unclear about what he bought for the occasion but in 1550 he spent the substantial sum of 55 scudi on firewood, 308 rockets and ten catherine wheels to mark the election of Julius III.[24] In Palazzo Monte Giordano, there were excellent reasons for rejoicing that night. Ippolito's role in the election had been crucial. Vargas, faced with what was for him a crushing defeat and determined to present the event in the best possible light, claimed to Philip II that Medici's election had been due to the hard work of Sforza and Farnese, making no mention of Ippolito, nor the French, nor even the two Carafa cardinals.[25] When the news arrived in Spain, the Florentine ambassador boasted that the Medici family now ruled supreme in Florence, Rome, France (Catherine de' Medici) and Spain, where the queen was Catherine's daughter.[26] Cosimo I himself, however, was more generous: in a letter to his son-in-law Alfonso II he wrote 'thanks be to God a new pope has been elected for which the palm of victory should be given to your uncle, who behaved so brilliantly in this final act'.[27]

On 27 December, the day after the election, Ippolito was summoned to a meeting with the new pope in the Vatican and he emerged from the papal apartments in jubilant spirits. 'Guise and I have been with the pope who showed much gratitude for the support he has received from our hands and we are extremely satisfied,' he wrote to his nephew Alfonso II.[28] Pius IV had announced that he intended to grant significant favours not only to the French crown 'which I hope will prove to be true', but also for Alfonso. 'He spoke many loving words towards you saying among other things that he hopes to see you in Rome,' Ippolito reported, adding 'I think you can take for granted that what you did for the election of the pope will result in great benefits and that he will lodge you at the Vatican, as he intends to do with the Duke of Florence when he comes.' To be lodged at the papal palace was indeed a signal honour, but there was

even better news. 'Among the other favours which we requested,' Ippolito continued, 'we asked him to give a red hat to Don Luigi' – Luigi was Alfonso's younger brother, whose promising career in the Church had been stalled when Ippolito was exiled by Paul IV – 'and this he promised very willingly' though it might not happen immediately, Ippolito counselled, as 'he also said that he intended to limit his first promotion of cardinals to his nephews'. And, of course, there were benefits for Ippolito himself. Pius IV promised to restore him to his posts as cardinal-protector of France and governor of Tivoli, the first of many favours a grateful pope would bestow on him and which would establish him at the heart of the new regime.

Ippolito had much to celebrate, not least the relief at no longer being confined in his cramped cubicle in the Sala Regia. Back amid the luxuries of Palazzo Monte Giordano, he could enjoy the parties, laughter and leisure instead of the gruelling conclave routine regulated by the irritating ringing of Firmano's little bell. He was a guest at the Vatican on 29 December, when his valet tipped 3 scudi to Pius IV's viol players; he paid out another 16 scudi in tips to those responsible for the noisy jollifications that marked the arrival of the New Year with the clamour of trumpets and drums, and the salvoes of artillery fired from great cannons by the bombardiers of Castel Sant'Angelo.[29] He had come a long way over the last twelve months: above all, he had played the role of kingmaker in the election of the new pope and returned to Rome in triumph after four long years of provincial exile.

9

⚜

Winners and Losers

JANUARY–DECEMBER 1560

Ippolito's high spirits were unlikely to have been dented by an attack of gout which started on New Year's Day. The rigours of the long conclave, the pressure of the election and the excesses of the feasting that followed, all seem to have taken their toll on his health and on 2 January he had to cancel a meeting with Pius IV. 'I have to tell you that on the night of 1 January I felt a few twinges of gout,' he informed his nephew a few days later, 'and I went to bed to try and cure it with peace and quiet but I was not able to avoid it coming on and the following night it got much worse and I am still suffering but, God be praised, it does seem to be beginning to get better.'[1] He was still too ill, however, to take part in the papal coronation on 6 January, which was performed in St Peter's by the senior cardinal-deacon Alessandro Farnese – and where, the Roman newssheets reported, some twenty-five people were crushed to death in the stampede to gather the coins which the new pope traditionally threw to the crowds waiting on the steps of the basilica.[2]

Back home in Palazzo Monte Giordano, Ippolito's household also celebrated. With their cardinal reinstated at the papal court, they could look forward to a prolonged stay in Rome – and a lot more work. Wardrobe master Diomede Tridapalle organized new ecclesiastical outfits for Ippolito and took material from the storeroom to make three surplices.[3] The tailor started work on outfits for Ippolito to wear while attending Pius IV's consistories: among the items he stitched were a new cassock of purple silk cloth with a matching cape of purple silk taffeta, and a purple satin bag to carry documents to the meetings.[4]

Perhaps the most eloquent evidence of Ippolito's restored prestige appears in treasurer Francesco Novello's ledgers where the cash-flow crisis now began to ease. Although it would take time for the issue of the relevant bulls restoring Ippolito to his position as cardinal-protector of France, and for the revenues to materialize, there is evidence that the revival of his fortunes had not gone unnoticed by Rome's shopkeepers, who were happy to wait for their invoices to be paid. Novello was able to satisfy several suppliers, such as Silvestro the poultry man and Antonio the butcher, with money on account.[5] Others were even more tolerant: Gaudenzio, for example, who had yet to be paid for any of the glasses and carafes that he had delivered every week since the start of the conclave, agreed to wait until the end of January for payment of his September invoice.[6]

Ippolito was also able to exploit his new prestige to borrow funds and on 31 December the bookkeeper recorded loans totalling 4,500 scudi to the cardinal.[7] Of this sum, 1,500 scudi was a loan from Alfonso II in Ferrara; 1,000 scudi came from an old friend, Giovanni Campeggio, Bishop of Bologna, who 'has kindly loaned this to Ippolito'; and a further 1,000 scudi also came from a friend, the wealthy Roman patrician Giulio Bufalini.

The final 1,500 scudi came from a much more surprising source: Battista Facianis, the grocer who had proved so accommodating about the late payment of Ippolito's bills in mid-November (see p. 154) – it seems that dried goods were a highly profitable trade. The ledger recorded that Facianis's loan was to be repaid by the end of February and although Ippolito missed that deadline, the loan was repaid on 21 March.[8]

Meanwhile the whole city watched and listened for signs that would indicate the nature of the new regime: tradesmen's profits, cardinals' careers, all were at stake. There were winners and losers after every election; and it would soon become clear to all what had actually happened inside the locked doors of the Vatican. How would Pius IV favour those who had supported him in the conclave? Would he honour those promises that had been made in the Vatican on his behalf? How would this pope from the progressive wing of the Church deal with the hard-line reformists? One of the most gruelling conclaves in history was over but it would be several months before its full impact began to unfold.

Aged sixty, Pius IV was generally in good health though, like Ippolito, he suffered from gout. He was a great believer in the beneficial effects of walking and took long daily tramps through the streets of Rome. He was a cheerful, amiable soul, a peacemaker who enjoyed the good things in life, a very different character to the severe Paul IV, though both men were noted for their impatience and for their dislike of opposition. Right from the start he sought to distance himself from his predecessor. He endeared himself to the Romans that January by lifting the restrictions Paul IV had imposed on the celebration of Carnival. After years of economic hardship and austerity the city's shopkeepers anticipated a surge in their profits, while artists and building workers anticipated opportunities on his ambitious plans for new streets, palaces and churches to transform the papal capital. Other more political differences between the two regimes soon emerged. All Paul IV's diplomats were recalled, and none was given a new posting. Pius lifted his predecessor's anti-Semitic legislation and, although he confirmed Cardinal Ghislieri as Inquisitor General, he severely restricted that institution's authority. Importantly, he also formally absolved Cardinal Morone of the charge of heresy that had been revived during the conclave.[9]

At his first consistory on 12 January, Pius IV announced his intention to reopen the Council of Trent that had been closed by Paul IV. He sent ambassadors to all the rulers of Europe to gain their support for this, a process that would take several months of political wrangling – as the cardinals well knew, it was tricky to get the rival crowns of France and Spain to agree. Vargas observed that the reopening of the council was a major priority for Pius IV. 'He repeatedly proposes to do so,' the ambassador informed Philip II on 25 February, 'and yesterday he assured me in the presence of eight cardinals that as soon as your majesty, the Emperor and the King of France were all in agreement on this matter, he would decide when and where the council was to open.'[10] While the diplomatic legwork was underway, he set up a commission to begin the moral reform of the Church – it was to meet every Thursday, the same day of the week that Paul IV had earmarked for his personal attendance at the trials of the Inquisition.

This commission was the first official sign of the new regime and Pius IV's choice of names gave Ippolito and his colleagues much food for thought. Following convention it contained most of the heavyweights in the college, men who had been cardinals for many years and only two of them were below the age of forty. Also unsurprisingly, a majority – eight of the thirteen – had been in the Spanish-imperial faction with Pius IV during the conclave: they included the two party bosses, Sforza and Madruzzo as well as Cueva, a senior Spaniard. But Pius had also included Morone, underlining the significance of his very public declaration of that cardinal's innocence of the trumped-up heresy charges. Equally unexpectedly, he appointed Carpi, who had notably attempted to stop Pius's election on Christmas Day, a shrewd move aimed at diluting hostility to the new regime. He had only named two French cardinals but his choice of Ippolito and Tournon, who had been the candidates of the French crown, showed an appropriate level of respect. Neither Guise nor Bellay were chosen: at thirty-one years old Guise was too young, and he was set on returning to France as soon as possible, while the unfortunate Bellay was still seriously ill and not expected to live long (he died in the middle of February). The other three members of the commission had all voted with Carafa: Alessandro Farnese, vice-chancellor of the Church and one of the leading figures in the college; Savelli who had earned his place as one of the four Italian cardinals who had joined the French to prevent the election of Pacheco in mid-December; and, in a nod to the hard-line reformist wing of the Church, Pius IV had also included the Franciscan Dolera.

It was the omissions, of course, that provided the most revealing evidence of the new pope's intentions regarding Church reform. A prominent figure not on the list was Gonzaga but he was later to play an important role: Pius IV would appoint him president of the Council of Trent in February 1561. More significantly, there were only two hardliners on the commission

– Carpi and Dolera. Understandably Pius had not nominated Truchsess, who had attempted to discredit him during the conclave with accusations of heresy. Nor was there any mention of Pacheco, who had so nearly been crowned with the papal tiara less than a month earlier – though if Pacheco had been elected, the cardinals would have been faced with a return to the squalor of the lockdown in the very near future as the elderly Spaniard died in early March. Finally, there was no mention of Inquisitor General Ghislieri who might have expected to play a leading role in moral reform. It was evident to all that the new pope intended to promote his own progressive views on the subject of Church reform.

The other telling omission was Carlo Carafa. There had been good reasons for excluding Guise but all the other party bosses had been nominated and Carafa, who had been the leader of the party that had enabled Pius IV's election, was very conspicuous by his absence. But the pope was careful to reassure Carafa. In late December he had dispatched Carafa's conclavist Fabrizio di Sangro to Spain with orders to negotiate with Philip II for compensation for Carafa for the loss of the duchy of Paliano. The ex-Duke Giovanni, however, was less sanguine: when the two brothers met in early January, Giovanni refused to enter Rome in case he was arrested on the charge of murdering his wife's lover and insisted on remaining outside the gates of the city.

Carafa was also reassured by the support of Vargas, by implication the favour of Philip II himself. It is unlikely that Vargas told Carafa of the letter he had received from the king reprimanding him in forceful terms for his behaviour during the conclave. Philip II had been furious that his ambassador had revealed his private opinion of Gonzaga – though it was a little unfair to blame Vargas for the postal service – but the king had also been appalled at Vargas's readiness to overstep his authority as envoy by making promises to Carafa on the king's behalf. When Pius IV was informed of this offer he had summoned Vargas to an audience and accused him of fraudulently making promises in the name of Philip II without the king's permission. The ambassador retorted angrily that it was only thanks to similar tactics that Pius IV himself had been elected, which indeed was true.[11] Still, Vargas must have counted himself lucky that he was still the Spanish ambassador to Rome and he spent the next few months canvassing hard on Carafa's behalf at the papal court.

Another important clue about the new regime emerged in the consistory on 31 January when Pius IV announced his intention of giving red hats to two nephews: Gian Antonio Serbelloni, aged forty, and Carlo Borromeo, who was just twenty-one. To the surprise of the college, it was Borromeo and not the elder Serbelloni who was nominated as senior cardinal-nephew. He was given the pope's old see of Milan and put in charge of running the Papal States; he was also nominated to the reform commission, its youngest member by several decades. But Borromeo was an exceptional character and Pius IV's faith in his nephew's probity was to be well rewarded. Borromeo was to play a pivotal role in his uncle's efforts to reform the Church and become one of the heroes of the Counter-Reformation. And he infuriated those hoping for favours by his refusal to be corrupted by high office and abuse his position for personal gain. He would be canonized in 1610, just twenty-five years after his death.

Inevitably after every conclave, men with even distant connections to the new pope flocked to Rome in the hope of obtaining posts in the administration. The son of a minor Milanese patrician, Pius IV was one of fourteen children, ten of whom survived to adulthood; and although three of his five sisters were nuns, his other siblings all had offspring. Several had married into families with imperial links: as the Ferrarese ambassador reported in early 1560, the pope's 'relations from Milan and Germany are multiplying every day'.[12] As was the custom, Pius gave his nephews the most prestigious secular posts in his regime. Cardinal Borromeo's brother, Federigo, was appointed captain-general of the Church; one of Cardinal Serbelloni's brothers was made castellan of Castel Sant'Angelo and the other became captain of the papal guard; and two sons of Pius IV's other sister, who had married into the Hohenems dynasty, were appointed as legates to Emperor Ferdinand I and to Philip II. There were also prestigious marriages: Federigo to Virginia della Rovere, daughter of the Duke of Urbino; Federigo's sister Camilla to Cardinal Gonzaga's nephew Cesare, Prince of Guastalla. These unions brought higher status to the pope's family, and they gave the della Rovere and Gonzaga families the prestige of familiar access to the papal court at the Vatican.

The other princely clan to benefit was the Medici. Pius IV had assigned a third red hat on 31 January, and the recipient's name came as a surprise to Vatican watchers: Giovanni, the fifteen-year-old son of Cosimo I. It was evident that Pius IV wanted to reward the duke for the decisive role he had played in the election and this exceptional favour convinced some that the new pope was going to be little more than Cosimo's poodle. This was certainly the boast of the Florentine ambassador in Spain who reported that Pius IV 'will be guided in everything by the advice and determination of Duke Cosimo'.[13] The duke had enjoyed a private audience with the pope in January and Ippolito informed his nephew they 'discussed things of great importance', and he foresaw 'a continuous series of favours and kindnesses from his Holiness who has honoured him as if he were a king'.[14]

A king was exactly what Cosimo aspired to be, and this was the reward he desired above all others. Pius, however, was very much his own man. Giovanni's red hat concealed his determination not to bow to pressure to make Cosimo king of Tuscany, a title that would have given him precedence over all Italian princes and caused a diplomatic uproar. The Medici dynasty was only thirty years old whereas the Este, for example, had ruled their state for over three centuries. Although Ippolito was delighted with the favours he had received from the pope, he was rather miffed that Giovanni de' Medici had been preferred over his own nephew – indeed it looked as if Cosimo I had been rewarded more prominently than himself. As he informed Alfonso II, 'considering that when [the pope] spoke to Guise and I at the beginning, he said that he did not intend to create anyone other than his own family... so we must do all we can to receive equal treatment for our own house'.[15]

The French were also satisfied. The elderly Bertrand had been well recompensed for his exhaustingly long journey from France with the pope's own titular church of Santa Prisca, a signal honour. Tournon was promoted to Cardinal-Bishop of Ostia and Robert de Lénoncourt became Cardinal-Bishop of Sabina in his place. In late January, Guise presented Pius IV with a list of requests from François II, which the pope granted without argument. 'Of the news here, there is little to tell you,' Ippolito informed his nephew on 26 January, 'except that Guise departed yesterday... highly satisfied with what his Holiness has done for France.'[16] But evidently this French aristocrat did not intend to endure another conclave. 'Despite all this,' Ippolito continued, 'he left not only determined never to return here but also, which is worse, he showed no sign of caring whether any of the other French cardinals stay here and it would be very bad if the others did the same.'

Guise was unwilling, apparently, to ride across the Alps in the middle of winter but travelled in comfort in his new coach, a present from Ippolito. The coach itself cost only 57.28 scudi though the furnishings and covers, which were made under Diomede's orders with expensive textiles from the wardrobe stores, added significantly to the costs.[17] The cardinal's luggage seems to have included six of Ippolito's silver plates: according to the inventory, five plates were 'stolen' and one 'lost', specifically 'on the day that Monsignor de Guise left Rome'.[18] He interrupted his journey north to spend several weeks as a guest of Alfonso II, tempted by the Carnival celebrations. Shrove Tuesday fell on 27 February that year and the celebrations were particularly lavish to welcome Alfonso's Duchess Lucrezia de' Medici, who made her formal entry into Ferrara earlier that month. 'I understand that Guise has postponed his departure [from Ferrara] because he would not have been able to get back to France in time to celebrate Carnival there,' Ippolito wrote to his nephew.[19] 'I am very pleased that you also are able to enjoy all the celebrations and pleasures that are done on this occasion and to enjoy them the more because here they are rather indifferent, so that it seems to be just a shadow of a Carnival, and very poor and meagre.' Ippolito evidently preferred the more aristocratic amusements such as tournaments, jousts, dancing and the performances of bawdy classical comedies that were on offer at the ducal court to the celebrations in Rome.

Ippolito's gout had improved enough for him to leave the comfort of his palace and sample the Carnival entertainments on offer on the streets.[20] It was the first time for five years that the Romans had been allowed to celebrate this feast in their traditionally boisterous and often coarse fashion with bullfights, horse races and cartloads of squealing pigs tumbled down a hill to be caught by lucky revellers waiting below. Ippolito's ledgers show he handed out tips to dancing girls, buffoons, street musicians and several poor people who gave him presents – a capon, for example, or a plate of trout – in the hope of some coins in return. He was much entertained by 'a German woman with no arms who did tricks with her feet'; on 27 February he watched the Shrove Tuesday revelries in Piazza Navona, giving the substantial sum of 6 scudi to a boy who performed the audacious feat of jumping off a torch holder.[21]

Ippolito gave visible expression to his renewed prestige by increasing the size of his entourage. Evidently what sufficed for a disgraced cardinal in exile was inadequate for one in a prominent position at the papal court. Several employees, notably his carver, who had not been needed during the conclave, were now summoned to Rome.[22] There were also forty new names in the ledgers that year, only five of whom replaced men who retired. Strikingly, thirty of these were directly concerned with Ippolito's public face: his valets, footmen, squires and dining staff (see table on p. 210). There were three new cooks, one of whom was described as a '*pottagiero francese*', or French chef responsible for the light broths and heavy stews served at table; there was also a laundress, a Slav named Anna, the only female to appear in the salary lists. Ippolito now took on a 'theologian', one Bartolomeo da Lugo, a Dominican friar and an appointment that reflected not only the cardinal's position on the commission for Church reform but also the importance Pius IV attached to the issue. The Dominican received a golden hello of 25 scudi and earned an annual salary of 100 scudi: this was less than Ippolito paid his philosopher (150 scudi) or treasurer Novello (130 scudi), but twice the salary of his valets (48 scudi).[23]

NEW STAFF IN IPPOLITO'S HOUSEHOLD, 1560[24]

Chamber staff	*Officials of the Mouth*	*Others*
valets 7	stewards 2	theologian 1
footmen 8	squires 7	wardrobe assistant 1
servants 1	larderers 1	laundress 1
cooks 3	bookkeeper 1	
servants & boys 1	misc officials 6	
Total 16	**Total 14**	**Total 10**

More compelling evidence of Ippolito's restored prestige emerges in his correspondence with his nephew Alfonso II. It was an important part of his job in Rome to use his influence on behalf of Ferrara – and to keep the duke informed of the political gossip doing the rounds at the papal court. Alfonso had been bombarding him with requests since the conclave closed: favours for Ferrarese citizens looking for jobs in a cardinal's household, for example, or with the new administration; others involved favours from the pope himself. A certain Giorgio de Gozzi, for example, 'is going to Rome in order to liberate himself from a marriage which, from what he has told me, he was fraudulently tricked into, deceived by the girl's family, and because he and his antecedents have always been in the service of our house and he deserves justice, on his part I cannot do more to recommend him to you and to beg you to do all you can to help him achieve a favourable outcome with the pope and his ministers.'[25]

One particular topic of discussion between the cardinal and the duke in early 1560 concerned a large consignment of wheat that Alfonso's father, Duke Ercole, had bought in September 1559, shortly before his death. Some of the grain had arrived 'but because all trading was then stopped on the orders of the College of Cardinals, the rest of the wheat, which amounts to one thousand sacks, is still in the hands of the [papal] treasurer,' he complained, 'as well as the money due on the contract.'[26] Ippolito had no luck here: Pius IV was understandably reluctant to give permission to release either the cash or the grain.

There were also favours Alfonso II could grant in return. Ippolito worried about the family of Cardinal Dandino, who had died during the conclave, and asked his nephew to do what he could to help them. 'Knowing, as you do, the affection I felt for the cardinal,' he explained, 'both for his qualities and for the love that he always showed towards me, you will not be surprised that the business of his descendants is close to my heart.'[27] Ippolito was determined to do all he could to make up for 'what they have lost by his death' so that 'at least they will not have lost the goodwill he deserved'. Ippolito himself bought several items of silver from Dandino's heirs, paying a total of 319 scudi for an ornamental gilded silver bread platter, two gilded salts, an elaborately decorated fruit bowl, a gilded dish warmer and an engraved goblet, which his inventory describes as 'in the German style'.[28]

Meanwhile, the favours for Ippolito from a grateful pope kept on coming. Two of his courtiers, destined for Church careers, received their first bishoprics: Ippolito's secretary Paolo Amanio was made Bishop of Anglona, while Provosto Trotti, the trusted friend who had been part of Ippolito's entourage since 1535, was made Bishop of St-Jean-de-Maurienne.[29] This last see, which had become vacant after Cardinal Capodiferro's death, was not French but part of Savoy so there was no 'tip' for Ippolito to charge but he did pay some of the expenses relating to his courtier's promotion.[30] 'I know you will be delighted to see one of your own men, and such an old servant of mine, thus honoured,' Ippolito wrote to Alfonso II later that same day.[31]

In April, Pius IV appointed his legates in the Papal States. 'Yesterday in consistory the pope finally appointed his legates, among whom he has appointed me to Viterbo', Ippolito enthused to his nephew. 'Although it is the least important of all, I wanted it more because of its advantages and the recreations that I can have there because it is so near Rome.'[32] Pleasure certainly came high on Ippolito's list of priorities. And this sinecure, which involved providing entertainment for important guests travelling to and from Rome, included woods and lakes rich in game, that would make for excellent hunting during the autumn, and plentiful hot sulphur springs, which are still considered to be unusually beneficial for gout.

Pius IV also granted Ippolito the gift of a substantial piece of land adjoining Palazzo Monte Cavallo, his villa on the Quirinal, which had been acquired by the papacy after its owner went bankrupt.[33] By early March there was a team of labourers at work clearing and digging the site, which would be transformed into one of the most beautiful gardens in Renaissance Rome.[*] Although a French visitor in Rome around 1560 praised the antique sculpture that ornamented Cardinal Carpi's villa as the more impressive, he did consider Ippolito's gardens to be far superior because of their 'quantities of beautiful trees'.[34]

---

[*] Sadly these sumptuous gardens no longer exist – they lie beneath the grounds of the Quirinal Palace, the official residence of the president of Italy.

Michelangelo, *Last Judgement*, 1536–41 (Vatican, Sistine Chapel). This fresco attracted controversy from the moment of its unveiling. While connoisseurs of art hailed it as a masterpiece, hardline reformers were appalled and Paul IV went so far as to cover several of the naked figures with fig leaves, and to clothe others in trousers.

Vatican, Cappella Paolina, begun 1538. Commissioned by Paul III as his private chapel, the lavish decoration of the Cappella Paolina was redolent of the power and wealth of the Church.

Jean Clouet, *Cardinal Charles of Lorraine* (Oxford, Ashmolean Museum). This senior French cardinal did not attend the conclave, but remained in France to take charge, with his elder brother the Duke of Guise, of the young King Francis II, who was married to their niece, Mary Queen of Scots.

Jean Clouet, *Cardinal Louis of Guise* (Oxford, Ashmolean Museum). The younger brother of Cardinal Charles of Lorraine, Louis of Guise did travel to France for the conclave and assisted Ippolito in the management of the French party.

Jean Clouet, *Cardinal Jean Bertrand* (Oxford, Ashmolean Museum).

Titian, *Cardinal Georges d'Armagnac and his secretary*, 1538–40 (Alnwick Castle, Collection of the Duke of Northumberland). Appointed cardinal by Paul III as a favour for Francis I, Armagnac was the French envoy to Venice, where he commissioned Titian to paint his portrait, before his appointment as ambassador to the papal court in Rome.

Michelangelo, *Crucifixion of St Peter* (overleaf) and *Conversion of St Paul*, (above) begun 1542 (Vatican, Cappella Paolina). The scenes were designed to celebrate the two great pillars of the Christian faith, both of whom had been martyred in Rome for their beliefs.

View of Tivoli from across the Roman Campagna. Situated in the Sabine hills to the east of Rome, Tivoli provided Ippolito, his courtiers and his household with welcome relief from the oppressive summer heat in Rome.

Tivoli, Villa d'Este, Fountain of the Cascade and Water Organ, begun 1566. Ippolito's villa at Tivoli was famous across Europe for its ingenious use of water to channel air into pipes and play music.

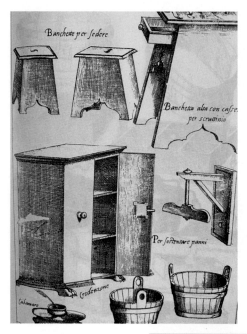

Miscellaneous items needed for the conclave, including stools, a writing desk for voting, an inkwell and a coathanger (from Scappi's *Opera dell'arte del cucinare*).

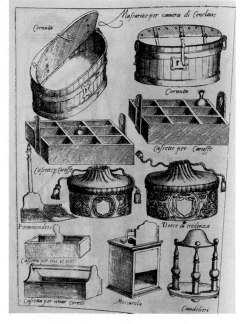

More miscellaneous items needed for the conclave, such as boxes for food and wine, cases for oil and vinegar, and another 'to clean knives' as well as a dustpan (from Scappi's *Opera dell'arte del cucinare*).

Ippolito used his income as cardinal-protector of France to finance his embellishment of the villa and its gardens, keeping track of revenues and expenditure in a special account book rather than the ordinary household ledgers. His income had markedly increased since Pius IV's election: in the four months from April to July 1560 he received a total of 51,486 scudi, some 4,000 scudi of which came from the protectorship.[35] Much of this latter money was the 'tip' he charged on appointments to French benefices, all of whom were required to pay a levy of fifteen per cent of the estimated value of their benefice, with a minimum charge fixed at 40 scudi. To give an idea of the sums involved: in March the new Bishop of Lisieux paid Ippolito 655 scudi for his promotion, while in November the new Archbishop of Bordeaux paid the same amount for his see and also an additional sum of 82 ducats to enable him to retain his income from a benefice in a different diocese.[36]

The bulk of the expenditure at the villa in 1560 was for the gardens, where Ippolito employed three full-time gardeners.[37] They were not solely ornamental: there was a large kitchen garden planted with a range of vegetables including spinach, broad beans, chicory, artichokes, cabbages, garlic and chives. The gardeners also took charge of tending the fragrant citrus, myrtle and orange trees, planted in great terracotta jars and in formal groves around the splendid fountains that were such a feature of sixteenth-century gardens. The ledgers record payments for bricks, lime, sand, lead, ironware, copperware, terracotta pipes and wood for scaffolding; for wages to the labourers digging the foundations of the fountains and salaries to the engineers who designed the pipework and oversaw the construction of the water storage system. There were also payments for coloured marbles, stuccoes, pieces of bright enamel, mother-of-pearl, clam shells and coral to decorate the fountains. It is evident that Ippolito wanted to rectify the lack of antique sculptures in his garden: the ledgers include payments to carters for the transport of antique marbles and statues to Monte Cavallo. He also took advantage of Bellay's death to acquire pieces from the cardinal's collection, paying his heirs the modest sum of 16 scudi for several unspecified items.[38]

Easter that year fell on 14 April and Ippolito had his tonsure done in Holy Week, tipping the barber 2 scudi. He gave alms to two poor men outside St Peter's on Good Friday when he also attended mass in the Sistine Chapel, where he 'offered 2 scudi to the Cross'.[39] Easter that year was particularly busy in Rome with official delegations arriving in the city from the rulers of the Empire, Spain, Portugal, Poland, France, Florence and Venice to pay their respects to the new pope and to begin negotiations for the reopening of the Council of Trent.

Among the visitors was Giovanni de' Medici, who was in Rome to receive his red hat from Pius IV and take part in the arcane ceremonies marking this rite of passage. The pope showed special favour by giving him the titular church of Santa Maria in Domnica, once held by the first Medici pope Leo X – a gesture that involved transferring its present holder to another title. The seventeen-year-old was widely fêted during his visit. Lavish hospitality and generous presents were useful tools in building up client networks at the courts of sixteenth-century Europe, and many cardinals took this opportunity to flatter their young colleague in anticipation of the next conclave. Alessandro Farnese, for example, entertained Giovanni to a magnificent banquet at the Villa Madama, complete with music and theatrical entertainments, and a game of billiards.[40] Carpi gave him a medal from his collection and a large porphyry table, which caused problems for the young cardinal's staff who had to arrange transport of this cumbersome object back to Florence.[41]

Not to be outdone by Farnese or Carpi, Ippolito also cultivated Giovanni's friendship – and he had the added advantage that his nephew, Alfonso II, was married to Giovanni's sister. Alfonso had already confided to Ippolito that he thought Lucrezia was pregnant, and this was confirmed in early April: 'I was most pleased to hear of your hopes that the duchess is pregnant, so you can imagine how much more pleased I am now that you can take it for certain,' Ippolito replied, in a postscript written in his own hand.[42] 'I sent your note round to Cardinal de' Medici and, although he has heard this news from Florence, your confirmation is of great joy to him and to all who have heard, and I send congratulations to you and to the duchess with the greatest affection and pray to God that this successful beginning will achieve the end for which we are all hoping' – a son, naturally, to continue the dynasty.

There were also generous presents for Giovanni, who was known to be fascinated by the art of ancient Rome – 'lost in antiquities and medals', as one contemporary recorded. Ippolito gave him eleven medals from his own collection including a silver Augustus and a cameo with the head of Aristotle set in gold.[43] He also presented him with a luxurious gilded coach, complete with purple velvet furnishings and matching horse covers. A magnificent present by any standards, the entries in Ippolito's ledger, together with an estimate of the cost of the textiles that all came out of Ippolito's wardrobe stores, suggest that it cost Ippolito just short of 700 scudi. He also supplied horses for it, a point that particularly impressed Giovanni who informed his father that the cardinal 'has given me a new coach with his horses that are perhaps the most beautiful that there are today in Rome'.[44]

A COACH FOR CARDINAL DE' MEDICI[45]

- to the under-stable master for expenses for the coach   16.86
- to a painter for gilding the coach   31.82
- to a sword-maker for gilding the ironware for the coach   23.55
- to a button-maker for 465 nails and 20 large chair studs   5.14
- to a fringe-maker for supplies   173.05
- 64 yards purple kermes velvet to make
  covers for coach and for horses   240.00 from wardrobe
- 33 yards purple kermes satin to
  line cover for coach   68.00 from wardrobe
- 9 lbs gold thread to make fringes etc
  for coach cover   132.00 from wardrobe

Total   690.42

Another visitor was Alfonso II, who arrived in Rome on 1 June to pay his respects to Pius IV – the duke had wanted to visit the city during Holy Week but Ippolito had discouraged this plan, explaining that the pope would 'be too busy with ceremonies' to spare time for a proper audience.[46] It had been part of Ippolito's duties as legate to Viterbo to arrange an escort for his nephew, and one of his valets was reimbursed with 207.36 scudi for the expenses incurred.[47] He hosted a splendid banquet at Palazzo Monte Cavallo and the poulterer's bill that month was almost three times that of April – it included 158 capons, 129 hens, 663 poussins, 708 pigeons and 126 geese.[48] The guests were entertained with a performance of a comedy written by Ippolito's secretary and ledgers record tips of 22 scudi to the actors, the singers and players who provided the musical accompaniment.[49]

It is unclear whether Alfonso II was a guest at the Vatican, as had been promised back in January, but he had several audiences with Pius IV. The pope evidently intended to honour his promise to give a red hat to the duke's younger brother, Luigi, and wrote a personal letter to the twenty-two-year-old guaranteeing that he would be among the next cardinals created – the promise was kept and Luigi was one of the eighteen men named in Pius IV's second creation of cardinals the following February. Ippolito himself had doubts about whether this worldly prince should pursue a Church career, though this was not an opinion he shared with the pope. Before Alfonso II's visit to Rome, he had suggested to his nephew that, 'I fear that not only the women in your city but also those in France will do all they can to wreck the project' – the women he meant were Luigi's mother Renée, the Protestant dowager duchess of Ferrara, and the French demoiselles with whom Luigi was notoriously intimate.[50] 'I think his inclination has unfortunately turned more towards the secular than the ecclesiastical,' Ippolito warned his nephew a month later, adding, rather crossly, 'I have not had a single word from him and he has still not sent one of his courtiers to see me.'[51]

Alfonso II had arrived in Rome to find the city buzzing with the news of the arrest of Cardinal Innocenzo del Monte – Julius III's ex-rent boy – and his imprisonment in Castel Sant'Angelo charged with the murder of two men while travelling to Rome for the conclave the previous August. He was found guilty but released in October after paying a huge fine of 100,000 scudi;

he was exiled from Rome in the company of two Jesuits who had orders to reform the cardinal's morals.[52] The duke was still in Rome in early June when the papal court was hit by another bombshell. There had been clues, for those who were looking, but they had been missed by most of the college. In mid-May a special envoy had arrived in Rome from Spain with instructions from Philip II to inform the pope that, although the king – up to his old diplomatic tricks – was giving every public sign of supporting the Carafa family, in private he had withdrawn his protection. Pius IV shrewdly adopted the same tactic.

In Rome too the Carafa family were lulled into a false sense of security. Reassured by the emollient promises of Vargas, Cardinal Carlo was unaware that the ambassador had been sidelined by his monarch; and his agent at the Spanish court, Fabrizio di Sangro, was also deceived. Indeed, Sangro had good news to report. 'I am enclosing copies of the letters that Fabrizio has sent from the [Spanish] court', Carafa informed his brother Giovanni on 1 June, full of optimism 'that, although his majesty has still not decided the matter of compensation nevertheless these negotiations do look as if they will turn out in our favour.'[53] Carafa was reassured, above all, that Pius IV himself was proving to be 'particularly well-disposed towards us, as he has been since the beginning, so I think you can rest at ease'. He urged Giovanni to come to Rome immediately as 'it appears that Fabrizio will be here very soon, not more than five or six days' time, and we then we will know more about the matter'. On 6 June Giovanni rode down to Rome, arriving after dark at his brother's palace, where their nephew Cardinal Alfonso was also staying. According to the newssheets, the family held a noisy party to celebrate 'the good news from Spain', with a description of the evening's scandalous revelries: 'they held a most beautiful banquet' and there was 'much laughter, music, dancing and theatrical entertainments and then they spent much of the night amusing themselves in the carriages with courtesans, singing and shouting with much joy'.[54]

The following morning the two cardinals rode to the Vatican for the weekly consistory. Ippolito was among those who witnessed what happened next, as were Sforza, Farnese, Carpi, Gonzaga, Madruzzo, Ghislieri, Dolera and several others who had been the target of Carafa's duplicity during the conclave. Carlo was first to arrive in the consistory hall and he was immediately summoned upstairs to the pope's private apartments. Assuming that Pius IV wanted to congratulate him about the news from Spain, he 'ran eagerly up the spiral staircase' and was soon joined by Alfonso, reported the Florentine ambassador, who was just leaving after his own audience with the pope.[55]

However, it was not the pope who was waiting for the cardinals at the top of the spiral staircase but the castellan of Castel Sant'Angelo, who arrested them. 'So this is my reward for all my good work,' shouted Carlo, while Alfonso 'looked confused and said nothing' – the newssheet account rather more colourfully reported that Alfonso 'seemed more dead than alive'.[56] Taken under guard to the fortress, they were joined by Giovanni, who was arrested at his brother's palace, which had been carefully searched for incriminating evidence. Among the crimes with which Carlo, Giovanni and Alfonso were charged were the murder of the Duchess of Paliano, theft of Church property and abuse of their authority during Paul IV's pontificate, not least with the invention of the Spanish 'plot' to poison the pope.

Ippolito and his colleagues were shocked. Pius IV appeared, 'looking very satisfied', and gave them a full account of what he had done and why it had been necessary. Ippolito, in agreement for once with both Carpi and Farnese, tried to persuade the pope to be lenient but the pope was resolute, much to the joy of the city of Rome. Vargas, despite specific orders from Philip II to the contrary, continued to plead for Carafa. Encountering the pope one day, the sidelined ambassador went down on his knees. 'Get up and get out of my way,' the usually affable pope replied in scorn.[57] The trial opened in Castel Sant'Angelo on 8 July and continued all summer before a committee of cardinals. There had been no place for Ippolito, Carpi or Farnese but Inquisitor General Ghislieri was on the panel, after letters to the Turkish and Protestant courts were found among Carlo's papers, providing evidence that the cardinal might also be guilty of heresy. The trial was important to the pope; according to the Venetian ambassador, 'his holiness cares about it more than any other matter'.[58] It evidently took priority over his plans to visit Ippolito. 'Regarding the arrival of his holiness here,' the cardinal informed Alfonso II on 17 August, 'I had a reply to my letter from Borromeo the day before yesterday and it seems that his holiness will not travel until everything is settled with the prisoners, which he judges will not be before the middle of next month.'[59] The trial continued to the end of September and Alfonso was released on the payment of a fine of 100,000 scudi but it took another five months for the College of Cardinals to agree on a punishment for Carlo and Giovanni. On 4 March the brothers were condemned to death and executed the following day; because of his rank the cardinal was allowed to die in the privacy of his cell.

It was most unusual for business at the papal court to continue through the summer. Normally everything ground to a standstill for four months, from the feast of St Peter and St Paul on 29 June to All Saints' Day on 1 November. Pope and cardinals alike sought relief from the sweltering heat in their villas in the nearby hills. This year Ippolito left for Tivoli on 13 July, an exodus that required much planning, not least the payment of all his outstanding bills the day before they left, the details of which covered three pages in the ledger. Before leaving Rome his tailor made several items for the holiday: two belted tunics in purple silk taffeta, two doublets in the same material and a matching peacock-feather hat.[60] It was a great cavalcade that rolled out of Rome for Tivoli, a journey of 20 miles: courtiers, valets, musicians, chefs, the *credenzieri* and the carver, mattresses, bed linen, saucepans and kitchen knives, chests of clothes, crates of silver and glass, boxes of napkins and tablecloths, rolls of tapestries and leather wall-hangings, and so on – all the trappings that were so essential to the life of a Renaissance prince. Relaxing inside the cool stone walls of the governor's palace, a shield bearing his coat-of-arms freshly painted over its portal, Ippolito complained about the exceptional heat.[61] 'Even here up in the hills it is extremely hot,' he wrote to Alfonso II on 10 August, 'and everybody is complaining about the extraordinary weather but at least it is not so bad here as it is in Rome' – a week later he was able to report that 'it has been raining a little', though this was not enough to bring an end to the heatwave.[62]

Tivoli was a small, walled town set against the backdrop of the stones and brush of the barren Sabine hills with magnificent views across the Roman Campagna. What a contrast to the lush green pastures of the Po valley where Ippolito had been in exile the previous year, and to the sweltering streets of Rome. The place was very much on the edge of civilization – Ippolito handed out tips to men for killing two wolves and to others for carcasses of mountain deer. He also tipped people for coins and fragments of antique statues, a reminder that centuries ago the area had been fashionable among the elite of ancient Rome. Still visible outside the town were the vast ruins of Emperor Hadrian's villa where Ippolito's antiquarian, Pirro Ligorio, had begun excavations that would inspire him to undertake his most famous project, transforming his modest governor's residence into the sumptuous Villa d'Este.

The location may have been primitive but Tivoli was Ippolito's own fiefdom. Among his papers is a ledger recording the fines handed out by his lieutenant for misdemeanours in the town.[63] Some were for petty pilfering, though more serious theft was punished by a prison sentence, but the bulk were for violence: a baker flogging his apprentice, for example; a housewife thrashing her servant; three women fighting; a man stoning a beggar; marital clashes; and many young men brawling. Despite the violence, Tivoli was a thriving town. Among the people named in the book of fines were a haberdasher, a sword-maker, a coppersmith, two millers, a washerwoman, plenty of workers in the building trade and several lawyers, who were paying the fines on behalf of their clients. The ledger recording household expenses that charts Ippolito's stay in the town during the summer of 1560 mentions a shoemaker, a locksmith, a greengrocer, a butcher and wine sellers.

However, the town was unable to provide the luxuries that Ippolito enjoyed in Rome. In his luggage he brought boxes of sweets and 2,000 toothpicks, a large supply for the two-month stay.[64] There was no shortage of onions, lettuces, green beans, parsley or other vegetables in Tivoli, and the butcher supplied the cheaper cuts of beef and mutton but not expensive veal, which had to be ordered from the regular butcher in Rome – surprisingly there is no evidence that the butcher charged extra for the forty-mile round trip on poor roads.[65] It was not just veal that was loaded onto carts in Rome: Ippolito's poulterer supplied fresh eggs, doves, pigeons and plump capons, while the grocer packed butter, parmesan cheese, almonds and dried fruit, and Gianino the fruiterer sent crates of peaches and pears, as well as 500 oranges, 272 melons and 107 lemons to Tivoli during July and August. Treasurer Novello settled all their bills when the household returned in September.[66]

Business was conducted at a leisurely pace. There were occasional items to transact in his capacity of cardinal-protector of France, and a lawyer came out from Rome on 25 August with documents for him to sign.[67] His ledgers also record regular tips to the footmen for running errands in Rome, and for taking letters to join the postal service to Ferrara and France.[68] Ippolito devoted most of his time to the pursuit of pleasure. There were lunch and dinner parties to host, and more parties to attend at the villas of his colleagues nearby. Sermoneta sent him several baskets of his favourite melons while Vitelli presented him with braces of partridge.[69] We can be sure that Ippolito indulged his taste for gambling at the card table, but perhaps there were also more edifying discussions with his philosopher, who had been given 8 scudi in July 'to buy books to take to Tivoli'.[70]

There were also plans to discuss for the conversion of the modest governor's palace into a grand villa. This converted medieval Franciscan convent was somewhat cramped and there was not enough room for all Ippolito's household, so he rented several houses in the town: one for the pages, another for guests and a third for the *credenzieri* to prepare their cold dishes for his dining-table.[71] Ippolito had long discussions with Ligorio and others about the design of the magnificent gardens he intended to lay out. He had already started buying up land for this project and work had begun on constructing an aqueduct to provide a proper supply of water for the spectacular fountains that would ornament the grounds.

While Ippolito was enjoying the cooler air in Tivoli, the builders continued to work at Palazzo Monte Cavallo. During August they started work on a new kitchen for this villa, where Ippolito hosted many of his sumptuous banquets, while a team of painters finished redecorating his apartments and frescoing the loggia beside the orange trees.[72] The carters brought regular deliveries of antique statues and marbles to the villa, as well as lime, sand and other supplies. The water carriers were particularly busy, laboriously carting their barrels from the banks of the Tiber up to the top of the Quirinal hill during the heatwave. Ippolito had left a skeleton staff behind in Rome including Iseppo, a footman who was given the responsibility of watering the vegetables in the kitchen garden as well as the tender orange, citrus and myrtle saplings. He was reimbursed for several payments he made to the water carriers during July and August amounting to the substantial sum of 11 scudi.[73]

Ippolito and his household returned to Rome, stopping for lunch at an inn where he watched a servant cut off the neck of a goose with a single strike of a sword and rewarded this impressive, if somewhat grisly, feat with a tip of 1 scudo.[74] With the end of the holidays and the start of the new term, Ippolito was soon back to his regular routine of parties, gambling, gossip, arranging favours and riding over to the Vatican for consistories. He lost money at cards and spent 18 scudi on a new marble fireplace for his rooms at Palazzo Monte Giordano, which he bought from the same nuns who washed his personal linen.[75]

That autumn, Ippolito had an unexpected problem. On 20 September his household expenses recorded this bizarre entry: 'To the Frenchman who brought news that two ships carrying wine from France have been captured by the Turks.[76] The wine, which came from Ippolito's own vineyards in the diocese of Narbonne – he was Archbishop of Narbonne – was being transported across the Mediterranean when the ships were seized off the Italian coast near Porto Ercole. Ippolito had to pay the pirates a ransom of 392 scudi for the return of the ships – their hire had already cost him over 380 scudi.[77] In addition, he also paid 26 scudi to the man who negotiated the deal and, when the French captains eventually arrived in Rome, the cargo had been depleted by twenty-six barrels, eighteen of which were kept by the Turks and eight requisitioned by the governor of Porto Ercole as a perk of his job.

The big social event in Rome that autumn was the state visit of Cosimo I, who arrived on 5 November with his duchess and their second son, Cardinal Giovanni. Ippolito had the privilege of receiving the ducal party. 'They were met at the gate of the city [Porta Santa Maria del Popolo] by two Most Illustrious cardinals, Sforza and Ferrara,' the master of ceremonies recorded, adding, evidently impressed with the show of wealth, that they made their grand entrance with 'thirty noble Florentine youths wearing outfits of purple velvet with many gold ornaments on their clothes and their hats'.[78] Ippolito entertained the visitors with several events including a display of dancing by four children and a banquet at Palazzo Monte Cavallo, grand enough to require him to take on extra kitchen staff for the occasion.[79] It is likely that it was for this occasion that he commissioned a splendid candelabra made from thirty-six pieces of his silver – cups, jugs, twenty-one plates and serving dishes, two spoons and half a fork – which were given to the goldsmith during November.[80]

Cosimo I's visit was not an unalloyed success. Although given every outward sign of favour, including guest apartments in the Vatican, Pius IV remained stubborn in his refusal to grant him the title of king. At the end of November, Cosimo fell ill. Ippolito informed Alfonso that 'the duke has unexpectedly suffered a slight fever... and his departure has had to be delayed as he cannot be moved'.[81] This caused the majordomo of the palace some logistical problems because he needed the guest apartments for Virginia della Rovere, Federigo Borromeo's young bride whose arrival was imminent. On 6 December, Ippolito wrote again to his nephew with the news that 'the duke's fever is gone and although he has taken a medicine that was very effective, his stomach was bad again this evening and he has some pain'.[82] But the duke still refused to move and, as Ippolito explained, Virginia della Rovere 'will make her entry into Rome the day after tomorrow and until the duke leaves she will be lodged in the Belvedere'. Cosimo did finally leave on 28 December but the proud boast made by the Florentine ambassador at the time of Pius IV's election that the Medici family now ruled Florence, Rome, France and Spain, and his belief that 'the pope will be guided in everything by Duke Cosimo's counsel and will', had proved wildly over-optimistic.[83]

Christmas represented more than just a Church feast in 1560. It was also the first anniversary of Pius IV's election, which he celebrated with the customary fireworks, bonfires and banquets. The feast in the Vatican was a particularly grand affair and among the guests were all the cardinals and members of Pius IV's family. According to his ledgers, Ippolito handed out 82 scudi in tips to nearly one hundred servants – the papal footmen as well as those of several of the guests, the papal musicians and *credenziero*, even the sommelier serving at the table where the cardinals were seated earned 1 scudo.[84] It would have been a lucrative night for the pope's dining staff;

and it was the culmination of a successful year for Pius IV and his allies. His pontificate would prove to be a landmark in the history of the Church and 1561 posed weighty problems, not least the challenge of uniting Europe's rulers behind his plans for reform.

10

France

JANUARY 1561–JUNE 1563

Pius IV's bull reconvening the Council of Trent, which was to spearhead his reform of the Catholic Church, was published on 29 November 1560 and although Europe's rulers all recognized it in principle, initially at least they showed some reluctance to go so far as to order their bishops to attend. To keep up the pressure, the pope dispatched legates across the Alps and in February he appointed Ercole Gonzaga as president of the council; but when the cardinal arrived at Trent on 16 April he found only ten bishops assembled in this small city-state at the foot of the Brenner Pass. Gradually over the summer, however, the numbers began to increase, especially after Philip II of Spain and the Italian powers instructed their bishops to attend. Emperor Ferdinand I gave his promise that he would send his bishops as soon as possible but refused to fix a date; in France, where violence between Catholics and Protestants had begun to cause serious problems, the situation was even less promising.

Protestantism had never become a significant threat in either Spain or Italy, thanks in large part to the tight control the

Inquisition exercised over religious beliefs. Here, opposition to the new sect had begun to harden and the voices of extremism calling for the total eradication of the heresy had started to drown out the moderates who counselled compromise. In northern Europe, by contrast, the movement was widespread and it had begun to challenge not only religious orthodoxy but also the political status quo. In the Spanish provinces of the Netherlands, Philip II threatened brutal measures to suppress the new religion. This was not an option in the Empire, where Ferdinand I could only maintain power by accepting the freedom of worship of his autonomous princes, several of whom had adopted the new religion – though he did oblige his son Maximilian to renounce his Protestant beliefs.

The situation in France was more complicated. The young Francis II had died in early December, just days after the publication of Pius IV's bull convening the council, and he had been succeeded by his ten-year-old brother Charles IX, under the regency of their mother, Catherine de' Medici. By Christmas she had radically altered the power structure of the French court, sidelining the staunchly Catholic Guise brothers – François, Duke of Guise and Charles, Cardinal of Lorraine – who had dominated the reign of Francis II, in favour of a more tolerant attitude towards the new religion. Writing to her daughter Elisabeth, Queen of Spain, soon after the privy council confirmed her appointment as regent, she insisted that her prime aim was 'to preserve my authority, not for myself but for the conservation of this kingdom and for the good of all your brothers'.[1] Her agenda was to create unity by healing religious differences and for this she needed to broker a compromise.

Catherine de' Medici decided to hold a colloquy – she was careful not to call it a council – at which both Catholics and

Protestants could openly discuss the differences between their faiths. As cardinal-protector of the French crown, Ippolito would have been involved in formulating papal policy towards her plan and by early March rumours were circulating that Pius IV intended to send him to France.[2] When his appointment as legate was finally confirmed on 2 June, it became clear that his brief extended beyond the protection of the Catholic faith in the kingdom. Ippolito was charged with persuading the regent to send her bishops to Trent and, more improbably, with making overtures to Elizabeth I in the hope of returning England to the Catholic faith.

Ippolito was an obvious choice for this tricky mission – certainly for the French aspects of it. His family were long-standing allies of France and he himself had spent many years at the royal court: he had been a favourite of both Francis I and Henri II, Catherine's dead husband, who had appointed him as cardinal-protector at the papal court. However, his appointment was not popular with the hard-line reformists in Rome and, as a sop to them, Pius IV agreed to include several Jesuits in the legation, including the general of the order, Diego Lainez. By a curious coincidence, the man who took over as general in Lainez's absence was Francisco Borja,* Ippolito's cousin and great-grandson of Alexander VI.

With Ippolito's departure planned for the end of the month, June was an unusually busy time at Palazzo Monte Giordano, especially for Ippolito's French tailor, Pierre. He cut and sewed several ecclesiastical outfits for Ippolito: two cassocks and coats, one in red taffeta and the other in crimson silk; a coat and a short cape, known as a *mozzetta*, in red silk that was specifically

---

* St Francisco Borja was canonized in 1671.

described as 'for riding'; and a raincoat cut from 5 metres of red cloth that had been specially treated with wax to make it waterproof, and cost the substantial sum of 35 scudi – just 1 scudo would buy four large capons.[3] There were also twenty-three white linen doublets to sew for Ippolito's footmen, pages and kennel men, and fifty mule covers.[4] On 27 June, Ippolito received his legatine cross from Pius IV in a noisy ceremony that involved tips of 38 scudi for the trumpeters and other musicians of both the pope and the government of Rome. Four days later, he left the city accompanied by an enormous cavalcade of mules laden with his personal possessions and horses carrying his courtiers and secretaries, his musicians, valets, stewards, squires, footmen and pages, an apothecary and a doctor, Pierre the tailor, two sommeliers, three chefs and a pastry cook, plus his stable boys who did the journey on foot.

The journey must have been arduous in the summer heat. He stopped for a fortnight in Ferrara, leaving behind his coachmen, his coach horses and some foals – one of the more unusual items among Ippolito's surviving papers is a ledger describing in meticulous detail the quantities and types of fodder given to each of these horses during Ippolito's absence in France.[5] On 8 August he left Ferrara, riding north to Mantua then through the Po plain to Turin and crossed the Alps via the Mont Cenis pass. Travelling as fast as possible, he rarely spent more than a single night in any one place and reached Chambéry on 30 August, where he was the guest of the Duke of Savoy. Four days later he had crossed the frontier into France and arrived at Lyon.

Ippolito's progress from Rome to Paris is charted in a ledger recording the sums he handed out each day on the road: tips to innkeepers for lunch, for example, or to the gate keepers, trumpeters and other officials in cities where he stayed the night; or alms to the poor.[6] Interestingly, it was only once he was in France that he made a show of his rank as papal legate. Unlike the first leg of the journey through Italy and Savoy, he now attended mass regularly, tipping the priest for the service, and gave one of the footmen 2 or 3 scudi each day to dispense in alms. In Lyon he ostentatiously dispensed 70 scudi in alms to various people and institutions, including 25 scudi to the hospital for poor Italians.[7] It could also be seen as an act of charity that Ippolito paid the expenses of Diego Lainez and his fellow Jesuits, who were part of the cavalcade travelling north to Paris, and he gave them 4 scudi every few days to enable them to make their own arrangements for accommodation.

Two days after leaving Lyon, Ippolito reached Roanne and the upper Loire. On 7 September he was at Varennes-sur-Allier, lodged at an inn, when a letter arrived from his niece Anna, Duchess of Guise, to warn him 'in the greatest secrecy' that she had heard he was 'not to be given lodgings in the castle' at Saint-Germain, where the royal court was currently in residence, 'not to receive a private audience, nor have his status [as legate] recognized'.[8] At La Charité-sur-Loire on 11 September he was the guest of the abbot – the rest of the party stayed at the inn – and he tipped not only the 'gentlemen of the house of the abbot' but also gave 2 scudi 'to the carpenters working in the abbey which has burned down', evidence perhaps of the escalating religious violence.[9]

On 13 September Ippolito was at Briare, south-east of Orléans – staying in a private house on this occasion, though, with the rest of the household at the inn – when a royal courtier arrived with orders that they needed to hurry as the colloquy had already opened at the Dominican convent at

Poissy, near Saint-Germain. More encouragingly, Ippolito was assured that he was to be given lodgings in the royal château and would be granted audiences with the regent, though his formal recognition as legate was proving more problematic among the Protestants at court.[10] The following day, he rode 25 miles north to Montargis, which had been a present to his Protestant sister-in-law Renée of France from Francis I. At this point Lainez and the Jesuits decided to continue the journey on their own and Ippolito gave them 11 scudi to cover their expenses – it is likely that they were in a hurry to reach Poissy, and they would have viewed spending even one night in this converted town with repugnance.

The papal legate had no such qualms, and stayed two nights at Montargis. Renée obviously enjoyed Ippolito's company and begged him to stay for longer ('but I must leave tomorrow and God willing I will arrive at court on Friday [19 September]', he informed Duke Alfonso).[11] Renée was a generous hostess. She 'has truly omitted nothing in her effort to honour me both as legate and as family', he continued, though he did add a sentence, in code: 'Regarding her religion, I found her to be most determined in her belief in the new sect.'

Meanwhile, Pierre the tailor was having difficulty finding the time to stitch the clothes needed for Ippolito's entry at Saint-Germain. By the time they reached Montargis the issue had become urgent, so he was sent off to Paris to finish the outfits with the wardrobe bookkeeper, Marcantonio Cambio, to do the necessary shopping. The tailor, who did not receive a salary from Ippolito but was paid for each item he made, sent in his bill in October listing each of the fifty-seven items he had sewn since leaving Ferrara, as well as travel expenses for himself and his horse for the three-day ride to Paris and the cost of accommodation for the eight days he spent in the capital.[12] In his own expenses, Cambio listed payments for candles to enable Pierre 'to work overnight on these items', and wages for the boys taken on in Paris to help.[13] In addition to the cloth, thread and other materials needed by Pierre, Cambio bought several mattresses, ten chairs, a fire screen, benches and other pieces of furniture to furnish Ippolito's apartments at court, perfumes to purify the air in the rooms and a ledger to record all these purchases as well as the cost of transporting them to Saint-Germain.[14]

The entry must have been a splendid sight. Ippolito himself was dressed in a new red satin cassock and coat, lined with silk plush to keep out the autumn chill, but the predominant colour worn by his muleteers, singers and pages was purple.[15] Pierre had made short quilted jerkins of purple cloth with matching hose for the muleteers, while the singers wore short purple jerkins over black hose and white doublets, and the pages were dressed in long quilted jerkins made of purple velvet over purple hose and white quilted doublets.

When the colloquy had opened at Poissy on 9 September, Ippolito had been in Nevers, still 150 miles away, and he had missed the first encounter between the rival religions. In the spirit of compromise, Catherine announced that anyone wishing to attend would be welcome and promised safe conduct for those travelling from Geneva, the hotbed of radical Protestant reform under John Calvin. Calvin himself did not attend but sent one of his ablest theologians, Théodore de Bèze, who arrived with a group of Protestant pastors at Saint-Germain on 23 August. They were received by both the regent and the king and allowed to preach sermons at court – and were housed, Bèze recorded, 'for their safety in a house belonging to Cardinal Châtillon' near the royal castle.[16]

At the first session, Bèze gave a detailed account of Protestant doctrine, finishing with the contentious issue of the Eucharist. For Catholics, the bread and wine received at communion were the body and blood of Christ, thanks to the miracle of transubstantiation that took place at the altar during the mass. For Protestants, however, no miracle took place; they believed that the bread and wine simply represented Christ. When Bèze concluded his discussion by saying 'the body of Christ is as far from bread and wine as heaven is from earth' there was an angry buzzing in the audience and murmurs of 'blasphemer'.[17] Cardinal François de Tournon, the elderly and devout Catholic whom Catherine de' Medici had appointed to preside over the proceedings, was heard to say to the regent: 'Is it possible that your majesty can tolerate such a sacrilege?'[18]

Ippolito also missed the second session on 16 September when the Cardinal of Lorraine robustly defended the Catholic position, but he did attend the third session on 24 September when Diego Lainez addressed the hall. Bèze recorded that the Jesuit hurled insults, calling Protestants 'monkeys and foxes', and his speech, which lasted for an hour, was 'a pile of insults and slander'.[19] The Jesuit also reduced Catherine de' Medici to tears by insisting that she must expel all Protestants before they destroyed the kingdom.[20] The antipathies on both sides were so intense that the meeting soon degenerated into a shouting match and it closed in early October. History has judged the Colloquy of Poissy a failure and it certainly did fail in its primary goal, to reach an understanding between French Catholics and Protestants. It was, however, an almost impossible task. A moderate herself, Catherine de' Medici did not understand the mindset of the fanatics on either side; they, in their turn, mistrusted her efforts at reconciliation, fearful that it cloaked her real intention of supporting the enemy's cause.

It is easy to see in hindsight how this mistrust thrived. While Catherine's faith was never in danger, she was not entirely unsympathetic to the Protestant cause. Several of her closest friends were Protestant; others were considered heretical for openly criticizing the Catholic Church. Her chancellor Michel de L'Hôpital was the object of particular hatred because of his insistence that the reform of the abuses in the Church could bring peace between the warring factions.[21] Despite the ban on translations of the Bible, Catherine owned one in French and the royal children were said to pray in their own language.[22] And Charles IX himself was rumoured only to attend mass to please his mother.[23]

While less sympathetic to Protestantism, Ippolito too was a moderate. Moreover, it is evident from his correspondence that both Pius IV and Cardinal Borromeo held similar views. All three churchmen had more experience of religious fanaticism than the regent. When Ippolito's attitude was condemned by the papal ambassador in France, instead of replacing his legate the pope recalled the envoy to Rome. The new ambassador was more amenable and reported to Rome on 31 October that Ippolito 'for his part is doing everything he can, losing neither time nor opportunity to deal with these princes'.[24] As legate, Ippolito's principal task was the protection of the Catholic Church in France but he went out of his way to help Catherine in her bid to bridge the gulf between the two religions. He urged Pius IV, for example, to agree to her request to allow communion of both kinds to the laity – at this stage the laity were only allowed to receive the bread at communion, with the chalice restricted to churchmen – and, remarkably, Cardinal Borromeo agreed with the legate.[25]

Above all, while extremists on both sides tended to see the problem exclusively in religious terms, Ippolito understood that for Catherine de' Medici the situation was much more complicated. As he explained in code to Duke Alfonso: 'The issue, as I have written to you many times before, is not solely to do with religion but to do with political power, which is the reason why these negotiations are so troublesome and difficult.'[26] Ippolito made an important point. It was not just religion that had split the kingdom: the enmity had become political as well and even divided the upper echelons of the royal court. The traditional rivalries between the houses of Bourbon, Montmorency and Guise were now potently spiced with religious fanaticism, pitting father against son, brother against brother and husband against wife, as well as creating some unlikely comrades.

Thanks to his many years in France, Ippolito had friends on both sides of the divide and understood its complex political and social background. He grasped, for example, the ramifications of the issue that gripped the gossips at court that autumn: the very public disintegration of the marriage of the philandering Antoine de Bourbon and the headstrong Jeanne d'Albret, the King and Queen of Navarre. The Bourbons were France's premier nobles, princes of the blood descended from Louis IX (1226–70). As the head of the family, Antoine was default heir to the French throne and Catherine de' Medici had made him lieutenant-general of France as a sign of his political and social status. However, the family was divided, its traditional loyalties destroyed by religious belief in a way that was emblematic of France itself. One of Antoine's brothers, Cardinal Charles de Bourbon, was a devout Catholic; the other, Louis, Prince of Condé, had converted to Protestantism. More ominously, Antoine himself had also started to display Protestant sympathies, while his wife, a close friend of the regent, had announced her conversion to the new religion on Christmas Day, 1560. However, Jeanne's robust efforts to persuade her husband to follow the same course had run into difficulties. The senior prince of the blood was being equally robustly courted by the opposition, and he was vacillating between the two. That he was keen for Ippolito's favour was evident on 3 November when he presented the legate with a valuable horse.[27]

Ippolito also had connections to the other two powerful families at court: the houses of Guise and Montmorency. Unlike the Bourbons, the Guises were newcomers: François, Duke of Guise, only acquired royal status in 1548 on his marriage to Ippolito's niece Anna d'Este, who was the granddaughter of Louis XII. Although Anna was the daughter of the Protestant Renée of France, the Guises were united in their militant opposition to the new religion – and the duke's brothers, Cardinal Charles of Lorraine and Cardinal Louis of Guise, had played key roles in the conclave that elected Pius IV.

Anne de Montmorency, the indomitable Constable of France, was also a staunch member of the Catholic party. He had been a favourite with Francis I and Henri II, one of the few, like Ippolito, to prosper under both monarchs. Like the Bourbons, Montmorency's relations were also split between the two faiths. Although his own sons belonged to the Catholic party, those of his sister did not. Gaspard de Coligny, Admiral of France, François d'Andelot, Colonel-General, and Cardinal Odet de Châtillon all owed their careers at court to their uncle but they had abandoned these ties of kinship and converted to the new religion. While Coligny and d'Andelot were openly Protestant, Cardinal Odet had been more circumspect – though many must have suspected where his sympathies lay when he played host to Théodore de Bèze and his Protestant colleagues during the Colloquy of Poissy.

The houses of Montmorency and Guise had been bitter rivals for decades so it had been all the more surprising when the constable and the Duke of Guise put aside their differences in early 1561 and, with Marshal Saint-André, formed a triumvirate dedicated to the defence of the Catholic faith against what they saw as the regent's suspiciously Protestant leanings. It was this triumvirate that was scheming to persuade the King of Navarre to take on the role of Catholic leader.

Above all, Ippolito was an old friend of Catherine de' Medici and, despite the warning from the Duchess of Guise that he would not be welcome at court, he was immediately admitted into the inner family circle. On 29 September, while the colloquy was still in progress, the cardinal lost 12 scudi playing cards with the eleven-year-old Charles IX and a week later lost another 5 scudi – surely these were expedient losses, Ippolito was normally a successful gambler at the card-table.[28] He had been twenty-six in 1536 when he first met Catherine, two Italians among so many French men and women at the royal court. She was not quite seventeen, the childless bride of Francis I's second son who, within weeks of Ippolito's arrival at the French court, was thrust suddenly into the limelight when the death of the king's eldest son made her husband heir to the throne. She had been a dutiful wife as dauphine and then queen, but now she had real power and one of her first acts on becoming regent was to commission her own seal as proof of her new status.[29] Although her influence had been somewhat curbed when Montmorency, the Duke of Guise and Marshal Saint-André formed the triumvirate, she was still the central figure at a court where the battle for control of the political and religious future of the kingdom was becoming increasingly vicious.

The failure of the colloquy in October 1561 was followed by an escalation in violence as fanatics on both sides of the religious divide took revenge for brutal attacks. Across southern France, Protestants destroyed Catholic churches, vandalizing images and relics; and the rumour mills were hard at work circulating stories such as the report that Protestants had started cutting off the ears of their opponents.[30] In Montpellier, they pillaged all sixty churches in the city, murdering 150 monks and priests; at Nîmes there was a public bonfire of precious relics and many nuns were killed in Castres.[31] Elisabeth of Valois, Queen of Spain, warned her mother that if she did not enter an alliance with Philip II against the Protestants, then the king would join up with the French Catholics to fight against her.[32]

It is a measure of just how far Ippolito was prepared to help Catherine de' Medici in her search for a solution that would achieve a level of peaceful co-existence between the rival religions that, in the middle of November, he actually agreed to attend a Protestant sermon. He explained to Duke Alfonso how this happened:

> I went with the Queen [Catherine de' Medici] to visit the Queen of Navarre [Jeanne d'Albret]... and we got into a discussion and the Queen of Navarre told me she had heard a sermon that morning from a new preacher who was very modest and had spoken without offending anyone and that it would give her great pleasure if I would agree to accompany

her to a sermon, and she invited me to dine with her. For her part the Queen Mother also urged me to do this... I was certainly in a quandary, more however for the allegations of people who knew nothing about, or would not accept, the reasons that move man, than for the essence of the thing; but in the face of this request I felt that I was unable to refuse and I extracted a promise from the Queen of Navarre that she and her court would accept an invitation to dine with me and to listen to a sermon from one of my theologians.[33]

So Ippolito accepted the royal invitation to listen to the sermon which was given by an unfrocked Franciscan who had converted to the new faith. 'It was very reasonable,' the legate reported to his nephew, 'addressing the issues in general terms and avoiding all controversy, so that neither I nor any of those with me were scandalized in any way.' The return invitation was delayed for a few days: first, the Queen of Navarre had a fever, then her husband had a cold, but eventually both consented to appear at Ippolito's table – though the queen, fearful of being poisoned, brought her own food.[34] Ippolito's inventory recorded that a gilded silver platter and knife with a silver handle were stolen at the banquet.[35] Again, in the interests of reconciliation, Ippolito ensured that his guests came from both sides of the politico-religious divide: in addition to the Protestant queen and her indecisive husband, he invited the king's two brothers, the Catholic Cardinal Bourbon and the Protestant Condé, as well as the closet Protestant Cardinal Odet de Châtillon and his openly Protestant brother, Admiral Coligny. After the meal they all listened to a sermon preached by a theologian in Ippolito's party, though the Queen of Navarre was seen to leave her seat during the sermon and rudely turn her back on the friar.[36]

The news that Ippolito had attended a Protestant sermon caused an uproar in Rome but he remained unrepentant: 'Even if I had known that my presence at the sermon would produce such malicious reactions, I have to say nevertheless that I would do it again.'[37] He must have been very relieved to hear from a friend that 'his holiness himself has chosen to defend me and he gave an explanation in consistory to demonstrate his support'.[38] In view of the later history of the Counter-Reformation, the pope's gentle reproof in a personal letter to Ippolito is fascinating. 'Even though you attended this sermon with good intentions and with prudence, nevertheless it would have been better if you had done it more privately and known to few, and that it had not become such a public scandal,' he wrote in a personal letter to Ippolito, adding with some sadness at the end, 'in the event, however, it seems to us that this tolerant approach is no longer possible.'[39] Nevertheless, it was revealing that the pope still made no attempt to replace Ippolito as legate; indeed he later wrote 'every day we are more satisfied with the diligence with which you are trying to find a solution.'[40]

Nor were Ippolito's other tasks as legate very easy. His attempt to persuade Catherine de' Medici to order the French bishops to attend the council in Trent had met with some success: she had agreed that she would do so but expediently refused to commit to a firm date. That autumn he sent an envoy to London to open talks – they were hardly negotiations – with Elizabeth I and, though the mission was not a success, at least it caused less controversy than Ippolito's dealings in France. Interestingly, with an entirely different agenda in mind, he sent his under-stable master Rigo Springalle with the mission to London. As he informed Duke Alfonso: 'I sent Rigo with [the envoy] so that he can look for a horse over there and I have given him orders above all to find one that is good enough to be able to serve in your stud, but although he has brought several small horses (jennets) he has not been able to find anything suitable for you.'[41] Rigo made other purchases in London, notably items of warm winter clothing for Ippolito, including two wool shirts and two pairs of woollen stockings, as well as four hunting horns and seven dog collars.[42]

Now that he was settled in France for the foreseeable future, Ippolito was in need of warm clothing. His ledgers list purchases of a pair of leather boots lined with sheepskin and of the materials for a kind of quilted bodywarmer that Pierre the tailor made from fine linen and filled with down.[43] During November and December, the wardrobe spent 520 scudi on furs in Paris, mainly sables, and bought two large chests covered with black leather that were fitted with locks to keep these valuable items safe.[44] In December, Pierre stitched a very expensive red satin coat and a matching cassock lined with fourteen sable pelts and trimmed with lynx: the satin cost 31 scudi, the sables 178 scudi, and another 30 scudi for the lynx trim.[45] He also spent 340 scudi on red satin for a set of bed hangings.[46] To give some idea of the price of these bed hangings, they cost the same as an expensive race horse, or the annual wages of six carpenters at work on Ippolito's villa on the Quirinal.[47] Life at the royal court was far from cheap and there were more expenses at Saint-Germain where Ippolito welcomed in the New Year – his ledgers list five pages of tips to the households of the king and his mother.[48]

Meanwhile, as the violence escalated across France, Catherine de' Medici redoubled her efforts to find areas of compromise between the two religions and, acting on the advice of Chancellor L'Hôpital, hosted a series of discussions early in 1562. Ippolito sent Borromeo an account of the debate over religious images, which the Protestants considered went against the Bible's explicit ban on 'graven images' and 'any likeness of any thing' (Exodus 20:4). 'The queen', wrote Ippolito, 'wanted to understand the opinions of all, particularly those who were most offended, and what the reasons and beliefs behind their opinions were.'[49] His own view was that Catherine was becoming increasingly sympathetic to the Protestant cause: 'I myself am doing as much as I can, daily struggling to persuade the queen that all the fault lies with our adversaries.'[50] On 24 January she issued the Edict of January*, allowing Protestants to worship in public for the first time. However, this significant gesture towards toleration was severely limited: these services could not be held within town walls and there were harsh penalties for any Protestant taking up arms in the cause of religion. At the same time, Catherine ordered the court to observe the Catholic faith or risk exile: on 3 February, Ippolito informed Duke Alfonso that she 'has told the Queen of Navarre that she can no longer hold services in the castle'.[51]

The Catholic party was far from reassured by Catherine's move. With the Queen of Navarre sidelined at court, the triumvirate now seized the opportunity to persuade the King of Navarre to join them. Using the threat that Philip II would expel him from Navarre unless he returned to the fold, Antoine de Bourbon bowed to pressure and committed himself to the Catholic cause. He denounced the Edict of January in forceful

---

* This edict is also known as the Edict of Saint-Germain or the Edict of Toleration.

terms, declaring all moderates at court to be heretics: 'The King of Navarre was never so earnest on the Protestant side as [he is] now zealous on the other.'[52] Ippolito reported a very public row between Bourbon and Cardinal de Châtillon: 'The King of Navarre said that if there had been a proper inquisition in France to supervise religious affairs as there is in other places, things would not be in the state they are; at which point the cardinal said that anyone advising the formation of such an inquisition in France cared nothing about this kingdom, to which the king retorted, with no little malice and using pungent words, that he himself had the interests of the kingdom far more to heart.'[53] And perhaps the most dramatic statement of his metamorphosis was his public repudiation of his Protestant wife, who was forced into exile.

The new influence of the Catholic party, and the importance of the King of Navarre, was soon evident at court where Catherine de' Medici, despite still being regent, had succeeded in forcing the heads of all three rival families – Bourbon, Montmorency and Guise – into agreement. On 22 February, Ippolito wrote enthusiastically to Alfonso II: 'I hope I am not deceived in believing that the conversion of the King of Navarre is the most powerful way of saving this kingdom.'[54] The legate admitted to his nephew that he was much relieved after the stress of the previous few weeks; and he congratulated himself on 'managing to stay healthy despite the turbulence of the affairs here… and I hoped to relax a little now and enjoy the results of my hard work but then I had an attack of gout, which just goes to show that nothing is perfect in this world'.

A week later events spiralled out of control, sparking off the outbreak of the religious wars that would split France until 1598. On 1 March, the Duke of Guise was travelling towards Paris with a troop of soldiers when he came across a group of unarmed Protestants worshipping in a barn next to the church inside the walls of Vassy and opened fire on them, leaving seventy-four dead and another hundred persons injured. The Catholic party was jubilant at the news of the massacre. Catherine de' Medici and her children left the castle at Saint-Germain on 6 March for the greater safety of Fontainebleau, the beautiful château built by Francis I some 50 miles south of the capital. 'In Paris,' Ippolito informed Borromeo, 'the King of Navarre accompanied by a great entourage of the leading supporters of the Catholic religion went to church after which they all dined together at the house of Constable Montmorency with much celebration.'[55]

By 23 March, Paris had become unsafe for the Prince of Condé, who had become leader of the Protestants after the defection of his brother, and he fled the city. A few days later, the Catholic victory seemed complete when Montmorency and Guise, with 1,000 horsemen, rode to Fontainebleau to force Catherine to return to Paris for her protection.[56] When the Protestants accused them of kidnapping the royal family, they issued a statement declaring that 'far from being held prisoners by the constable and the princes of the house of Guise, they live in complete freedom in Paris, which is the capital of their realm', Ippolito informed Borromeo.[57]

The Protestants, however, were far from beaten. On 2 April Condé, who had joined forces with Admiral Coligny soon after fleeing Paris, seized Orléans, imposing the new religion on the city, stripping its churches of their decorations and burning relics. Four days after the conquest, Condé published a manifesto from his new power base outlining his key aims: to free the royal family from the 'protection' of the Catholics and to secure freedom of worship for all Protestants in France. The war had started and Ippolito's letters to Rome now concentrated on the need to raise funds and troops. It was an indication of the seriousness of the situation that there was no more talk of reconciliation: he was more firmly in the Catholic camp. So, it would seem, was Catherine de' Medici. As he wrote to Borromeo on 4 April: 'Above all, given what has happened, the best is that the regent and the King of Navarre are closely united with the Catholics and they all have the same goal which is to pacify the troubles of this kingdom for the common good of all its subjects.'[58] Moreover, Ippolito was evidently in favour at court: when Cardinal de Tournon died on 21 April, Catherine agreed to appoint him Archbishop of Lyon in Tournon's place.

Catherine's initial attempts to negotiate with Condé through the Bishop of Orléans met with little success, so in early June she decided to talk to the prince herself. Their first meeting was planned for 9 June at the small town of Toury, north of Orléans, but Condé failed to turn up. His advisors thought it unsafe, Ippolito informed Borromeo, 'giving the reason that the queen's entourage was so large that they were secretly worried that some violence was planned against the prince'.[59] The next attempt a few days later was more successful. Accompanied by an escort of just 100 horsemen, the regent and Condé 'spoke for three-quarters of an hour, exchanging the usual compliments but when they moved on to the details the prince refused to negotiate'.[60] Further meetings also ended in failure. Finally, Catherine told Condé, 'since you rely on your forces, we will show you ours'.[61] On 5 July, Ippolito informed Borromeo that she 'has satisfied God and her conscience that she has shown these [Protestants] and the whole world that her desire is to protect the subjects of the king her son and to save them from these troubles'.[62]

Much of Ippolito's correspondence with Rome that spring and summer concerned Catherine's need for money. Hoping to persuade Pius IV to agree to a loan, she gave orders for the French bishops to be ready to leave for Trent and included in the party Cardinal Charles of Lorraine, France's senior churchman since the death of Cardinal de Tournon in April. There would be time later to find excuses delaying their departure: fears that their dioceses might fall into the hands of the Protestants was one; the bad weather was another. Pius IV's first offer was generous – a gift of 100,000 scudi and the loan of another 100,000 scudi – but there were severe conditions attached. Catherine was to annul the concessions granted to the Protestants in the Edict of January and to expel all adherents to the new religion, whether open or secret, from her court, including Chancellor L'Hôpital; and finally she had to promise not to make any accord with the enemy in future.

It was Ippolito's rather unwelcome task to reveal these conditions to the regent, who was understandably furious at this diktat that severely undermined her authority. She refused to consider cancelling the edict or exiling any of her loyal courtiers. As the legate informed Borromeo: 'When I asked her about the chancellor, as the pope had expressly asked me to do, she replied more angrily than before that all these issues were the plots of interested parties and she absolutely would not be guided in this by the wishes of others.'[63] But she needed the money. In August, she sent the Bishop of Auxerre to Rome to negotiate on her behalf and Pius IV was persuaded to tone down his previous offer, agreeing in particular not to force her to exile her courtiers; and in November the French bishops arrived at Trent.

Meanwhile, Ippolito was increasingly keen to leave France. It is not entirely clear what was wrong – he might have had enough of the complexities of French politics, but equally stress was not good for his gout, or maybe he dreaded another northern winter and just wanted to be back in Italy. He asked Pius IV several times to replace him as legate but the pope always refused. That September, for example, the pope wrote: 'About your wish to return, we cannot agree to your request because we desire first to see the outcome of this war, or at least that its end is in sight, and then similarly that the business of the council [at Trent] must be quietly and safely on its way to completion.'64 There was no sign that the war in France would end any time soon. Over the summer, the Protestants had made substantial advances, seizing the cities of Poitiers, Troyes, Tours, Bourges, Lyon and Rouen. Condé had more success than Catherine at raising funds: on 20 September his envoys signed a treaty with Elizabeth I at Hampton Court in which the queen promised to supply men and money in exchange for the Channel port of Le Havre. However, the Catholics had begun to fight back, taking Blois and Poitiers in July while Bourges fell to Saint-André in August.

In late September, the Catholic army led by the King of Navarre set siege to Rouen. Catherine de' Medici travelled north to the army camp to see the action and when warned by Montmorency and Guise that it was dangerous, she replied 'my courage is as great as yours'.65 Ippolito was also a spectator at the siege though he had left most of his household behind, some in Paris and others at the Abbey of Chaalis, one of his benefices north of the capital. One of the few who accompanied the legate to Rouen was the long-suffering Pierre the tailor, who needed the help of two boys in Rouen to make a dark red satin coat lined with sable to go with a pair of matching velvet breeches for Ippolito in October – evidently, watching war was easier in secular clothes than in cardinal's robes.[66]

Unfortunately, on 16 October Navarre was wounded in the shoulder by an arquebusier. Initially it did not appear serious. 'The King of Navarre is improving continually, every day he is a little better,' Ippolito informed Borromeo ten days after the incident.[67] The following day he wrote again to Borromeo, this time with the exciting news that Rouen had fallen – the legate was particularly impressed by the efficiency of the mines that had facilitated the victory, and by the bravery of the Duke of Guise, 'who put himself in danger as if he were a mere captain'.[68] However, Navarre's improvement did not last. When the court finally left for Paris on 12 November, his fever was worse and it was decided 'to put him on a barge to travel up [the Seine] to Paris as he has the greatest desire to be gone from here', Ippolito informed his nephew, 'and I left one of my men with the king in order to be informed hour by hour of the progress of his illness'.[69] Sadly, the king died before reaching the capital; and Ippolito was again obliged to delay his departure 'because of this accident and because of the dangers of the road now that the enemy soldiers are everywhere'.[70]

While the Catholics were celebrating their success at Rouen, and mourning the death of Navarre, Condé and his troops unexpectedly left Orléans and marched north with the intention of making an attack on Paris. Unfortunately for Condé, the Duke of Guise was warned about the threat and managed to reach the capital before him. On 19 December Condé's army was intercepted at Dreux by Montmorency's troops. The result was a Catholic victory – and it is likely that the payment Ippolito made to one of his squires on 15 January 'for having two drawings made of the battle' refers to Dreux.[71] But it was a particularly bloody encounter; as many as a third of all those fighting were killed or wounded. Marshal Saint-André died, as did one of Montmorency's sons; Montmorency himself was made a prisoner by the Protestants, while the Catholics managed to capture Condé, though both were later released.

Early in the new year, encouraged by their recent successes, the royal army laid siege to the Protestant headquarters at Orléans and the court moved to the royal château at Blois to be close to the army camp. Ippolito suffered an attack of gout in January and a carpenter in Paris made him a special gout chair but he was not well enough to leave for Blois until early February.[72] Shortly before leaving he wrote to Duke Alfonso, attaching a copy of the letter he had just written to Cardinal Borromeo, explaining just how dangerous travel was at this time:

> I am now well enough, God be thanked, to be able to start for the court, despite the uncertainty and difficulty of the journey because of the roads... though the regent has given orders to Marshal Montmorency [the constable's eldest son] to escort me with his company of one hundred men-at-arms as far as Chartres where the Duke of Guise will arrange an escort for me to the camp.[73]

The marshal's men received 12 scudi from Ippolito 'for their journey back to Paris'.[74] Most significantly, the letter to his nephew revealed his conviction that the journey to Blois would be the first leg of his return home: 'I am of the firm hope that I will be able to leave from there for Italy on the second day of Lent.'

Ippolito's plans were to be further interrupted. Ash Wednesday, which fell on 24 February that year, saw the legate still at Blois. Indeed, he had arrived there six days earlier and had been much encouraged by the state of the roads, which he considered good enough 'to allow me to leave the court in a few days and start my journey to Italy', as he informed Duke Alfonso.[75] Unfortunately, the day Ippolito rode into Blois, 18 February, the Duke of Guise was wounded in an assassination attempt at Orléans. 'I must remain here for a few more days to see how the wound develops and although the reports that arrive here every hour suggest it is getting better, he is such an important person with such close ties to our house that I must put aside my own wishes at this moment.' He did not send the letter immediately so was able to add a postscript on 24 February: 'It is with the greatest regret that I must give you the news of the death today of the Duke of Guise.' And in a copy of the letter to Borromeo that he enclosed in the dispatch, he wrote of his sadness 'not only at the great damage this has done to the realm but also to see my niece the Duchess of Guise with all her small children in such distress'. There was some small consolation in the fact that the assassin, a Protestant noble named Poltrot de Méré, had been caught 'more thanks to God than to the industry of man because, having had two nights and a day to escape from the camp, he had only managed to get five leagues away', a distance of less than 10 miles.

Huge crowds gathered in Catholic Paris to watch the assassin's execution on 18 March and to witness the funeral of the Duke of Guise the following day. The war had been expensive. In the space of three months, the Catholics had lost three of their ablest leaders (the King of Navarre, Marshal Saint-André and the Duke of Guise); and they were now forced to accept a very unfavourable peace. The terms of the Pacification of Amboise, published on 19 March, included an amnesty for Protestant nobles and the freedom of worship for Protestants in all cities where the new religion was already established, though this freedom would not extend to Paris nor to the court. 'It is greatly to be regretted that the queen has been forced by necessity to agree to this accord but her adversaries stubbornly insisted on their sermons and services at least in certain places,' Ippolito informed his nephew, and this was the only way 'to free the kingdom from the terrible destruction and ruin it is suffering and to regain the occupied lands for the crown'.[76]

Although the fighting had mostly stopped, it was not until late April that it was safe enough for Ippolito finally to leave for Italy. If his ledgers are anything to go by, then it was a most pleasant month.[77] The court was first at Amboise, where the peace was announced on 30 March and Good Friday celebrated on 9 April; and on Easter Monday they moved to Chenonceau,* the château built by Henri II's mistress that Catherine had confiscated after her husband's death. Among the entries are some 60 scudi that Ippolito lost playing cards on various occasions with Charles IX and with his mother; a tip of 2 scudi to the queen's gardener at Amboise for a present of asparagus and salad; and one of 4 scudi to the 'many builders who are working for her majesty at Chenonceau'.

On 20 April the royal embroiderers arrived from Tours to deliver two sets of embroideries for Ippolito's beds, and he paid

---

* The town is Chenonceaux but traditionally the château is known as Chenonceau.

them 6 scudi for the expenses of their journey to Chenonceau, about 18 miles.[78] One of these sets depicted the story of Jacob and cost Ippolito 156 scudi; the other, which recounted that of Vulcan, the crippled god who was cuckolded by his wife Venus, was more elaborate and cost him 364 scudi.[79] Other purchases that spring included 762 scudi on necklaces, frustratingly with no information as to who they were for, and 5 scudi on 'a silver jewel case for a lady'.[80] He commissioned two clocks from Renée of France's clockmaker (80 scudi) and a spinet (19 scudi), as well as several books of music for his singers, one of which was intended as a present for his nephew Alfonso, which was decorated with the ducal coat-of-arms picked out in gold.[81]

Ippolito was also inundated with presents of horses and dogs from various members of the Guise and Bourbon families.[82] He received horses from the Prince of Roche-sur-Yon, a cousin of the King of Navarre, from Cardinal Louis of Guise, brother of the dead duke, and from his niece Anna. There were dogs from another Guise brother and a prized Spanish hunting dog from Marshal Montmorency, who had provided his escort from Paris to Chartres back in February. Ippolito had acquired a lot of dogs during his stay in France: in January 1563 before leaving Paris, one of his staff had been sent out to buy bread for forty dogs, and while he was at Chenonceau he tipped Catherine de' Medici's kennel man after one of the queen's dogs covered one of Ippolito's bitches.[83]

That June, Ippolito arranged for twenty-five dogs to be taken back to Ferrara from Paris and the details of their journey, in the charge of a French kennel man and three boys, are listed in the bill the kennel man submitted to Ippolito's factor after they reached Ferrara.[84] It took the party thirty-four days to complete the journey, a distance of 700 miles, and the expenses listed included a daily allowance for accommodation for the four men, which came to 38 scudi, as well as the purchase of shoes for two of the boys who were too poor to have their own, and the daily amounts of giblets, sheep's heads and milk to feed the dogs, wine to wash their paws, lard to rub into their pads and eight pairs of shoes for dogs who developed sores.

Ippolito himself left Chenonceau on 22 April: 'The queen with the king and all the lords here showed me all the kindness I could have desired on my departure from court.'[85] His journey, which took almost the same length of time as that of the dogs, was unusually tedious because of the need to avoid marauding bands of Protestants. Instead of travelling across France to reach the safety of the Duke of Savoy's capital Chambéry via Lyon, he was obliged to avoid that city and all large towns, travelling cross-country from Romorantin to Bourg-en-Bresse, a route that was obscure enough to require the hire of guides in addition to troops of armed guards for most of the way to Chambéry. Fortunately, he had had the foresight to acquire funds to pay for these extra expenses: before leaving Amboise he borrowed 700 scudi from a Polish priest, signing a chit so that the priest could recoup the money from Ippolito's agent in Paris.[86]

Ippolito spent two nights at Chambéry as a guest of the Duke of Savoy, no doubt enjoying the luxuries of court after two weeks on the road, and reached Ferrara at the end of May. There was little time for Ippolito to recover from the journey, nor for his household. Within days Cardinal Charles of Lorraine arrived from Trent for talks with the legate; and Pierre the tailor made yet more outfits for his master, and the rest of the staff prepared to move back to Palazzo Monte Giordano. On 9 June Ippolito, accompanied by his nephew Cardinal Luigi and Lorraine, left for Rome where Pius IV welcomed him:

I know you will have heard from your ambassadors of my return to Rome... nevertheless I wanted to send you this account in order that you can hear from myself how in truth I was received with much kindliness by his holiness and with an extraordinary courtesy from almost all this court. Today I was present at a public consistory and was honoured with the greatest compliments I could possibly desire.[87]

❧

Roma Resurgens

JULY 1563–JANUARY 1566

I ppolito must have been astonished as he made his way along the familiar streets from the Porta del Popolo to see the amount of building work that was going on in Rome. Thanks to Pius IV the city had become one enormous construction site. The pope commemorated his ambitious programme of urban renewal in a medal inscribed with the words *Roma resurgens*, evidently conceiving this project as a visual counterpart to his equally ambitious goal of reforming the Catholic Church itself. Bridges and aqueducts were being renovated, new streets laid out and churches repaired, some financed from the papal coffers but others paid for by the cardinals who had been ordered by Pius IV to restore their titles. At the Capitol, work had restarted on Michelangelo's innovative designs for the piazza, a project that had been abandoned by the puritanical Paul IV, while at Castel Sant'Angelo builders were busy updating the defensive capabilities of this papal stronghold. The work at the castle cost over 130,000 scudi, much of it raised in levies on milling and on the slaughter of animals for sale in the city markets: the measures were unpopular with the Romans, though the papal projects themselves provided employment for hundreds of workers in the building trades.[1]

Once again there were workers swarming over the scaffolding at St Peter's, another project that had come to a standstill under Paul IV. The prime symbol of papal power and still unfinished sixty years after the demolition of the old basilica, this was one of Pius IV's main priorities. At the Vatican he repaired the halls where the drama of his election had taken place and decorated the bare walls of the Sala Regia, designed for the reception of kings and emperors, with scenes of rulers from Charlemagne onwards bowing to papal authority. He commissioned a series of maps and landscapes for the Loggia della Cosmographia to celebrate his achievements across Christendom – though, curiously, there was no indication whatsoever that some of the countries, notably England, had actually severed all connections with Rome. He transformed the great interior courtyard of the palace into a huge theatre, described by a visitor as 'an atrium of pleasure', where tiers of seats were erected for the tournaments and other spectacles with which he entertained his guests.[2] In the gardens of the papal palace he built an elegant *casina** (literally, little house), designed by Ippolito's architect Pirro Ligorio to provide a peaceful retreat with fishponds, a fountain and a loggia for alfresco dining, decorated with *all'antica* stuccoes and statues that proclaimed Pius IV's pontificate as a new golden age.[3] There was also construction work going on around the Vatican where Pius IV was building the Borgo Pio, a new residential district between St Peter's and Castel Sant'Angelo, centred on a new road, the Via Angelica, and a new gate in the city walls, the Porta

---

* The Casina di Pio IV is now the seat of the Pontifical Academy of Sciences.

Angelica – both names were derived from the pope's baptismal name, Angelo.*

Ippolito would not have missed the construction work at the Porta del Popolo, the main entrance into the city for travellers from the north, for which Pius IV had commissioned a new facade. Designed by Michelangelo, its solid Doric columns gave an appropriate welcome to the pilgrim arriving at this city of St Peter, the rock on which Christ had built his church.[4] Nor would Ippolito have missed the building work going on near his villa, the Palazzo Monte Cavallo, where the narrow road that ran alongside his garden wall was being transformed into a broad straight thoroughfare, the Via Pia,† to link the Quirinal to the Via Salaria and the Via Nomentana with another new gate, the Porta Pia, also designed by Michelangelo, set in the city walls.

The new road also ran past the ruins of the Baths of Diocletian, where Pius IV was building a new church, Santa Maria degli Angeli, also designed by Michelangelo. The pope made much of the terrible reputation of this emperor, famous above all for the brutal persecution of Christians, who were forced as slaves to build the baths, and he commissioned a medal with the inscription: 'What once was pagan is now a temple to the Virgin, founded by Pius; fly away demons'.[5] According to the Venetian ambassador, Pius IV's Rome was conspicuously Christian:

> In public [the cardinals] stand apart from all sorts of amusement. They are no longer seen riding or driving masked in the company of ladies; at most they sometimes ride in coaches,

---

* Via Angelica is now the Borgo Angelico, while the Porta Angelica was destroyed in 1890 to make way for the Piazza del Risorgimento.

† Now the Via XX Settembre.

but without any retinue. Banquets, games, hunting parties, liveries, and all forms of external luxury are at an end... and priests now go about in the dress of their order so that reform is visible to the eye.[6]

Contrary to the ambassador's account quoted above, life in Rome was not entirely without 'external luxury', as we shall see below, but there had definitely been a change in tone since Ippolito left for France back in the summer of 1561. Pius IV's gracious reception of the cardinal on his return was at variance with the views of others in the college, many of whom were openly critical of his performance as legate. In his absence, the political and religious rivalries dividing the papal court had hardened: those in the Spanish party accused him of using his legation to promote his own interests in France, while the hard-line reformers argued that he had shown excessive favour towards Protestant heretics. They denounced Catherine de' Medici for her reluctance to deal harshly with the Protestants among the French nobility, insisting that this was about heresy not about politics. In particular, they accused Ippolito of protecting Cardinal Odet de Châtillon, whose leanings towards the new religion were well known. In the end, Pius IV was obliged to order the French cardinal's case to be examined by the Inquisition, which was still in the hands of the ascetic Dominican Michele Ghislieri. In January 1563, after much procrastination, Ippolito had finally delivered the summons against Châtillon; three months later the Frenchman was charged with heresy and deprived of his red hat.

In the more devout atmosphere of Pius IV's Rome, even the pope was exasperated by Ippolito's inability – or unwillingness, as the cardinal's enemies put it – to control the behaviour of his wayward nephew Luigi, who had been made a cardinal two years earlier. It was Ippolito's private opinion that the boy – aged twenty-two when he received his red hat – was not cut out for a career in the Church and he was soon proved correct. Luigi had taken up residence with his uncle at Palazzo Monte Giordano where, during the autumn of 1563, some of his men got into a fight and killed a senior policeman. The pope was furious and ordered the young cardinal to be put under house arrest; he also sharply upbraided Ippolito in a public consistory on 2 November, reminding him of the many favours he had shown him, not least giving Luigi a red hat as well as supporting him after the affair of the Protestant sermon.[7]

The Council of Trent was to have a decisive impact on the Church. By the time it closed in December 1563, it had drawn up decrees encompassing the complete reform of the Church and its government. Among its reforms was the obligation that all cardinals be ordained priests in contrast to the tradition whereby cardinals from princely houses were allowed to remain in minor orders in case they were needed to provide their family with heirs. Ippolito was ordained in March 1564, along with Alessandro Farnese and several others, and on 13 November of that year Pius IV issued the bull *Professio fide*, which defined the basis of the Catholic faith in the context of the Protestant reformation that had rejected many of its key beliefs, notably that of papal supremacy. And the impact of the council would be felt not only on religious life but also on society, art, architecture, music and literature.

Pius IV himself was a prominent patron of religious as well as secular scholarship: he ordered new editions of the works of the Church Fathers and other Christian authors, adding significantly to the ecclesiastical collections of the Vatican library. He also sponsored a new forum for the discussion of Christian knowledge, the Academia Vaticana, founded in 1562 by his nephew Carlo Borromeo. The academy held regular evening meetings in the papal palace, where Borromeo and a group of like-minded friends and mentors discussed ancient literature and philosophy as well as contemporary science in the context of Christian truth.

Borromeo provided the model of how a cardinal was expected to comport himself in the new Rome. He placed great stress on the Christian virtue of humility – the word appeared four times in his coat-of-arms – and, despite family pressure after the death of his older brother in 1562, he refused to abandon his ecclesiastical career for the prestige of a secular title.[8] In line with the regulations governing the behaviour of churchmen published by the Council of Trent in December 1563, his court at Rome became increasingly austere. 'They must understand,' the council exhorted, that they had not been appointed to acquire 'riches or luxury but to labour and care for the glory of God'.[9] Borromeo conspicuously observed the ruling, dispensing eighty per cent of his annual income of around 100,000 scudi in alms.[10] He moved out of his grand palace at Santi Apostoli, sold much of its valuable furnishings and took up residence in the modest house attached to his titular church, Santa Prassede. He reduced the size of his household to just one hundred and required all his courtiers to be both modest and celibate. Even more strikingly, he ignored the social conventions whereby a cardinal, like a secular prince, ate separately from the rest of his household and insisted not only on sitting at the same table as his men but also eating the same dishes.

Not all cardinals went as far as Borromeo. Alessandro Farnese, the wealthy vice-chancellor, for example, continued to spend lavishly on secular projects, notably his villa at Caprarola and the Palazzo Farnese in Rome, which he inherited in 1565 and embellished with antique statuary.[11] However, in the 1560s, alongside this worldly extravagance, he began to display a more spiritual image.[12] Following Pius IV's order, he renovated his titular church, San Lorenzo in Damaso, on which he had spent little beyond supplying it with an altarpiece in the three decades since he had been made cardinal, preferring to spend his money embellishing his residence Palazzo della Cancelleria next door. At about this time he also began his patronage of the Jesuits, and his offer in 1561 to pay for a new church for the order in Rome would culminate with the building of the Gesù, which was finally begun in 1568.

Even Ippolito's patronage showed signs of the new spirituality, though not at his titular church, Santa Maria in Aquiro, which dated back to the eighth century and may have required more than mere repair work – it was completely rebuilt in the 1590s. Soon after his return from France, he started work on a lavish chapel at Palazzo Monte Giordano: the ledgers list payments for building materials, including travertine window frames, nails, pigments and gold as well as wages for the team of twelve painters employed in its decoration.[13] He supported new developments in the musical field too. A lifelong patron of music, his household contained several singers, lutenists and other players, and in the late 1560s he appointed Giovanni Pierluigi da Palestrina as the master of his chapel. Palestrina, who had become famous at master of the chapels at the Roman basilicas of San Giovanni in Laterano and Santa Maria Maggiore, dedicated his first book of motets (1569), with its music for each of the major feasts of the Christian year, to the cardinal.

At Palazzo Monte Cavallo, Ippolito continued to embellish the grottoes, fountains and gardens. He built a new dovecote, planted apricot and cherry trees, flowering plants such as cyclamen and vegetables including artichokes, garlic, fennel, chicory, broad beans and cabbages.[14] One of the tasks of his doctor, Giuliano Cecchini, was the purchase of antiquities for the gardens: during 1565 he bought seven statues – two terms (busts that morph into their pedestals), an Aesculapius, a Commodus, 'a Venus, a faun and a Diana'.[15] He spent a total of 208 scudi on the statues – of which the Commodus, at 75 scudi, was the most expensive – a sum that also included payments for the transport of the statues to the Quirinal and wages to sculptors to carry out repairs. Ippolito's ledgers also provide evidence that showed how he benefitted from Borromeo's austerity drive, buying several items from the cardinal including two carpets, a pair of brass fire guards and six pieces of tapestry decorated with 'woodland scenes and animals'.[16]

Ippolito's papers suggest that the new climate in Rome was not as devoid of pleasure as the Venetian ambassador had suggested. There were certainly banquets: Ippolito's staff managed to lose several large silver dishes during one party at Palazzo Monte Cavallo in the summer of 1566.[17] When a large shipment of wine from his French benefices arrived at the wharf in Rome earlier that year, Ippolito sent five large barrels to Pius IV and distributed a further twenty-two 'as presents to various cardinals and ambassadors'.[18] Intriguingly, he also had eighty-four salamis sent in boxes from Ferrara to Rome, perhaps as more presents for the papal court.[19]

Ippolito also continued to do personal favours for Catherine de' Medici and Charles IX, whose majority had been declared on 17 August 1563. In 1565, the king sent Ippolito 1,640 scudi to buy horses in Italy and to pay for their transport back to France – one of these was a racehorse costing 400 scudi.[20] The following year, Ippolito sent a carriage to France as a present for Catherine. The carriage itself was built in Ferrara at a cost of 64 scudi but unfortunately we know little of how it was furnished, though Ippolito's embroiderer was paid just over 10 scudi for what must have been quite extensive work embellishing the hangings.[21] It was transported to France with a party of men including a chaplain and one of Ippolito's gardeners, both of whom were going into service with the Queen Mother.[22] The travellers left Ferrara in October, riding mounts supplied by Ippolito, who spent 53 scudi on four horses for this purpose – these were inexpensive hacks, far cheaper than the king's thoroughbred racehorses.[23] Another member of the party was a muleteer who was in charge of the four mules pulling the carriage, which had been carefully covered with lengths of waxed cloth to protect it against the autumn weather.[24] Ippolito was also sending ten horses to France – five for the king, four for the queen and one for an unnamed courtier – and the prestige of the recipients of these presents was underlined by the fact that Ippolito had entrusted the mission to his own senior trainer, who was given the substantial sum of 210 scudi to cover the expenses of the journey.[25]

Pius IV died in December 1565 from the complications of gout, having achieved an astonishing amount in a pontificate that lasted only six years. The conclave to elect his successor bore scant resemblance to the one that had chosen him. Nearly half of the cardinals who had voted in 1559 were now dead and of the sixteen members of the French party, only five – Ippolito and the other four Italians, Pisani, Simoncelli, Sermoneta and Crispi – made it to Rome. Lorraine, Armagnac, Strozzi and Guise remained in France; and Guise proved true to his word, refusing to attend this or any future conclave. Other absentees were Camerlengo Sforza and Ippolito's enemy Carpi, both of whom had died in 1564, the latter despite being fortified a few days earlier with one of Scappi's nourishing capon broths.[26]

It was not only the cardinals themselves who had changed. In 1562, while Ippolito had been in France, Pius IV issued the bull *In eligendis* to curb the chicanery that had made his own election such an anarchic affair. Visitors were banned, so were letters and so was the enjoyable practice of betting on the result; security was a priority and all walls, ceilings and floors of all the rooms in the conclave were to be inspected regularly; and the number of conclavists was limited to two, a courtier and a menial servant, both of whom had to be members of the cardinal's household.[27] The atmosphere was very different: the discovery of a letter hidden in a coat belonging to Innocenzo del Monte, which would have been a commonplace event in 1559, now caused a scandal.[28] In another significant change, Pius IV decided that the Sistine Chapel should no longer be used as a dormitory but become the place where the cardinals conducted the election, as indeed it still is today.

Pius IV's bull might have regulated behaviour inside the Vatican but it could do little to change the nature of the election. The conclave, which opened on 19 December, promised to be the usual ill-tempered power struggle between the various factions in the college – the French pitted against the Spanish; moderates against hardliners; and the playing out of personal animosities between individuals, not least between Ippolito and his great rival Vice-Chancellor Alessandro Farnese. Pius IV had made careful plans for this election with his nephew. The previous year, he had created twenty-three new cardinals with the intention of giving Borromeo a large enough majority to enable the election of Giovanni Morone as his successor. He advised Borromeo to pre-empt the conclave with a surprise bid to elect Morone by acclamation before the scrutinies got underway – in much the same way as the Spanish had attempted to elect Carpi six years earlier. Unfortunately, this scheme was foiled that first night by Inquisitor Ghislieri who, perhaps wakened by voices outside his cubicle, was determined to ruin the chances of a man he personally considered guilty of heresy.

Ippolito must have been surprised when a visitor asked to be admitted to his cubicle so late, even more so to discover that it was Ghislieri and that this hard-line reformer wanted his help to stop Morone's election. Overnight, a very unlikely coalition was negotiated between Ippolito, Ghislieri and Farnese and the next morning it successfully scuppered Borromeo's plan to elect Morone. After the excitement of 20 December, the conclave settled into its normal routine as the various factions jostled for power and by the end of the year plenty of strong candidates had begun to emerge. On 29 December, Farnese received thirty-two votes, just three short of the necessary two-thirds majority; close behind him was Giovanni Ricci, the candidate of Cosimo I, with twenty-nine votes; Morone had twenty-eight, Ippolito had twenty-six and even Ghislieri, who was the favoured candidate of Philip II of Spain, received ten votes.[29] One by one, the bids were destroyed by one faction or another. Ricci's chances were ruined by Borromeo, who urged the cardinals to consider the unsuitability of electing this man who was the father of several children. Farnese's vote count continued to hold up until rumours that the Roman mob was planning to riot and declare Farnese, their hero, as the next pope, did not go down well inside the Vatican, while Ippolito's chances, given the absence of the French cardinals, were never very high.

The conclave continued into the new year, apparently wide open, but the cardinals were in for a surprise on the morning of 7 January. Overnight, Borromeo and Farnese had done a deal that saw Ghislieri led into the Sistine Chapel to be elected by acclamation. Out of gratitude to Borromeo, he chose the name Pius V. The election of the grim Inquisitor General, protégé of Paul IV, was an important victory for the hard-line reformist wing of the Catholic Church. Strict, untiring and ascetic, very much in the mould of his mentor, Pius V would be a fierce opponent of Protestantism.* However, there was no question of a return to the policies of the detested Carafa pope. The Church had changed out of all recognition in the past six years: thanks to the progressive policies of Pius IV, it had been jolted out of its medieval complacency and modernized for its own time, a fact that Ghislieri himself must have implicitly recognized in his choice of name. Out of loyalty to Paul IV, however, one of his first acts was to declare that the sentences imposed on the pope's nephews, Giovanni and Carlo Carafa, had been unjust; and he built a massive tomb for Paul IV in Santa Maria sopra Minerva, the mother church of the Dominicans in Rome. On the wider political front Pius V gave unqualified support to those rulers who enforced the Catholic faith in their dominions. He applauded Philip II's brutal suppression of the Protestant revolt in the Netherlands; he excommunicated Elizabeth I; and in

---

* Pius V was canonized in 1712.

France his policies ensured the failure of Catherine de' Medici's plans for avoiding further war between the religions.

Nor was Ippolito optimistic about the election of Pius V, and Pius IV's pontificate would prove to be the Indian summer of his career. Like other worldly cardinals, he was rapidly sidelined from the papal court – and the new pope revived the accusations made by his mentor Paul IV against Ippolito, charging him once again with simony in the conclave. Although he was forgiven, it was perhaps fortunate for Ippolito that he was needed in Ferrara. In December 1565, Alfonso II had married Barbara of Austria, the sister of Emperor Maximilian, and part of the agreement between the two men had been a promise that the duke would join the imperial army to fight the Turks who continued to harry the borders of the Empire. So, in July 1566 Ippolito, with all his household, moved back home to act as regent with the inexperienced duchess while Alfonso was away. He returned to Rome the following year but increasingly spent his time at Tivoli, more interested in the embellishment of his lovely villa than in political affairs. In August 1572, just four months after Pius V's death, news reached Rome of the St Bartholomew's Day massacre that saw the butchering of Protestants on an appalling scale across France. By now, Ippolito was in Tivoli, increasingly ill with gout, which finally killed him three months later. His career had spanned seven pontificates and the transformation of the Church through the Council of Trent and the Counter-Reformation. The Renaissance was truly over.

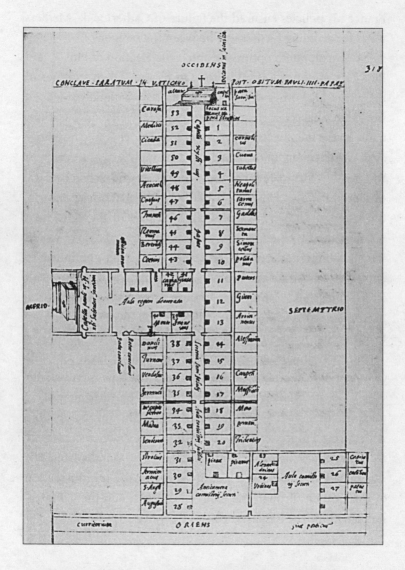

A photograph of the original list compiled by the master of ceremonies days before the conclave opened in September 1559 and stored in the Vatican archives.

Appendix

Cardinals Attending the 1559 Conclave

Listed in order of precedence

				date created	age in 1559	died
Bellay	Jean du Bellay	bishop	Ostia	1535	67	1560
Tournon	François de Tournon	bishop	Sabina	1530	70	1562
Carpi	Rodolfo Pio da Carpi	bishop	Porto	1536	59	1564
Pisani	Francesco Pisani	bishop	Frascati	1517	65	1570
Cesi	Federigo Cesi	bishop	Palestrina	1544	59	1565
Pacheco	Pedro Pacheco	bishop	Albano	1545	71	1560
Gonzaga	Ercole Gonzaga	priest	S Maria Nova	1527	53	1563
Sermoneta	Niccolò Caetani da Sermoneta	priest	S Eustachio	1536	33	1585
Lénoncourt	Robert de Lénoncourt	priest	S Cecilia in Trastevere	1538	74	1561
Morone	Giovanni Girolamo Morone	priest	S Maria in Trastevere	1542	50	1580
Madruzzo	Cristoforo Madruzzo	priest	S Cesareo	1542	47	1578
Cueva	Bartolomé de la Cueva	priest	S Croce in Gerusalemme	1544	60	1562
Armagnac	Georges d'Armagnac	priest	S Lorenzo in Lucina	1544	58	1585

				date created	age in 1559	died
Truchsess	Otto Truchsess von Waldburg	priest	S Sabina	1544	45	1573
Crispi	Tiberio Crispi	priest	S Agata dei Goti	1544	61	1566
Medici	Giovanni Angelo Medici	priest	S Prisca	1549	60	1565
Monte C	Cristoforo del Monte	priest	S Prassede	1551	75	1564
Corgna	Fulvio della Corgna	priest	S Stefano Rotondo	1551	41	1583
Saraceni	Gianmichele Saraceni	priest	S Anastasia	1551	60	1568
Ricci	Giovanni Ricci	priest	S Vitale	1551	60	1574
Mercurio	Giovanni Andrea Mercurio	priest	S Ciriaco alle Terme	1551	41	1561
Puteo	Jacques de Puy	priest	S Maria in Via	1551	64	1563
Cicada	Gianbattista Cicada	priest	S Clemente	1551	49	1570
Dandino	Girolamo Dandino	priest	S Marcello	1551	50	1559
Scotti	Bernardino Scotti	priest	S Matteo in Merulana	1555	81	1568
Carafa D	Diomede Carafa	priest	S Martino ai Monti	1555	67	1560
Rebiba	Scipione Rebiba	priest	S Pudenziana	1555	55	1577
Suau	Jean Suau de Reumes	priest	S Giovanni a Porta Latina1555	1555	56	1566
Capizucchi	Giovanni Antonio Capizucchi	priest	S Pancrazio	1555	43	1569
Gaddi	Taddeo Gaddi	priest	S Silvestro in Capite	1557	39	1561

				date created	age in 1559	died
Strozzi	Lorenzo Strozzi	priest	S Balbina	1557	35	1571
Bertrand	Jean Bertrand	priest	SS Nereo & Achilleo	1557	77	1560
Ghislieri	Michele Ghislieri	priest	S Maria sopra Minerva	1557	55	1572
Dolera	Clemente Dolera	priest	S Maria d'Aracoeli	1557	58	1568
Farnese	Alessandro Farnese	deacon	S Lorenzo in Damaso	1534	38	1589
Sforza	Guido Ascanio Sforza	deacon	S Maria in Via Lata	1534	40	1564
Este	Ippolito d'Este	deacon	S Maria in Aquiro	1538	50	1572
Savelli	Giacomo Savelli	deacon	S Maria in Cosmedin	1539	36	1587
Capodiferro	Girolamo Capodiferro	deacon	S Giorgio in Velabro	1544	57	1559
Farnese R	Ranuccio Farnese	deacon	S Angelo in Pescheria	1545	29	1565
Rovere	Giulio della Rovere	deacon	S Pietro in Vincoli	1547	26	1578
Monte	Innocenzo del Monte	deacon	S Onofrio	1550	27	1577
Corner	Alvise Corner	deacon	S Teodoro	1551	42	1584
Guise	Louis of Guise	deacon	S Tomaso in Parione	1553	31	1578
Simoncelli	Girolamo Simoncelli	deacon	SS Cosma & Damiano	1553	37	1605
Carafa	Carlo Carafa	deacon	SS Vito & Modesto	1555	42	1561
Carafa A	Alfonso Carafa	deacon	S Maria in Domnica	1557	19	1565
Vitelli	Vitellozzo Vitelli	deacon	S Maria in Portico	1557	28	1568

Acknowledgements

Giles Bancroft, Jules Bancroft, Elisabeth de Bièvre, David Chambers, Flora Dennis, Sarah Douglas-Pennant, Andrea Gáldy, Charles Handy, Min Hogg, Chris Hollingsworth, Rosamund Hollingsworth, John Kenyon, Julian Kliemann, Sally Laurence Smyth, Neil MacGregor, Ann Matchette, Christopher Newall, John Onians, Rui Paes, Miles Pattenden, Carol Richardson, Clare Robertson, Graham Rust, Henry Saywell, Rupert Shepherd, Thomas Tuohy, Maria Antonietta Visceglia and Arno Witte.

I would also like to thank the staff at Head of Zeus, especially my courteous editor Richard Milbank. I also owe a special debt to my agent Andrew Lownie for his untiring encouragement and support.

Conclave 1559 is a sequel to *The Cardinal's Hat* (London 2004). While the first part of the book is based on my *Conclave* (London 2013), I have amended and amplified the text, adding several chapters, all based on the letters and ledgers of Cardinal Ippolito d'Este which have survived in the state archives at Modena.

Bibliography and Sources

Abbreviations

ASMo, CDAP   Archivio di Stato di Modena, Camera Ducale, Amministrazione Principi

ASMo, CS   Archivio di Stato di Modena, Casa e Stato

BHO, Venice   *British History Online*, Calendar of State Papers Relating to English Affairs in the Archives of Venice, vol. 7: 1558–80

Bibliography

Antonovics, A., 'Counter-Reformation Cardinals 1534–90', *European Studies Review* 2, 1972, pp. 301–28.

Bèze, Théodore de, *Histoire Ecclésiastique des Églises Réformées au royaume de France*, 2 vols (Toulouse, 1882).

Catena, Giovanni Battista, *Lettere del Cardinale Giovanni de' Medici figlio di Cosimo I Gran Duca di Toscano non più stampate* (Rome, 1752).

Cavallo, Sandra, 'Health, beauty and hygiene', in Marta Ajmar-Wollheim and Flora Dennis (eds), *At Home in Renaissance Italy*, London, 2006, pp. 174-87.

Chambers, David S., 'Papal Conclaves and Prophetic Mystery in the Sistine Chapel', *Journal of the Warburg and Courtauld Institutes* 41, 1978, pp. 322–6.

Coffin, David R., *The Villa d'Este at Tivoli* (Princeton NJ, 1960).

——*The Villa in the Life of Renaissance Rome* (Princeton NJ, 1979).

——*Pirro Ligorio* (University Park PA, 2004).

Colomer, Josep M. and Iain McLean, 'Electing Popes: Approval

Balloting and Qualified-Majority Rule', *Journal of Interdisciplinary History* 29, 1998, pp. 1–22.

Davidson, Bernice F., 'The Decoration of the Sala Regia under Pope Paul III', *Art Bulletin* 58, 1976, pp. 395–423.

Davila, H. C. (ed.), *Negotiations, ou Lettres d'Affaires Ecclesiastiques et Politiques. Ippolito d'Este* (Paris, 1658).

Dickinson, Gladys, *Du Bellay in Rome* (Leiden, 1960).

Döllinger, J.J.J. von, *Beiträge zur politischen, kirchlichen, und Kulturgeschichte der sechs letzen Jahrhunderts* (Regensburg, 1862).

Duruy, George, *Le Cardinal Carlo Carafa (1519–1561): Étude sur le Pontificate de Paul IV* (Paris, 1882).

Ehrle F. and H. Egger, 'Die Conclavepläne. Beiträge zu ihrer Entwicklungsgeschichte', in *Studi e documenti per la storia del Palazzo Apostolico Vaticano*, fasc. 5 (Vatican City, 1933).

Eubel, Konrad, *Hierarchia Catholica Medii et Recentioris Aevi*, 9 vols (Regensburg, 1898–2002).

Faccioli, Emilio (ed.), *L'Arte della cucina in Italia* (Turin, 1992).

Ferrière, Hector de la, *Lettres de Catherine de Médicis*, 8 vols (Paris, 1880).

Fosi, Irene, 'Court and City in the Ceremony of the *possesso* in the sixteenth century', in Gianvittorio Signorotto and Maria Antonietta Visceglia (eds), *Court and Politics in Papal Rome 1492–1700*, Cambridge, 2002, pp. 31–52.

Franceschini, Chiara, 'La corte di Renata di Francia (1528–1560)', in Alessandra Chiappini et al (eds), *Storia di Ferrara vol. VI: Il Rinascimento. Situazioni e personaggi*, Ferrara, 2000, pp. 186–214.

Frommel, Christoph Luitpold, 'Antonio da Sangallos Cappella Paolina. Ein Beitrag zur Baugeschichte des Vatikanischen Palastes', *Zeitschrift für Kunstgeschichte* 27, 1964, pp. 1–42.

——'La villa e i giardini del Quirinale nel Cinquecento', in L. Morozzi (ed.), *Restauri al Quirinale* (special volume of *Bollettino d'Arte*), 1999, pp. 15–62.

Gáldy Andrea, 'Lost in Antiquities: Cardinal Giovanni de' Medici (1543–1562)', in Mary Hollingsworth and Carol M. Richardson (eds), *The Possessions of a Cardinal*, University Park PA, 2010, pp. 153–65.

Gattico, Gianbattista, *Acta Selecta Caeremonialia Sanctae Romanae Ecclesiae*, 2 vols (Rome, 1753).

Gilio, Giovanni Andrea, *Dialogue on the errors and abuses of painters,* (eds) Michael Bury, Lucinda Byatt and Carol M. Richardson (Los Angeles, 2018).

Grieco, Allen, 'Meals', in Marta Ajmar-Wollheim and Flora Dennis (eds), *At Home in Renaissance Italy*, London, 2006, pp. 244–53.

Guerzoni, Guido, 'Servicing the *Casa*', in Marta Ajmar-Wollheim and Flora Dennis, *At Home in Renaissance Italy*, London, 2006, pp. 146–51.

Guidoboni, Francesco and Antonia Marinelli, 'Un progetto del 1559 per la vigna d'Este a Monte Cavallo', in Marina Cogotti and Francesco Paolo Fiore (eds), *Ippolito II d'Este. cardinale, principe, mecenate*, Rome, 2013, pp. 185–204.

Hollingsworth, Mary, *Patronage in Sixteenth-Century Italy* (London, 1996).

——*The Cardinal's Hat* (London, 2004).

——'A Cardinal in Rome: Ippolito d'Este in 1560', in Jill Burke and Michael Bury (eds), *Art and Identity in Early Modern Rome*, Aldershot, 2008, pp. 81–94.

——'A Taste for Conspicuous Consumption. Ippolito d'Este and his Wardrobe, 1555–1566', in Mary Hollingsworth and Carol M. Richardson (eds), *The Possessions of a Cardinal*, University Park PA, 2010, pp. 132–52.

Hurtubise, Pierre, 'La table d'un cardinal de la Renaissance', *Mélanges de l'école française de Rome* 92, 1980, pp. 248–82.

Jones, Pamela M., 'The Court of Humility: Carlo Borromeo and the Ritual of Reform', in Mary Hollingsworth and Carol M. Richardson (eds), *The Possessions of a Cardinal*, University Park PA, 2010, pp. 166–84.

Jong, Jan L. de, 'An Important Patron and an Unknown Artists: Giovanni Ricci, Ponsio Jacquio, and the Decoration of the Palazzo Ricci-Sacchetti in Rome', *Art Bulletin* 74, 1992, pp. 135–56.

Knecht, Robert J., *Catherine de' Medici* (London and New York, 1998).

——*The French Renaissance Court* (New Haven and London, 2008).

Kuntz, Margaret, 'Designed for Ceremony. The Cappella Paolina at the Vatican Palace', *Journal of the Society of Architectural Historians* 62, 2003, pp. 228–55.

Langdon, Gabrielle, *Medici Women* (Toronto and London, 2006).

Müller, Theodor, *Das Konklave Pius' IV. 1559* (Gotha, 1889).

Occhipinti, Carmelo, *Carteggio d'arte degli ambasciatori estensi in Francia (1536–1553)* (Pisa, 2001).

Onians, John, *Bearers of Meaning* (Princeton NJ, 1988).

Pacifici, Vincenzo, *Ippolito d'Este, Cardinale di Ferrara* (Tivoli, 1920).

Pastor, Ludwig von, *The History of the Popes from the Close of the Middle Ages*, 29 vols (London, 1894–1951).

Petruccelli della Gattina, Ferdinando, *Histoire Diplomatique des Conclaves* (Paris, 1864).

Ribier, Guillaume, *Lettres et Mémoires d'Estat, des Roys, Princes, Ambassadeurs, et autres Ministres, sous les règnes de François premier, Henri II et François II*, 2 vols (Blois, 1667).

Robertson, Clare, *Il Gran Cardinale* (New Haven and London, 1992).

Roelker, Nancy Lyman, *Queen of Navarre. Jeanne d'Albret 1528–1572* (Cambridge MA, 1968).

Scappi, Bartolomeo, *Opera dell'arte del cucinare* (Venice, 1570); reprinted (Bologna, 2002).

Shearman, John, 'The Vatican Stanze: Functions and Decoration', *Proceedings of the British Academy* 57, 1971, pp. 369–424.

Vasari, Giorgio, *Le opere di Giorgio Vasari*, Gaetano Milanesi (ed.), 8 vols (Florence, 1981).

Visceglia, Maria Antonietta, 'Factions in the Sacred College in the sixteenth and seventeenth centuries', in Gianvittorio Signorotto and Maria Antonionetta Visceglia (eds), *Court and Politics in Papal Rome 1492–1700*, Cambridge, 2002, pp. 99–131.

——*Morte e elezione del papa: Norme, riti e conflitti. 2: L'età moderna* (Rome, 2013).

Endnotes

Chapter 1
Ferrara

1. ASMo, CDAP, 969, f. 21v.
2. Franceschini, pp. 196–8.
3. ASMo, CDAP, 885, ff. 135r–143r.
4. Hollingsworth, 'A cardinal in Rome', p. 82.
5. ASMo, CDAP, 924 (1535) & 928 (1555).
6. ASMo, CS, 149, doc. 1709-xvi/44.
7. ASMo, CDAP, 969, f. 29r.
8. ASMo, CS, 150, doc. 1709-xxiii/42.
9. On Ippolito at the French court, see Hollingsworth, *Cardinal's Hat, passim*.
10. Ribier, 2: p. 220.
11. Hollingsworth, 'A cardinal in Rome', pp. 82–3.
12. ASMo, CDAP, 901, 904; on his household in 1536, see also Hollingsworth, *Cardinal's Hat*, pp. 30–62.
13. ASMo, CDAP, 928, f. 92 Usc; on Ligorio, see Coffin, *Pirro Ligorio*.
14. Pacifici, p. 372.
15. Hollingsworth, 'A taste', pp. 141–2.
16. Pacifici, pp. 120–1, n. 4.
17. ASMo, CDAP, 928, ff. 238-42, 273-5, 290, 293-4, 307, 344.
18. Pacifici, pp. 113–14 n. 1.
19. Pastor, 13:63–5.
20. Pastor, 13:63 n. 2.
21. Coffin, *The villa*, p. 132; Pastor, 11:356 n. 2.
22. Dickinson, p. 68.
23. ASMo, CS, 149, doc. 1709-xx/24.
24. Hollingsworth, 'A taste', p. 138.
25. ASMo, CDAP, 913, f. 14v
26. ASMo, CS, 149, doc. 1709-xx/43.
27. ASMo, CDAP, 893 (1558), 969 (1559); see also Hollingsworth, 'A taste', p. 138.
28. ASMo, CDAP, 928, f. 239u.
29. ASMo, CDAP, 968, ff. 21v, 38v; 969, f. 14v.

30. ASMo, CDAP, 968, ff. 17r,
    21r, 22r, 22v, 23v, 26v, 30v.
31. ASMo, CDAP, 893 *passim*.
32. ASMo, CDAP, 893, ff. 180r-v.
33. ASMo, CDAP, 893, ff.
    185r-186v *passim*.
34. For details of this trip, see
    Hollingsworth, 'A taste', p.
    139.
35. ASMo, CDAP, 936, f. 1/3r;
    928, f. 293 Usc.
36. ASMo, CDAP, 893, ff. 40r,
    40v; Hollingsworth, 'A taste',
    p. 139.
37. ASMo, CDAP, 928, f. 71 Usc;
    968, ff. 17r, 21v, 23v.
38. ASMo, CDAP, 968, ff. 27r-31r
    passim.
39. ASMo, CDAP, 928, ff. 71 Usc,
    f. 75 Usc; 968, *passim*; 969, ff.
    14r, 15r, 26v.
40. Petruccelli, 2:111.
41. Pastor, 14:265-8 *passim*.
42. ASMo, CDAP, 928, ff. 157-61;
    see also Occhipinti.
43. Pastor, 14:299.
44. Jong, p. 135.
45. Duruy, pp. 296-7 n. 4.
46. Pastor, 14:228-9.
47. Pastor, 14: 236-7, 412.
48. ASMo, CDAP, 928, ff. 239
    Usc, 240 Usc, 294 Usc.
49. Pastor, 14:413 n.1.
50. Petruccelli, 2:118.
51. ASMo, CDAP, 936, f. 1/10r;
    969, f. 31r; 1005, f. 22r.
52. ASMo, CS, 150, doc.
    1709-xxiii/43.
53. ASMo, CDAP, 928, ff. 83 Usc,

288 Usc.
54. ASMo, CDAP, 969, f. 31v.
55. ASMo, CDAP, 929, 1/31-35
    Usc.
56. ASMo, CDAP, 1005, 12r-40r
    passim.
57. ASMo, CDAP, 969, f. 32v; on
    the gout, see CS, 149, doc.
    1709-xxi/10.
58. ASMo, CDAP, 969, f. 31v.
59. ASMo, CS, 79, doc.
    1654-xxiii/41.

Chapter 2
Rome

1. Ribier, 2:827-8.
2. Petrucelli, p. 118.
3. ASMo, CS, 148, doc. 1709-
   xv/2.
4. For a collection of the
   pasquinades, see Dickinson,
   pp. 155-206.
5. Dickinson, p. 185.
6. Dickinson, pp. 181-2.
7. Dickinson, pp. 165-7.
8. Duruy, pp. 316-17.
9. Pastor, 15:159.
10. ASMo, CDAP, 989, f. 13v;
    1005, f. 42r.
11. ASMo, CDAP, 1005, f. 39v.
12. ASMo, CDAP, 1005, f. 39v;
    913, ff. 28r, 28v.
13. ASMo, CDAP, 989, ff. 13r-v.
14. ASMo, CDAP, 989, f. 9r.
15. ASMo, CDAP, 913 *passim*;
    1005 *passim*.
16. ASMo, CDAP, 1005, 18v-19v.

17. ASMo, CDAP, 1005, f. 11r.
18. ASMo, CDAP, 1005, ff. 11r-14v.
19. ASMo, CDAP, 1005, f. 15v.
20. ASMo, CDAP, 935, f. 7v; 989, f. 102v.
21. ASMo, CDAP, 1005, f. 36v.
22. ASMo, CDAP, 989, 102v.
23. ASMo, CDAP, 989, ff. 103r, 105r.
24. ASMo, CDAP, 989, f. 104v.
25. Hurtubise, p. 267 and n. 100.
26. Pastor, 14:479, doc. 8.
27. Visceglia, 'Factions', p. 104.
28. Pastor, 15:10.
29. Hollingsworth, *Cardinal's Hat*, pp. 122–3, 131, 140, 199.
30. Ribier, 2:830.
31. Ferrière, 1:123-4.
32. BHO, Venice (8 September 1559).
33. BHO, Venice (8 September 1559).
34. ASMo, CS, 79, doc. 1654-xix/39.
35. ASMo, CS, 149, doc. 1709-xxi/10.
36. ASMo, CS, 79, doc. 1654-xix/39.
37. ASMo, CS, 149, doc. 1709-xxi/10.
38. ASMo, CS, 149, doc. 1709-xxi/11.
39. ASMo, CS, 79, doc. 1654-xix/39.
40. Dickinson, pp. 186–9.
41. Chambers, *passim*.
42. Hollingsworth, 'A cardinal in Rome', p. 89 n. 11.
43. ASMo, CDAP, 928, f. 171 Ent.
44. ASMo, CDAP, 984, f. 37r.
45. ASMo, CS, 150, doc. 1709-xxiii/44.
46. BHO, Venice (22 September).
47. Ribier, 2:830.
48. Ribier, 2:830-1.
49. Ribier, 2:830-1.
50. ASMo, CDAP, 1005, ff. 17r, 39r, 39v.
51. ASMo, CS, 150, doc. 1709-xxiii/44.
52. Gattico, 1:332.
53. Visceglia, *Morte e elezione*, p. 268.
54. Gattico, 1:332.
55. ASMo, CS, 149, doc. 1709-xxi/10.

Chapter 3
Inside the Vatican

1. Frommel, 'Antonio da Sangallo', *passim*.
2. Davidson, p. 418.
3. ASMo, CDAP, 969, f. 38r.
4. Gattico, 1:309-10.
5. Onians, pp. 199–200.
6. ASMo, CDAP, 913, f. 27v; on prices, see Hollingsworth, 'A cardinal in Rome', p. 89 n.4.
7. Dickinson, pp. 187–8.
8. Gilio, p. 157; for the treatise see idem, pp. 85–239.
9. Pastor, 12:659-70 doc. 9; Vasari, 7:211.

10. Vasari, 7:65.

11. Gattico, 1:311.

12. Ribier, 2:830.

13. Gattico, 1:332.

14. Ehrle and Egger, tavola 5.

15. Gattico, 1:332 (8 September).

16. Pastor, 15:17 n. 2.

17. ASMo, CS, 149, doc. 1709-xxi/12.

18. Pastor, 15:382.

19. Pastor, 15:17; for voting tables, see pp. 382–9.

20. Müller, p. 33.

21. Petrucelli, p. 134.

22. Pastor, 15:20 n.2.

23. Pastor, 15:389-90 doc. 2.

24. ASMo, CS, 149, doc. 1709-xxi/13.

Chapter 4
Cubicle Life

1. ASMo, CDAP, 881, ff. 71r-80v.

2. Gattico, 1:309.

3. ASMo, CDAP, 933, f. 9r.

4. ASMo, CDAP, 928, ff. 119 Ent, 213 Ent.

5. ASMo, CDAP, 929, f. 1/4 Ent.

6. ASMo, CDAP, 928, f. 101 Usc.

7. ASMo, CDAP, 928, f. 77 Ent.

8. Gattico, 1:310.

9. ASMo, CDAP, 928, ff. 115 Usc, 175 Usc.

10. Gattico, 1:240.

11. ASMo, CDAP, 928, f. 101 Usc.

12. Pastor, 15:21 n. 1.

13. Ribier, 2:833-5.

14. Ribier, 2:834-5.

15. ASMo, CS, 150, doc. 1709-xxiii/45.

16. ASMo, CS, 150, doc. 1709-xxiii/45.

17. Pastor, 15:22-3 n. 2.

18. Petrucelli, p. 136.

19. Ribier, 2:833-5.

20. Petrucelli, p. 136.

21. Pastor, 15:23 n. 4.

22. Gattico, 1:332 (26 September).

23. BHO, Venice (7 January 1560).

24. Döllinger, 1:290-4 doc. 76.

25. Döllinger, 1:265-8 doc. 70; 270-4 doc. 72.

26. Döllinger, 1:265-8 doc. 70.

27. BHO, Venice (11 December 1559).

28. Pastor, 15:24 n. 2.

29. Pastor, 15:28-30.

30. Müller, pp. 130–1.

31. Pastor, 15:30.

32. Döllinger, 1:268-70 doc. 71.

33. BHO, Venice (30 January 1560).

34. Döllinger, 1:268-70 doc. 71.

35. ASMo, CS, 85, doc. 1655-xx/7 (mistakenly filed as a letter from Alfonso II).

36. ASMo, CS, 150, doc. 1709-xxiv/1.

37. ASMo, CS, 152, doc. 1709-xxxix/1.

38. ASMo, CS, 79, doc. 1654-xxiii/45.

Chapter 5
Banquets

1. ASMo, CS, 152, doc. 1709-xxxix/2.
2. Döllinger, 1:270, doc. 72.
3. Petrucelli, p. 126.
4. Ribier, 2:837-8.
5. ASMo, CS, 85, doc. 1655-xx/7 (mistakenly filed as a letter from Alfonso II).
6. Gattico, 1:332-3 (2 October).
7. Gattico, 1:333 (2 October).
8. Gattico, 1:333 (3 October).
9. Gattico, 1:333 (5 October).
10. Gattico, 1:333 (8 October).
11. ASMo, CDAP, 1005, f. 39r.
12. ASMo, CDAP, 929, ff. 1/3-4 Ent, 1/7 Usc.
13. ASMo, CDAP, 1005, f. 37v.
14. Faccioli, p. 243.
15. Hurtubise, p. 273.
16. Hurtubise, p. 269.
17. Pastor, 17:46ff.
18. Scappi, 2:240r.
19. Scappi, 2:239r.
20. Scappi, 2:239v-40r.
21. ASMo, CDAP, 1005, ff. 36v, 37v.
22. ASMo, CDAP, 1005, ff. 12r, 21r, 38r.
23. ASMo, CDAP, 1005, f. 24r; vol. 913, f. 23v.
24. Scappi, 2:395.
25. Scappi, 2:ff. A3r-A4r.
26. Scappi, 2:f A3v.
27. Scappi, 2:A4r.
28. Gattico, 1:333 (9 October).
29. Gattico, 1:333 (10 October).
30. Gattico, 1:333 (11 October).
31. Pacifici, 107 n. 1.
32. ASMo, CS, 150, doc. 1709-xxiv/1.
33. ASMo, CDAP, 928, ff. 121 Usc, 299 Usc.
34. Gattico, 1:240-1.
35. For the voting figures in mid-October, see Pastor, 15:384-5, 388-9.
36. Pastor, 15:384-5, 388-9.
37. Pastor, 15:32-3.
38. Ribier, 2:837-8.
39. Ribier, 2:837-8.
40. ASMo, CS, 150, doc. 1709-xxiv/3.
41. ASMo, CS, 152, doc. 1709-xxxix/2.
42. Ribier, 2:835-7.
43. Ribier, 2;837-8.
44. Pastor, 15:33-4.
45. Döllinger, 1:274-6, doc. 73.
46. Ribier, 2:837-8.
47. Pastor, 15:15.
48. ASMo, CS, 150, doc. 1709-xxiv/2.
49. ASMo, CS, 150, doc. 1709-xxiv/4.
50. Ribier, 2:835-7.
51. Döllinger, 1:276-82 doc. 74.
52. ASMo, CDAP, 1005, f. 13v.
53. Ribier, 2:837-8.
54. Gattico, 1:333-4 (25 October).
55. Gattico, 1:334 (26 October).

Chapter 6
Letters from Spain

1. ASMo, CS, 150, doc. 1709-xxiv/7.
2. Pastor, 15:385.
3. Gattico, 1:334 (31 October).
4. ASMo, CDAP, 929, f. 1/12 Ent.
5. ASMo, CDAP, 928, ff. 121 Usc, 131 Ent, 131 Usc, 133 Usc; 929, f. 1/12 Ent.
6. ASMo, CDAP, 929, f. 1/15 Ent.
7. ASMo, CDAP, 1005, f. 27r.
8. ASMo, CS, 152, doc. 1709-xxxix/3.
9. ASMo, CS, 150, doc. 1709-xxiv/6.
10. ASMo, CS, 150, doc. 1709-xxiv/7.
11. Langdon, pp. 143–4.
12. ASMo, CS, 150, docs. 1709-xxiv/8-10; 152, docs. 1709-xxxix/4-5.
13. Döllinger, 1:282-90 doc. 75.
14. Döllinger, 1:282-90 doc. 75.
15. ASMo, CDAP, 989, ff. 18r, 27r, 31r; 1005, f. 26v.
16. ASMo, CDAP, 928, ff. 121 Usc, 124 Usc, 174 Usc, 205-7 Usc, 224-5 Usc, 294 Usc.
17. ASMo, CDAP, 928, ff. 248 Ent, 249 Ent; 1005, f. 16r-v.
18. ASMo, CDAP, 928, ff. 112 Usc, 248 Usc, 249 Usc; 989, f. 11r.
19. ASMo, CDAP, 928, f. 38 Usc.
20. ASMo, CDAP, 928, ff. 83 Usc, 123 Ent.
21. ASMo, CDAP, 928, ff. 122 Ent, 136 Ent.
22. ASMo, CDAP, 928, ff. 83 Usc, 125 Ent.
23. ASMo, CDAP, 928, ff. 112 Usc, 248 Usc, 249 Usc.
24. Petrucelli, pp. 127–8.
25. BHO, Venice (14 November 1559).
26. BHO, Venice (11 December 1559).
27. Ribier, 2:838-9.
28. Döllinger, 1:294-307 doc. 77.
29. Pastor, 15:39 n. 2.
30. Döllinger, 1:294-307 doc. 77.
31. Ribier, 2:838-9.
32. Pastor, 15:389.
33. Ribier, 2:838-9.
34. ASMo, CS, 152, doc. 1709-xxxix/6.
35. Petrucelli, p. 150.
36. Petrucelli, p. 139.
37. Pastor, 15:43.
38. ASMo, CDAP, 989, f. 12r.
39. ASMo, CDAP, 989, f. 9r.
40. ASMo, CDAP, 1005, ff. 28v, 30v.
41. ASMo, CDAP, 989, f. 13r; 1006, f. 31r.
42. ASMo, CDAP, 989, f. 102v.

Chapter 7
Fraying Tempers

1. ASMo, CDAP, 1005, ff. 2r-v, ff. 11r-21r.

2. ASMo, CDAP, 989, ff. 7r, 10r-11r, 18r, 27r.
3. ASMo, CDAP, 859, f. 41r; 1006, f. 71v.
4. ASMo, CDAP, 989, f. 4r.
5. ASMo, CDAP, 1005, ff. 20v, 25v.
6. ASMo, CDAP, 989 *passim*.
7. ASMo, CDAP, 1006, f. 63v.
8. ASMo, CDAP, 989, f. 7v.
9. Pastor, 15:43-4 n. 8.
10. Gattico, 1:334 (29 November).
11. Pastor, 15:44.
12. Pastor, 15:42 n. 5.
13. ASMo, CDAP, 881, f. 96v.
14. Pastor, 15:42 n. 5.
15. Petrucelli, p. 154.
16. Döllinger, 1:294-307 doc. 77.
17. Pastor, 15:41 n. 1.
18. Petrucelli, p. 152.
19. ASMo, CS, 50, doc. 1709-xxiv/13.
20. ASMo, CS, 50, doc. 1709-xxiv/15.
21. BHO, Venice (13 December 1559).
22. Pastor, 15:41 n. 1.
23. Döllinger, 1:294-307 doc. 77.
24. ASMo, CS, 150, doc. 1709-xxiv/13.
25. ASMo, CS, 150, doc. 1709-xxiv/15.
26. Pastor, 15:387.
27. Gattico, 1:334 (5 December).
28. Pastor, 15:45 n.1.
29. ASMo, CS, 150, doc. 1709-xxiv/16.
30. Pastor, 15:48-9 n. 1.
31. Pastor, 15:48-9 n. 1.
32. Pastor, 15:47.
33. Pastor, 15:48-9 n. 1.
34. Pastor, 15:48-9 n. 1.
35. Pastor, 15:48-9 n. 1.
36. Pastor, 15:49 n. 1.
37. Döllinger, 1:316-23 doc. 81.
38. ASMo, CS, 150, doc. 1709-xxiv/16.
39. Ribier, 2:839.
40. ASMo, CS, 150, doc. 1709-xxiv/16.
41. Ribier, 2:839-40.

Chapter 8
Election

1. Pastor, 15:51.
2. Pastor, 15:51.
3. ASMo, CS, 150, doc. 1709-xxiv/18.
4. Pastor, 15:52 n. 1.
5. Pastor, 15:51-2 n. 6; BHO, Venice (30 January 1560).
6. Döllinger, 1:316-23 doc. 81.
7. Pastor, 15:53 n. 1.
8. ASMo, CS, 152, doc. 1709-xlvii/1.
9. Coffin, *The villa*, p. 131.
10. ASMo, CDAP, 1005, ff. 28v, 35r.
11. Pastor, 15:55.
12. Gattico, 1:334-5 (25 December).
13. ASMo, CDAP, 969, f. 32r.
14. Pastor, 15:60 n. 2.
15. Gattico, 1:335 (25 December).
16. Pastor, 15:62.

17. Gattico, 1:335 (25 December).
18. Ribier, 2:840.
19. ASMo, CS, 150, doc. 1709-xxiv/19.
20. Gattico, 1:335 (25 December).
21. ASMo, CDAP, 969, f. 38r; 1005, f. 39r.
22. ASMo, CDAP, 928, ff. 115 Usc, 121 Usc, 175 Usc, 276 Usc, 283 Usc, 299 Usc; 929, f. 1/4 Usc, f. 1/31 Usc, f. 1/32 Usc.
23. ASMo, CDAP, 913, f. 35v.
24. Hollingsworth, 'A cardinal in Rome', p. 84.
25. Döllinger, 1:323-4 doc. 82.
26. BHO, Venice (30 January 1560).
27. Pacifici, 286 n. 1.
28. ASMo, CS, 150, doc. 1709-xxiv/20.
29. ASMo, CDAP, 969, f. 32r, 33v.

Chapter 9
Winners and Losers

1. ASMo, CDAP, CS, 150, doc. 1709-xxiv/22.
2. Eubel, 3:36 n. 3.
3. ASMo,CDAP, 928, f. 78 Usc.
4. ASMo, CDAP, 928, ff. 15 Ent, 18 Ent, 104 Usc.
5. ASMo, CDAP, 989, f. 16v.
6. ASMo, CDAP, 1005, ff. 40v-41v.
7. ASMo, CDAP, 1005, ff. 3v-4v.
8. ASMo, CDAP, 989, f. 26v.

9. Pastor, 16:305, 307, 309.
10. Pastor, 15:181.
11. Pastor, 15:65 n. 1.
12. Pastor, 15:96 n.1.
13. BHO, Venice (30 January 1560).
14. ASMo, CS, 150, doc. 1709-xxiv/27.
15. ASMo, CS, 150, doc. 1709-xxiv/28.
16. ASMo, CS, 150, doc. 1709-xxiv/25.
17. ASMo, CDAP, 1005, f. 35r.
18. ASMo, CDAP, 928, ff. 240 Usc, 294 Usc.
19. ASMo, CS, 150, doc. 1709-xxiv/39.
20. Hollingsworth, 'A cardinal in Rome', pp. 84-5.
21. ASMo, CDAP, 969, ff. 35v, 36r.
22. ASMo, CDAP, 1005, f. 39r.
23. ASMo, CDAP, 905, *passim*; 957, f. 62r.
24. ASMo, CDAP, 989, ff. 127r-128r.
25. ASMo, CS, 85, doc. 1655-xx/18; Hollingsworth, 'A cardinal in Rome', p. 91 n. 50.
26. ASMo, CS, 85, doc. 1655-xx/13; Hollingsworth, 'A cardinal in Rome', p. 91 n. 49.
27. ASMo, CS, 150, doc. 1709-xxiv/23.
28. ASMo, CDAP, 928, f. 294 Ent; 989, f. 29r.
29. Hollingsworth, 'A cardinal in Rome', p. 85.
30. ASMo, CDAP, 969, f. 39r.

31. Hollingsworth, 'A cardinal in Rome', p. 92 n. 55.

32. ASMo, CS, 150, doc. 1709-xxiv/46.

33. Frommel, 'La villa', p. 29; see also Guidoboni and Marinelli, *passim*.

34. Coffin, *The villa*, p. 207.

35. ASMo, CDAP. 957, ff. 2v-5r; 1005, ff. 2r-4r; 1006, f. 22v.

36. ASMo, CDAP, 957, ff. 3v, 6r.

37. ASMo, CDAP, 957 *passim* for the expenditure.

38. ASMo, CDAP, 957, 78v-79r.

39. ASMo, CDAP, 969, ff. 37r, 38r.

40. Coffin, *The villa*, p. 256.

41. Gáldy, p. 158.

42. ASMo, CS, 150, doc. 1709-xxiv/46.

43. Hollingsworth, 'A cardinal in Rome', p. 98 n. 61.

44. Catena, 84–5. I am very grateful to Andrea Gáldy for this reference.

45. ASMo, CDAP, 1006, ff. 4v, 5v, 6r, 18v; 928, ff. 104 Usc, 249 Usc, 290 Usc.

46. ASMo, CS, 150, doc. 1709-xxiv/25.

47. ASMo, CDAP, 989, f. 39r.

48. ASMo, CDAP, 989, ff. 31v, 37v.

49. ASMo, CDAP, 969, ff. 41v, 43r.

50. ASMo, CS, 150, doc. 1709-xxiv/43.

51. ASMo, CS, 150, doc. 1709-xxiv/48.

52. Pastor, 15:174.

53. Pastor, 15:392-3 doc. 4.

54. Pastor, 15:394-7 doc. 7.

55. Pastor, 15:393-4 doc. 6.

56. Pastor, 15:144.

57. Pastor, 15:15, 150 n. 1.

58. Pastor, 15:401 docs. 9-10.

59. ASMo, CS, 150, doc. 1709-xxiv/72.

60. ASMo, CDAP, 928, ff. 42 Usc, 187 Ent, 285 Usc.

61. ASMo, CDAP, 1006, f. 43v.

62. ASMo, CS, 150, docs. 1709-xxiv/69, 71.

63. ASMo, CDAP, 1008 *passim*.

64. ASMo, CDAP, 1006, f. 35r.

65. ASMo, CDAP, 1006, ff. 39r, 42v, 47r.

66. ASMo, CDAP, 1006, ff. 41v-42r.

67. ASMo, CDAP, 969, f. 47v.

68. ASMo, CDAP, 969, ff. 44v-48r.

69. ASMo, CDAP, 969, ff. 45r-v.

70. ASMo, CDAP, 969, f. 43v.

71. ASMo, CDAP, 1006, f. 34v.

72. ASMo, CDAP, 957, ff. 62r-67r.

73. ASMo, CDAP, 957, ff. 63r-64v.

74. Hollingsworth, 'A cardinal in Rome', p. 94 n. 80.

75. Hollingsworth, 'A cardinal in Rome', p. 87.

76. ASMo, CDAP, 1006, f. 27r.

77. ASMo, CDAP, 1006, ff. 49r-v.

78. Coffin, *The villa*, p. 150.

79. Hollingsworth, 'A cardinal in Rome', p. 87.

80. Hollingsworth, 'A taste', p. 136.
81. ASMo, CS, 150, doc. 1709-xxv/8.
82. ASMo, CS, 150, doc. 1709-xxv/10.
83. BHO Venice (30 January 1560).
84. ASMo, CDAP, 969, f. 56r.

Chapter 10
France

1. Knecht, *Catherine de' Medici*, p. 73.
2. Pastor, 16:163 n. 1.
3. ASMo, CDAP, 928, ff. 282 Usc, 285 Usc; 1023, wardrobe ledger (18 June 1561); 1006, f. 30v.
4. ASMo, CDAP, 928, f. 270 Ent (sic); 1023, wardrobe ledger (30 May-10 June 1561).
5. ASMo, CDAP, 1007.
6. ASMo, CDAP, 1022.
7. ASMo, CDAP, 1022, ff. 38v-39r.
8. ASMo, CS, 150, doc. 1709-xxvi/41.
9. ASMo, CDAP, 1022, f. 43r.
10. ASMo, CDAP, 1022, f. 44r; CS, 150, doc. 1709-xxvi/42.
11. ASMo, CS, 150, doc. 1709-xxvi/42.
12. ASMo, CDAP, 930, 4r-v.
13. ASMo, CDAP, 930, ff.2r, 6v.
14. ASMo, CDAP, 930, 2r-3v.
15. ASMo, CDAP, 930, 4r-v.
16. Bèze, 1:267.
17. Bèze, 1:281.
18. Pastor, 16:170.
19. Bèze, 1:325.
20. Knecht, *Catherine de' Medici*, p. 82.
21. Knecht, *Court*, p. 247.
22. Knecht, *Catherine de' Medici*, pp. 54, 83.
23. Roelker, p. 171.
24. Pacifici, 301 n. 4.
25. Pastor, 16:173-4.
26. ASMo, CS, 150, doc. 1709-xxvii/11
27. ASMo, CDAP, 1022, f. 48v.
28. ASMo, CDAP, 1022, ff. 47r, 47v; Hollingsworth, *Cardinal's Hat*, 201-3.
29. Knecht, *Catherine de' Medici*, p. 73.
30. Pastor, 16:174.
31. Pastor, 16:179; Knecht, *Catherine de' Medici*, pp. 83-4.
32. Knecht, *Catherine de' Medici*, p. 83.
33. ASMo, CS, 150, doc. 1709-xxvi/44.
34. Roelker, p. 170.
35. ASMo, CDAP, 929, f. 1/51 Usc.
36. Roelker, p. 170.
37. ASMo, CS, 150, doc. 1709-xxvii/1.
38. ASMo, CS., 150, doc. 1709-xxvi/45.
39. Pacifici, p. 304 n. 1.
40. Pacifici, p. 306 n. 1.
41. ASMo, CS, 150, doc.

1709-xxvii/8.

42. ASMo, CDAP, 930, f. 27v.
43. ASMo, CDAP, 930, f. 8v.
44. ASMo, CDAP, 930, ff. 3v, 5v, 6r, 7v.
45. ASMo, CDAP, 930, ff. 7v, 8r.
46. ASMo, CDAP, 930, f. 7r.
47. ASMo, CDAP, 941, f. 79v; 958, f.29r.
48. ASMo, CDAP, 1022, ff. 51r-53r.
49. Davila, p. 48.
50. Davila, p. 57.
51. ASMo, CS, 150, doc. 1709-xxvii/8.
52. Roelker, p. 177.
53. ASMo, CS, 150, doc. 1709-xxvii/10.
54. ASMo, CS, 150, doc. 1709-xxvii/9.
55. Davila, pp. 120–1.
56. Knecht, *Catherine de' Medici*, p. 88.
57. Davila, p. 154.
58. Davila, p. 135.
59. Davila, pp. 234–5.
60. Davila, p. 235.
61. Knecht, *Catherine de' Medici*, p. 89.
62. ASMo, CS, 150, doc. 1709-xxvii/27; Davila, p. 293.
63. Davila, p. 241.
64. Pacifici, p. 321 n. 1.
65. Knect, *Catherine de' Medici*, p. 90.
66. ASMo, CDAP, 930, f. 29v.
67. ASMo, CS, 150, doc. 1709-xxviii/18.
68. ASMo, CS, 150, doc.

1709-xxviii/19.

69. ASMo, CS, 150, doc. 1709-xxviii/22.
70. ASMo, CS, 150, doc. 1709-xxviii/17.
71. ASMo, CDAP, 959, f. 12r.
72. ASMo, CDAP, 871, f. 30.
73. ASMo, CS, 151, doc. 1709-xxix/2.
74. ASMo, CDAP, 959, f. 15r.
75. ASMo, CS, 151, doc. 1709-xxix/3.
76. ASMo, CS, 151, doc. 1709-xxix/6.
77. ASMo, CDAP, 959, ff. 18v-20r.
78. ASMo, CDAP, 930, f. 41r; 959, f. 19r;
79. ASMo, CDAP, 930, f. 41r.
80. ASMo, CDAP, 871, f. 31; 959, f. 13v.
81. ASMo, CDAP, 959, f. 12v-13r.
82. ASMo, CDAP, 959, ff. 14r, 17r, 19r, 19v.
83. ASMo, CDAP, 959, ff. 12r, 19r.
84. ASMo, CDAP, 886, f. 131v.
85. ASMo, CS, 151, doc. 1709-xxix/8.
86. ASMo, CDAP, 871, f. 2.
87. ASMo, CS, 151, doc. 1709-xxix/11.

Chapter 11
Roma Resurgens

1. Pastor, 16:415.
2. Pastor, 16:415.

3. Coffin, *Ligorio*, p. 41.
4. Onians, p. 328.
5. Pastor, 16:445.
6. Antonovics, p. 303.
7. Pacifici, p. 325.
8. Jones, p. 167.
9. Jones, p. 168.
10. Jones, pp. 168–9.
11. Robertson, pp. 137–41.
12. Robertson, pp. 160–2.
13. ASMo, CDAP, 991, *passim*.
14. ASMo, CDAP, 896, ff. 4r-10r *passim*.
15. ASMo, CDAP, 896, ff. 8v, 23v; 940, ff. 10v,11v; 991, f. 12r.
16. ASMo, CDAP, 869, f. 74v.
17. ASMo, CDAP, 933, ff. 38v.
18. ASMo, CDAP, 941, ff. 65r, 66r.
19. ASMo, CDAP, 828, f. 19r; 1023, loose sheet (5 May 1566).
20. ASMo, CDAP, 896, f. 49r; 941, f. 101v.
21. ASMo, CDAP, 828, f. 16v; 869, f. 117r.
22. ASMo, CDAP, 869, f. 116v.
23. ASMo, CDAP, 869, 61r.
24. ASMo, CDAP, 869, f. 116v.
25. ASMo, CDAP, 869, f. 88r.
26. Scappi, 2:395r-v.
27. Pastor, 16:69-72; Visceglia, *Morte*, pp. 158–61.
28. Pastor, 17:8.
29. Pastor, 17:31-2 n. 5.

Picture Credits

Index